POLYCARP AND PAUL

SUPPLEMENTS TO

VIGILIAE CHRISTIANAE

Formerly Philosophia Patrum

TEXTS AND STUDIES OF EARLY CHRISTIAN LIFE
AND LANGUAGE

EDITORS

J. DEN BOEFT — R. VAN DEN BROEK — W.L. PETERSEN
D.T. RUNIA — J.C.M. VAN WINDEN

VOLUME LXII

POLYCARP AND PAUL

AN ANALYSIS OF THEIR LITERARY & THEOLOGICAL RELATIONSHIP IN LIGHT OF POLYCARP'S USE OF BIBLICAL & EXTRA-BIBLICAL LITERATURE

BY

KENNETH BERDING

BRILL

LEIDEN · BOSTON · KÖLN

2002

This book is printed on acid-free paper.

BR
65
.P653
E653
2002

Library of Congress Cataloging-in-Publication Data

Library of Congress CIP data is also available.

Die Deutsche Bibliothek – CIP-Einheitsaufnahme

Berding, Kenneth:
Polycarp and Paul : an analysis of their literary & theological relationship
in light of Polycarp's use of biblical & extra biblical literature / by
Kenneth Berding. – Leiden ; Boston ; Köln : Brill, 2002
  (Supplements to Vigiliae Christianae ; Vol. 62)
  ISBN 90–04–12670–8

ISSN   0920-623X
ISBN   90 04 12670 8

PRINTED IN THE NETHERLANDS

CONTENTS

ACKNOWLEDGMENTS

Special thanks are due to those who have guided me through this study. Stephen S. Taylor and Dan G. McCartney carefully read earlier drafts of this work, prodding me to think more deeply and communicate more clearly. Thanks also are due to Donald A. Hagner and Alain Le Boulluec for reading this manuscript later in the process and for their perceptive recommendations.

I also want to extend my thanks to the library staff at Westminster Theological Seminary, and, in particular, to Grace Mullen and Gail Barker for their untiring patience as I requested numerous difficult-to-locate books and articles.

My father, Drew Berding, deserves special thanks for helping me with the statistical analysis that appears in the appendix.

Finally, my deepest appreciation belongs to my wife, Trudi, for her inexhaustible encouragement and the strength she continues to extend to me as I study and write. I also cannot leave out Lydia and Grace, my two daughters, who (literally) cheered for me each time I completed another stage in the process.

ABBREVIATIONS

ABD	*The Anchor Bible Dictionary*
ATR	*Anglican Theological Review*
BBR	*Bulletin for Biblical Research*
BHT	Beiträge zur historischen Theologie
CBQ	*Catholic Biblical Quarterly*
CP	*Classical Philology*
CQR	*Church Quarterly Review*
CTM	*Currents in Theology and Mission*
CTR	*Concordia Theological Quarterly*
ExpTim	*The Expository Times*
HTR	*Harvard Theological Review*
JBL	*Journal of Biblical Literature*
JECS	*Journal of Early Christian Studies*
JSNTSup	Journal for the Study of the New Testament Supplement Series
JTS	*Journal of Theological Studies*
NTS	*New Testament Studies*
NIGTC	*The New International Greek Testament Commentary*
QJS	*The Quarterly Journal of Speech*
RB	*Revue Biblique*
TS	*Theological Studies*
TU	*Texte und Untersuchungen*
TZ	*Theologische Zeitschrift*
VC	*Vigiliae Christianae*
WUNT	Wissenschaftliche Untersuchungen zum Neuen Testament

CHAPTER ONE

INTRODUCTION

> "I continue to be impressed and surprised by the high and indeed unique status which Polycarp accords both to Paul and to his epistles."[1]

This study will explore the literary and theological relationships between the only extant letter(s)[2] of Polycarp of Smyrna and those of the Apostle Paul. The inquiry into these relationships will be built upon an analysis of Polycarp's quotations from and allusions to earlier (especially Christian) writings upon which he often depends. Since Polycarp is largely dependent upon the New Testament[3] writings, and the letters of Paul in particular, greater attention will be focused there. Upon this base our study of the relationship of these two famous Christians will be built.

The most important findings of this study include the following:

1. Polycarp is primarily dependent upon NT writings in his letter to the Philippians (henceforth, Pol. *Phil.*). His dependence upon OT writings is light (though evidently present in a few instances). There are a number of literary affinities between Pol. *Phil.* and *1 Clement*. Some general influence by the letters of Ignatius seems to exist, but individual allusions to his letters are debatable. In the NT, Polycarp is primarily dependent upon the letters of Paul, secondarily upon 1 Peter and the sayings of the Lord (probably via Matthew and Luke along with the oral tradition) and in a couple places upon 1 John (almost certainly), Acts (probably), and Hebrews (possibly). There is no evidence that any of these sources are cited from written manu-

---

[1] Charles M. Nielsen, 'Polycarp and Marcion: A Note,' *TS* 47 (1986): 298.

[2] The question of whether Polycarp's letter to the Philippians is one letter or two letters will be discussed later in the Introduction. When 'letter' in the singular is used in this study, it designates the majority of the letter, chs. 1-12 (and possibly ch. 14 as well); that is, what P. N. Harrison, *Polycarp's Two Epistles to the Philippians* (Cambridge: Cambridge University Press, 1936) called Polycarp's 'second letter' or 'crisis letter.'

[3] Henceforth NT. OT will be used for books found in our present Hebrew Bible/Old Testament. The short form, HBOT, seems inappropriate for a study of Polycarp since there is no evidence that Polycarp ever relies upon a Hebrew text or that he, for that matter, knows Hebrew. The use of OT, however, should not be construed to mean that Polycarp thinks in terms of a fixed Old Testament canon.

scripts. All the evidence suggests that Polycarp quoted from memory in all instances.

2. Polycarp has purposely imitated Paul in the composition of his letter *because he is writing to a church founded by Paul*. He has imitated Paul both literarily and in terms of Paul's ethical example. Polycarp's letter, however, is in no way pseudepigraphic; he emphatically contrasts himself to the person of Paul (3.2) while at the same time modeling his own letter after those of Paul.

3. Polycarp has unwittingly told us through the way that he clusters allusions to Paul's writings around the name of Paul (including two from 1 Timothy and one from 2 Timothy) that he considered 1 and 2 Timothy to have been written by Paul.

4. Polycarp shows significant dependence upon Paul in his theological statements (the few that exist). His letter, however, evinces a period of transition where Polycarp, while resonating with many of Paul's emphases, has moved away from others.

5. In light of Polycarp's use of imitation in the composition of his letter – a strong value among Graeco-Roman rhetoricians – the prejudice against Polycarp repeated time and again by modern scholars that Polycarp was uncreative and lacking in intelligence will have to be overturned.[4]

The need for this study will be evident to anyone who has studied the Apostolic Fathers in general and Polycarp in particular. There still exists no full-length study devoted to an analysis of Polycarp's citations and allusions from the NT writings for their own sake. To my knowledge, the question of whether Polycarp is in any way imitating Paul has never been studied. The recognition that Polycarp has clustered allusions to Paul's writings around the name of Paul and its relevance to Polycarp's understanding of Pauline authorship of 1 and 2 Timothy has never been observed. Various writers have commented upon one or more of Polycarp's theological positions (to the degree that they can be ascertained) but have disagreed on the extent to which he has diverged from Paul in terms of theology. Finally, the time has come for someone to point out the scholarly bias against Polycarp's intelligence and rectify it. That problem will be clarified now.

---

[4] See discussion immediately below.

Modern Scholars' Recognition of Polycarp's Importance and the Tendency to Regard Him as Unintelligent

Modern scholarship has repeatedly recognized the importance of the person of Polycarp of Smyrna in second-century Christianity. Only a few examples can be given:

R. Grant says, "The importance of Polycarp of Smyrna for the study of early Christian life in (*sic*) second century cannot easily be overestimated."[5]

Torrance calls Polycarp "the most venerable of the Apostolic Fathers, and perhaps the chief depository of the primitive Gospel tradition."[6]

Campenhausen comments, "In this connection Polycarp of Smyrna especially plays a paradigmatic role; for quite apart from his personal standing as a revered bishop and martyr he forms, on account of his unusually great age, a living link between the apostolic era and the third, or even the fourth, post-apostolic generation."[7]

Koester refers to Polycarp as "doubtlessly the most significant ecclesiastical leader of the first half of II C.E."[8]

Finally, P. N. Harrison points out that the early church contained "a group of problems, each in its own way fundamental, to which Polycarp was probably better qualified than any other man that ever lived to give authoritative solutions."[9]

The church after Polycarp resonates with these statements on the importance of Polycarp. Some of the prestige and influence of Polycarp in his own day may be adduced from the record of what the crowd is purported to have said at his martyrdom, "This is the teacher of Asia, the father of the Christians, and the overthrower of our gods, he who has been teaching many not to sacrifice, or to worship the

---

[5] Robert M. Grant, 'Polycarp of Smyrna,' *ATR* 28 (1948): 137.

[6] Thomas F. Torrance, *The Doctrine of Grace in the Apostolic Fathers* (n.p.: Oliver and Boyd Ltd., 1948; repr. Pasadena: WIPF & Stock Publishers, 1996), 90.

[7] Hans von Campenhausen, *Ecclesiastical Authority and Spiritual Power in the Church of the First Three Centuries*, trans. J. A. Baker (Stanford: Stanford University Press, 1953), 163.

[8] Helmut Koester, *History and Literature of Early Christianity*, vol 2: *Introduction to the New Testament* (Philadelphia: Fortress Press and Berlin: Walter de Gruyter, 1982), 308.

[9] P. N. Harrison, *Two Epistles*, 3.

gods."[10] Even allowing for exaggeration from those who composed *Mart. Pol.* it is still significant that these Christians (if not also their enemies) referred to Polycarp as "the teacher of Asia" and "the father of the Christians." Irenaeus looked to him as the living link between his generation and that of the apostolic age.[11] It is clear from Jerome's comments that the letter of Polycarp was known and read during his time.[12]

The irony is that while both Christians in the period immediately after Polycarp as well as modern scholars have recognized the importance of Polycarp, modern scholarship has a decided prejudice against his intelligence, creativity, and style:

Hort says, "The letter itself has no such vivid personal interest as those of Ignatius. The good Polycarp was a much more commonplace person."[13]

Lightfoot writes that the style of Pol. *Phil.* lacks "originality." He says, "The thoughts and words of others are reproduced with little or no modification, because the writer's mind is receptive and not creative. The Epistle of Polycarp is essentially common place, and therefore essentially intelligible. It has intrinsically no literary or theological interest."[14]

Torrance comments, "On the other hand, it may be that a mind such as that of Polycarp, essentially receptive by nature and lacking in originality, was not one to grasp best the principles of the new faith."[15]

Batiffol remarks, "The literary interest of the epistle is mediocre,

---

[10] *Mart. Pol.* 12.2.

[11] *Adv. Haer.* 3.3.4.

[12] *De Vir. Ill.* 17 (written in 383 C.E.).

[13] Fenton John Anthony Hort, *Six Lectures on the Ante-Nicene Fathers* (London: Macmillan and Co.), 42.

[14] J. B. Lightfoot, *The Apostolic Fathers: Clement, Ignatius and Polycarp*, 2d ed., part 2, vol. 1 (London: Macmillan and Co., 1890; repr., Peabody, Mass.: Hendrickson Publishers, 1989), 597. Note that his comment that "the writer's mind is receptive and not creative" has been repeated time and again. It should be noted that Lightfoot has a reason to exaggerate the simplicity of Polycarp's style. This passage is found in a comparison of Polycarp's letter with the letters of Ignatius. By showing Pol. *Phil.* to be commonplace, he is able to show it could not have been written by a forger who also forged the Ignatian letters. Thus, their *differences* argue for the *genuineness* of both. While agreeing that Polycarp and Ignatius differ significantly in terms of style, it is not necessary (nor accurate) to argue against Polycarp's intelligence to demonstrate the differences.

[15] Torrance, *Doctrine of Grace*, 90-91. He also refers to 'his lack of originality' on p. 91.

especially if it is compared with the exceptional value of the Ignatian epistles. The style of the bishop of Smyrna is without personal character."[16]

Dibelius opines, "The letter of *Polycarp to the Philippians* is quite lacking in originality."[17] And again, "Just as Polycarp's letter lacks originality in content so also it is decidedly insignificant in its form."[18]

According to Harrison, Polycarp's "mind was conservative rather than creative."[19]

Barnard says, "Polycarp was a rather unimaginative, conservative writer whose outlook and diction was steeped in the traditional Christian vocabulary."[20]

Nielsen calls Polycarp uncreative and receptive[21] and speaks of him having "some limits of intelligence."[22] "Granted that he was not clever enough to become acquainted with all the dimensions of Old Testament thought, it is also obvious enough that he did not have the ability to grasp everything the apostles said either."[23]

Miller waxes eloquent about Polycarp's so-called lack of creativity, "Polycarp is not noted for his originality; he had no creative genius; he was a transmitter and not a maker; he did not dig wells; he only carried the water."[24]

There are many others, but these should suffice to demonstrate a marked negativity toward Polycarp in terms of his style, creativity and intelligence. And what is thought to be true about the letter, is frequently extended to the man himself. Scholars have tripped over each other to paint Polycarp as a simpleton. Nor has this prejudice

---

[16] Pierre Batiffol, 'Polycarp', in *Dictionary of the Apostolic Church*, vol. 2, ed. James Hastings (Edinburgh: T. & T. Clark, 1918), 245.

[17] Martin Dibelius, *A Fresh Approach to the New Testament and Early Christian Literature* (New York: Charles Scribner's Sons, 1936), 179.

[18] Ibid., 181. And again on pp. 180-181, "...we are faced by the fact that he left behind a letter quite lacking in originality, which was very insignificant although well intentioned, whereas the much less important Ignatius left very valuable and original writings."

[19] P. N. Harrison, *Two Epistles*, 6.

[20] L. W. Barnard, *Studies in the Apostolic Fathers and Their Backgrounds* (Oxford: Basil Blackwell, 1966), 35.

[21] Charles M. Nielsen, 'Polycarp, Paul and the Scriptures,' *ATR* 47 (1965): 200.

[22] Ibid., 205.

[23] Ibid.

[24] W. Landon Miller, 'An Anthology of the Theology of the Apostolic Fathers' (Ph.D. diss., Southwestern Baptist Theological Seminary, 1948), 101.

against Polycarp been unrecognized by others.[25] Shepherd notes that in general, "Modern critics are fond of calling him 'unoriginal.'"[26]

A few scholars disagree.[27] Lindemann comments, "One might well conclude that Polycarp was not very independent as a theological author but took most of what he had to say from his sources. But the character of his letter may be a function of its purpose."[28] Lindemann, however, does not develop this thought much either in this article or in his book about the reception of Paul.[29] Nevertheless, the arguments of this dissertation support Lindemann's suggestion – the character of Polycarp's letter *is* a function of its purpose.

I will suggest in ch. 3 that the Philippians had requested that Polycarp write to them about 'righteousness,' perhaps even alluding to the fact that Paul had previously written such a letter to them and asking Polycarp to do the same. I will argue that Polycarp, breathing the air of Graeco-Roman ideas of the value of imitation, purposely modeled his letter after Paul. If in fact Polycarp is imitating Paul, and if he is successful in doing so, then he is not unoriginal at all when judged by the standards of his day. Rather, when judged by second century standards, he perhaps should be considered more successful in his literary activity than Ignatius. Perhaps

---

[25] See, for example, Annegreth Bovon-Thurneysen, 'Ethik und Eschatologie im Philipperbrief des Polykarp von Smyrna,' *TZ* 29 (1973): 241 and Boudewijn Dehandschutter, 'Polycarp's Epistle to the Philippians: An Early Example of "Reception,"' in *The New Testament in Early Christianity: La réception des écrits néotestamentarios dans le christianisme primitif*, ed. Jean-Marie Sevrin (Leuven: Leuven University Press), 275.

[26] Massey Hamilton Shepherd, ed. and trans., 'The letter of Polycarp, Bishop of Smyrna,' in *Early Christian Fathers*, ed. Cyril C. Richardson (New York: Collier Books, 1970), 123. Shepherd himself agrees on p. 123, "It is true; he shows not the slightest interest in theological or philosophical speculation."

[27] Dehandschutter has argued that even if Pol. *Phil.* is simply an example of 'reception' and passing on the teaching of early Christian literature, that in and of itself should not cast a writer as being unoriginal. "Polycarp's reception is nothing other than a demonstration that his ethical teaching is in continuity with the traditional Christian faith, guaranteed by the words of the Lord and the writings of the apostles. Why should this be considered as *un*original?" Dehandschutter, 'Polycarp's Epistle,' 280 (also 291).

[28] Andreas Lindemann, 'Paul in the Writings of the Apostolic Fathers,' in *Paul and the Legacies of Paul*, ed. William S. Babcock (Dallas: Southern Methodist University Press, 1990), 43.

[29] Andreas Lindemann, *Paulus im ältesten Christentum: Das Bild des Apostels und die Rezeption der paulinischen Theologie in der frühchristlichen Literatur bis Marcion*, BHT 58 (Tübingen: J. C. B. Mohr [Paul Siebeck], 1979).

this is why there is evidence that Polycarp's letter was valued in the early church until the time of Jerome, whereas there is no such continuing evidence for the letters of Ignatius.

The ease with which Polycarp cites from memory Christian writers would have sent a message to his readers, not that he was a simpleton, but that he was intelligent, for the ability to memorize would have been highly *valued*. It's not surprising that Polycarp would be remembered as a person with an outstanding memory of names.[30] It also should be noted that Polycarp is highly successful at bringing together a wealth of allusions to other writings in a brief compass. The letter is far less awkward than one would expect from a writer who alludes to earlier literature in almost every sentence.

Thus, to judge Polycarp an unoriginal thinker may be to anachronistically judge him by the standards of our age rather than his own. Nor can generalizations about Polycarp's intelligence be asserted based only upon the evidence of a single letter, particularly if he is modeling his writing after Paul. All that can be said is that Polycarp is following a particular procedure in this particular letter; if he had been writing to a church founded by John, he may have composed his letter differently.

One of the results of this prejudice is a tendency to overlook Polycarp's letter in favor of his big brothers 'Clement' and Ignatius. Both *1 Clement* and the letters of Ignatius taken together are longer. Both are earlier (*1 Clement*, c. 96 C.E. and Ignatius, some time before 117 C.E.), particularly if one accepts the dates of Harrison for Polycarp's 'second' letter (which I do not – see discussion pp. 13-24). Polycarp's letter also does not have as many scholarly difficulties to untangle such as the authorship of *1 Clement* or 'Clement's' discussion of the Phoenix bird[31] or Ignatius's fixation on martyrdom[32] and monepiscopacy.[33] Another reason Pol. *Phil.* has often been neglected is that it is often studied as an extension of studies of the letters of Ignatius. Though historically they are interrelated, it seems

---

[30] *FrgPol* among the Harris Fragments has this comment about Polycarp, "Moreover, he had this gift, that he never (f)orgot any w(ho) had come into contact with him." Here I have employed the translation of Frederick W. Weidmann, *Polycarp & John: The Harris Fragments and Their Challenge to the Literary Traditions* (Notre Dame, Ind.: University of Notre Dame Press, 1999): 44. Cf. also the similar comment in *Mart. Pol.* 8.1.

[31] *1 Clem.* 25-26.

[32] See, for example, Ign. *Rom.* 4-5.

[33] See, for example, Ign. *Smyrn.* 8-9.

that Polycarp was the more significant character of the two for the churches moving toward orthodoxy, particularly when one considers the length and location of his ministry in Asia. And if Harrison is correct that Pol. *Phil.* is actually two letters rather than one,[34] the letter as we now know it cannot be viewed merely as a cover letter for the collection of the Ignatian letters (which could make it seem less important in its own right).

One example will have to suffice as evidence of the relative neglect of Pol. *Phil.* in many analyses of the Apostolic Fathers. Mackinnon's tome, *The Gospel in the Early Church* discusses each of the Apostolic Fathers in turn, devoting a separate section to each. Clement of Rome earns seven pages, Ignatius of Antioch nine pages, Barnabas more than six, Hermas fourteen and the Didache together with Papias four.[35] One searches in vain for a discussion of Polycarp's letter. All that exists is a single paragraph at the *end* of the discussion of Ignatius and begins with these words, "The Epistle of Polycarp, bishop of Smyrna, to the Philippians may be treated as a sort of appendix to those of Ignatius."[36]

The need for fresh studies of Pol. *Phil.* is illustrated by such summaries. The following study will seek in small measure to rectify this situation.

Polycarp the Man[37]

The few facts about Polycarp's life that are known are summarized below:

1. He was born around the time of the destruction of Jerusalem, perhaps in 69 C.E.[38]

---

[34] A position I support, see discussion of date and unity pp. 13-24.

[35] James Mackinnon, *The Gospel in the Early Church: A Study of the Early Development of Christian Thought* (London: Longmans, Green, and Co., 1933), 257-299.

[36] Ibid., 275.

[37] For more background information about the man Polycarp, the city of Smyrna and the church in Smyrna, refer to the discussion in Howard Carroll, 'Polycarp of Smyrna – With Special Reference to Early Christian Martyrdom' (Ph.D. diss., Duke University, 1946), 1-73 who pulled together and summarized scholarship up until 1946.

[38] Based upon *Mart. Pol.* 9.3 where Polycarp is reported to have said at his martyrdom, "For eighty-six years I have been his servant and he has done me no wrong." He may have been older if he was not dating from the time of his birth but from the time of his conversion.

2. He was always associated with the city of Smyrna. It is not known whether he lived anywhere else in his youth.[39]

3. He was said by Irenaeus and Eusebius and *FrgPol* in the Harris Fragments to have been a disciple of a certain John. It is disputed whether this was John the Apostle or a separate John the Elder.[40]

4. Ignatius in the early part of the second century visited Smyrna, and subsequently wrote at least one letter to the church in Smyrna and at least one letter to Polycarp himself.[41]

5. Polycarp collected the letters of Ignatius at Ignatius's request (perhaps for the church in Antioch[42]) and forwarded them along with a cover letter to the church in Philippi.[43]

---

[39] Smyrna (modern day Izmir, Turkey) was a beautiful city set at the end of an enclosed harbor. It had a temple erected for Tiberius, a theater, many baths, a public library, an altar to Zeus and schools of rhetoric and medicine. Set as it was beside a natural bay, it was known in the ancient world for its beauty. See A. E. Welsford, *Life in the Early Church: A.D. 33 to 313* (London: National Society and S.P.C.K., 1951), 136.

[40] The statements by Irenaeus (*Adv. Haer.* 3.3.4), Eusebius (*H.E.* 4.14) and *FrgPol* in the Harris fragments (cf. Wiedmann, *Polycarp & John*) that Polycarp knew John the Apostle has not convinced many scholars. Many have thought that Irenaeus was mistaken about the identity of John and others simply followed him. See comments in Michael W. Holmes, 'Polycarp of Smyrna,' in *Dictionary of the Later New Testament & Its Developments*, ed. Ralph P. Martin and Peter H. Davids (Downers Grove and Leicester: InterVarsity Press, 1997), 934. It is interesting that Irenaeus does not say Polycarp was taught by John (an interesting omission since it would have helped his argument) but that John lived in Ephesus until the time of Trajan, thus implying that Polycarp would have been acquainted with him. Theodore Zahn, *Introduction to the New Testament*, vol. 2 (Grand Rapids: Kregel Publications, 1953), 437 argues that Polycarp's John was John the Apostle. He argues that Papias's reference to John as a μαθητὴς τοῦ κυρίου, does not mean simply a Christian but refers to one who actually heard the Lord – a personal disciple of Jesus. Pierre Nautin, *Lettres et Écrivains Chrétiens des IIe et IIIe Siècles* (Paris: Cerf, 1961), 82 n. 2 and 92 disagrees, saying that it was inevitable that the connection to the Apostle John would be made eventually, but suggests that the John of whom Irenaeus spoke was probably not the Apostle John, but was probably John the Elder that Papias mentions (*H.E.* 4.39.4). J. N. Sanders, *The Fourth Gospel in the Early Church: Its Origin & Influence on Christian Theology up to Irenaeus* (Cambridge: Cambridge University Press, 1943), 14 agrees, commenting that Polycarp's probable quotation of 1 John 4:2-3 in Pol. *Phil.* 7.1 and the lack of any definitive allusion to the Gospel of John are evidence that Polycarp may have been a disciple of John the Elder, who was different from the Apostle John. It seems that, lacking new evidence, it cannot be definitively demonstrated which view is correct.

[41] It seems very likely that Polycarp himself played a role in Ignatius' writing of his letters. See Edgar J. Goodspeed, *A History of Early Christian Literature*, rev. Robert M. Grant (Chicago: The University of Chicago Press, 1966), 27.

[42] Pol. *Phil.* 13.1.

[43] Pol. *Phil.* 13.2.

6. He wrote at least one letter, to the Philippians.[44] The plural 'letters' mentioned by Irenaeus may indicate that he wrote more.[45]

7. As a child, Irenaeus knew him and heard him teach.[46]

8. Polycarp knew Papias.[47]

9. In his old age Polycarp was involved in the Quartodeciman controversy and visited Anicetus in Rome.[48]

10. During his lifetime he had to contend with docetists (Pol. *Phil.* 7) and Valentinians and Marcionites.[49] It may be that toward

---

[44] There is no good reason to doubt that the letter was written from Smyrna though it cannot be proven. The fact that Polycarp was writing to respond to the Philippians' request makes it likely that he at least received their request in Smyrna. He may have been travelling, of course, but the likelihood, in the absence of contrary evidence, is that Polycarp would have been at home in Smyrna when he penned this letter.

[45] We do not know whether Polycarp wrote other letters and if he did why only Pol. *Phil.* is extant. We do know that Ignatius charged him to write letters in Ign. *Pol.* 8.1. Ignatius wanted him to write to 'the churches on this side' (ταῖς ἔμπροσθεν ἐκκλησίαις) probably a reference to the churches between Smyrna and Antioch. See J. B. Lightfoot, J. R. Harmer and Michael W. Holmes, trans. and eds., *The Apostolic Fathers: Greek Texts and English Translations of Their Writings*, 2d ed. (Grand Rapids: Baker Book House, 1992), 201, n. 33. It is unlikely that Polycarp would have ignored such a request from the esteemed martyr, Ignatius, after his death. On the other hand, the lack of extant letters *may* be explained thus: Polycarp *collected* Ignatius's letters and *circulated* them instead of writing his own. If this reconstruction is correct, and Polycarp collected Ignatius's letters and sent them to the churches between Antioch of Syria and Smyrna as Ignatius requested, ch. 13 of Pol. *Phil.* may represent the request from the Philippians to be included in that circulation (since they were not among those designated by Ignatius). Note also that Greek literature has a number of examples of the plural ἐπιστολαί when it is in fact referring to a single letter. See Stirewalt, *Studies*, 77. This also may be a valid observation for Polycarp's comment in Pol. *Phil.* 3.2 that Paul wrote to the Philippians ἐπιστολάς (plural).

[46] A careful reading of Eusebius, *H.E.* 5.20 indicates that Irenaeus was probably a child or a youth when he (repeatedly) heard Polycarp. He refers to what 'children' learn and retain when they grow up. He speaks of specifics ('the place where Polycarp sat,' 'the appearance of his body') which may suggest that he was trying to add credence to his relationship with Polycarp when in fact he was not a 'disciple' of Polycarp in any formal sense. There is no reason, however, to dispute his claim that he heard him regularly as a child and remembered much of what was said.

[47] According to Irenaeus, *Adv. Haer.* 5.23.4.

[48] He supported the celebration of Christ's crucifixion on the 14th day of the Jewish month Nisan, whatever day of the week it happened to fall upon. He visited Rome and discussed it with Anicetus, and though they disagreed it seems they separated without strife – agreeing to disagree. Anicetus continued to allow the celebration of the Lord's Supper by the Asiatics who were in Rome. See Eusebius, *H.E.* 5.24.

[49] Irenaeus, *Adv. Haer.* 3.3.4.

the end of his life he contended with Montanists, or at least some form of proto-Montanism.[50]

11. He probably gradually moved from a position as one of multiple elders of the church in Smyrna (before there was a single bishop) to becoming its singular bishop. It is not at all clear when he came to be recognized as the bishop of Smyrna. Whether he was in fact a bishop when he penned his letter to the Philippians is still debated.[51]

12. When he was at least 86 years old he was martyred and his martyrdom was detailed by eyewitnesses in *Martyrdom of Polycarp*.[52]

---

[50] Gerd Buschmann, *Das Martyrium des Polykarp* (Göttingen: Vandenhoeck and Ruprecht, 1998) argues that the whole of *Mart. Pol.* bears the mark of a conflict with Montanism (or perhaps 'proto-Montanism,' 52). If this is the case, this may point toward a conflict with which Polycarp himself had to deal during his later years.

[51] Polycarp addresses the church of Philippi, not as a special bishop, it seems, but as one of the elders. But Robert Grant, *An Introduction*, vol. 1, The Apostolic Fathers: A New Translation and Commentary, ed. Robert M. Grant (New York: Thomas Nelson & Sons, 1964), 172 points out that this does not prove that Smyrna did not *have* a bishop. Elsewhere Grant argues that this is because Valens *is* the bishop of Philippi (note esp. Pol. *Phil.* 11.2 and its connection to 1 Tim 3:5) who has been deposed. Therefore Polycarp is encouraging submission to the elders and the deacons, not emphasizing his own role as bishop. See Robert M. Grant, *After the New Testament* (Philadelphia: Fortress Press, 1967), 53-54. In general it should be noticed that the idea of centralization of authority of the bishop which is so predominant in Ignatius is not nearly so pronounced in Pol. *Phil.* See Hans von Campenhausen, 'Polykarp von Smyrna und die Pastoralbriefe,' chap. in *Aus der Frühzeit des Christentums: Studien zur Kirchengeschichte des ersten und zweiten Jahrhunderts* (Tübingen: J. C. B. Mohr [Paul Siebeck], 1963), 231-232. In contrast to Ignatius, who clearly wanted a hierarchical system with bishops above the presbyters and deacons (Ign. *Smyrn.* 8.1), Polycarp tells the church at Philippi "to be subject to the presbyters and deacons as to God and Christ." (Pol. *Phil.* 5.3). Ignatius clearly addressed the church in Smyrna as though Polycarp was their singular bishop (Ign. *Smyrn.* 8-9), but it is not clear whether this represents the situation as Ignatius observed it when he passed through Smyrna or whether it was just how Ignatius *wanted* to view it. As to the church in Philippi, Eric G. Jay, 'From Presbyter-Bishops to Bishops and Presbyters. Christian Ministry in the Second Century: a Survey,' *SecCent* 1 (1981), 142 argues, "Throughout the letter(s) [Pol. *Phil.*] there is nothing to suggest monepiscopacy in Philippi." It is probably best to understand Polycarp living during a period of transition. He was in his early period one of the elders, but was the ruling bishop by the end of his life. See Carroll, 'Polycarp,' 39-42.

[52] He probably died on February 22, most likely in 156 C.E. P. Nautin, *Lettres*, 72 n. 1 (following P. Braun) is typical of the censensus of most scholarship and assumes that the '86 years' in *Mart. Pol.* 9.3 is Polycarp's age, rather than the period of time since his baptism. On problems associated with dating Polycarp's death see Timothy D. Barnes, 'A Note on Polycarp,' *JTS* 18 (1967): 433-437 and Boudewijn Dehandschutter, 'The Martyrium Polycarpi: A Century of Research.'

Authenticity and Manuscripts

Most scholars[53] since Lightfoot did his detailed historical analysis of the letters of Ignatius and Polycarp[54] have accepted Pol. *Phil.* as authentic.[55] The authenticity of Pol. *Phil.* rests primarily on the following grounds.

1. The intimate connection between the Ignatian letters and Pol. *Phil.* makes them stand or fall together.

2. The style of Polycarp's letter (its themes, emphases, tone, and frequency of biblical allusions) is so different from the Ignatian letters that it cannot have been forged by the same hand.[56]

3. Externally, Irenaeus recommends to his readers a certain letter written from Polycarp to the Philippians. This is strong evidence since, as we know, Irenaeus claims to have personally been acquainted with Polycarp when Irenaeus was young.[57] He very likely would have been in a position to know whether Polycarp was or was not the author. Eusebius also mentions the letter in connection with the Ignatian letters and quotes at length from chs. 9 and 13.[58]

Only nine Greek manuscripts preserve portions of the letter. The most important of these is the 11th century manuscript Codex

---

ANRW 2 (1993): 485-522. *FrgPol* in the Harris Fragments (see Weidmann, *Polycarp & John*, 84-86) may suggest that the dating should be reckoned neither from birth, nor from baptism, but rather from the time Polycarp's youth is finished (say age 18 or 19). *FrgPol* explicitly says that Polycarp lived to 104. Still, as Weidmann points out, this could simply be a reckoning based upon the '86 years' mentioned in *Mart Pol* 9.3.

[53] Note particularly the exception of R. Joly, *Le Dossier d'Ignace d'Antioche*, Université libre de Bruxelles, Faculté de Philosophie et Lettres 69 (Brussells: Éditions de l'Université de Bruxelles, 1979).

[54] Lightfoot, *The Apostolic Fathers*, part 2, vol. 1. Note esp. the discussion on pp. 578-603.

[55] For a history of criticism *before* Lightfoot, see summary in P. N. Harrison, *Two Epistles*, 28-42.

[56] Also Dibelius, *A Fresh Approach*, 181 and Otto Bardenhewer, *Geschichte der Altkirchlichen Literatur*, vol. 1 (Frieburg: Herdersche Verlagshandlung, 1913), 166-167. Kleist, comparing Ignatius and Polycarp, says, "There is also a decided difference in their style of writing. Ignatius is fiery, abrupt, and impetuous, while Polycarp is calm and sedate, more akin to Clement of Rome." James A. Kleist, *The Didache, the Epistle of Barnabas, the Epistles and the Martyrdom of St. Polycarp, the Fragments of Papias, the Epistle to Diognetus*, vol. 6, Ancient Christian Writers, ed. Johannes Quasten and Joseph C. Plumpe (Westminster, Md.: The Newman Press, 1948), 69.

[57] *Adv. Haer.* 3.3.4.

[58] *H.E.* 3.36.

Vaticanus Graecus 859. It is evident that all the manuscripts are derived from the same literary tradition, since they all contain chs. 1-9 and are abruptly followed by the fifth chapter of Barnabas. They all end with καὶ δι' ἡμᾶς ὑπὸ in our texts of Pol. *Phil.* 9.2 and are followed without a break by the words of *Barn.* 5:7 τὸν λαὸν τὸν καινὸν...[59]

Eusebius of Caesarea copied chs. 9 and 13 into *H.E.* 3.36.[60] The Greek texts in our printed editions follow him where there are no other Greek texts.

There are also a few quotations in Monophysite or semi-Monophysite writings from the fifth to the seventh centuries.

The remainder of the text (chs 10-12 and ch. 14, including the last line of ch. 13) is preserved only in Latin texts. For English translation, I have often simply adopted the excellent translation of Lightfoot, Harmer and Holmes,[61] though I have not hesitated to deviate when clarity or accuracy seemed to demand it.

Date and Unity

Since the question of the date and the question of the unity of Pol. *Phil* are inextricably linked they will be dealt with together here.

The document referred to as Polycarp's letter to the Philippians was written some time in the first half of the second century C.E. But the exact date of the letter is much more difficult to determine. There is no external evidence which can help us date Polycarp's letter; as Harnack notes, "...the letter may have been written any time between A.D. 100-155."[62]

Harnack himself had considerable difficulty dating the letter, as Harrison would later comment, somewhat tongue-in-cheek, "In 1878 it was after 140, in 1886 after 130, in 1897 '110-117 or perhaps 117-125'; in 1920 he had come right round to Lightfoot's opinion, 'Trajan's time'. If he had lived a few years longer, who can say that

---

[59] Lightfoot, *The Apostolic Fathers*, part 2, vol. 3, 316-317.

[60] M. J. Suggs, 'The Use of Patristic Evidence in the Search for a Primitive New Testament Text,' *NTS* 4 (1957-1958): 139-147 comments concerning Eusebius's quotation habits that "...he is, in general, quite trustworthy."

[61] Lightfoot, Harmer and Holmes, *The Apostolic Fathers: Greek Texts*.

[62] Adolf von Harnack, 'Lightfoot on the Ignatian Epistles: II. Genuineness and Date of the Epistles,' *The Expositor*, third series, vol. 3 (1886): 185.

he would not have changed his mind again?"[63]

Lightfoot's contribution to the historical understanding of the letters of Ignatius and the letter of Polycarp was enormous.[64] One of his chief contributions was to confirm the authenticity of the Ignatian epistles (middle recension) and Polycarp's letter. This is significant, because the date of Polycarp's letter, if a unity, or the first letter (chs. 13 or 13-14) if divided, is based upon the date of the martyrdom of Ignatius, which Eusebius placed in the eleventh year of Trajan (108 C.E.) (*H.E.* 3.33.2-3 with 3.36.2). It has been suggested that perhaps Eusebius was mistaken about the date, but, as Schoedel comments, "The date is under a cloud, but few seem disposed to challenge the suggestion that it was within Trajan's reign (A.D. 98-117) that Ignatius was martyred."[65] Since Ignatius and Polycarp knew one another (Ignatius addressing one of his letters to Polycarp, and both referring to each other in their letters), and since Pol. *Phil.* (at least ch. 13) was written as a cover letter for a collection of the letters of Ignatius (13.2), the dating of Pol. *Phil.* is related to the date of the martyrdom of Ignatius. If we assume that Eusebius was correct in placing the martyrdom of Ignatius in Trajan's reign, 117 C.E. becomes the last possible date for the composition of Polycarp's letter (if a unity) or chs. 13/13-14 (if two letters).[66]

---

[63] P. N. Harrison, *Two Epistles*, 9. The main reason for Harnack's vacillation was the question of whether Polycarp's polemic was against Marcion or not. The early Harnack thought it was directed against Marcion (Harnack, 'Lightfoot,' 185-192) but later was persuaded of Lightfoot's view.

[64] J. B. Lightfoot, *The Apostolic Fathers*, part 2.

[65] William R. Schoedel, *Polycarp, Martyrdom of Polycarp, Fragments of Papias*, vol. 5 of *The Apostolic Fathers: A New Translation and Commentary*, ed. Robert M. Grant (Camden, N.J.: Thomas Nelson & Sons, 1967), 4.

[66] Hübner rejects the common connection between the letters of Ignatius and Polycarp. Reinhard M. Hübner, 'Thesen zur Echtheit und Datierung der sieben Briefe des Ignatius von Antiochien' *Zeitschrift für Antike Christentum* 1 (1997): 44-72. Hübner argues for a date of perhaps ca. 170 for the letters of Ignatius. To accomplish this, though, he appears to follow a line of investigation which is tentative at best. He must reject Eusebius's suggestion of the dating of Ignatius's martyrdom under Trajan (*H.E.* 3.33.2-3 and 3.36.2) (pp. 45-48). Few scholars doubt that Eusebius has filled in various gaps in his historical knowledge, but Hübner's suggestion as it stands must assume that Eusebius knew almost *nothing* reliable at all about this period. In addition, (following Lechner) Hübner must accept *both* that Pol. *Phil.* 1.1 δεξαμένοις to 1.2 καὶ *and* Pol. *Phil.* chapter 13 were later interpolations (pp. 48-50). These interpolations were, according to Hübner, added to Pol. *Phil.* to bring credibility for the letters of Ignatius. What this means is that, when taken as a whole Lightfoot's historical reconstruction is still less intrusive than Hübner's. Lightfoot has on his side the manuscript tradition linking Polycarp to

The first issue which must be addressed to determine a proper date of Pol. *Phil.* is whether or not the letter is a unity (in interaction with P. N. Harrison's thesis that the letter is actually two letters[67]). If it is one letter, it must all be dated in conjunction with the date of the martyrdom of Ignatius (based upon ch. 13). But if it is in fact two letters, the second letter may be dated later. I will attempt to support Harrison's thesis that ch. 13 (or 13+14) is a cover letter for a collection of Ignatian letters sent by Polycarp to Philippi within weeks of Ignatius's journey to Rome, and that chs. 1-12 (or 1-12+14) are a second letter composed at a later time. I do not support Harrison's thesis that the best date for chs. 1-12 is c. 135 C.E. Rather, a date of about 120 C.E. will be argued, based upon various considerations.[68]

Two Letters or One?

P. N. Harrison's book *Polycarp's Two Epistles to the Philippians* is, alongside the work of Lightfoot, probably the most significant piece of scholarship on Pol. *Phil.* Harrison's thesis is that our present letter from

---

Ignatius whereas Hübner must rely upon hypothetical text reconstructions in Pol. *Phil.* Moreover, the variant readings Hübner prefers over Lightfoot's in Ign.*Eph.* 1.2 and *Mgn.* 8.2 (pp. 50-52), even if correct, do not *prove* anything about the date; they only give a hint of an argument toward a historical setting which itself has been speculatively reconstructed. For, the fact of the matter is that the paucity of literature from the early to middle second century does not allow us with any confidence to make generalizations about what could *not* have been taught (particularly with the kind of certainty Hübner projects). Also, if Hübner's suggestion that Ignatius is directly dependent on Noetus of Smyrna (who we *only* know via Hippolytus) (pp. 52-59) is correct, we will have to answer the question of why Ignatius's writings were received as orthodox whereas Noetus's were taken to be heretical *in Smyrna* within the same generation. In addition, the exceptions Hübner lists (John 20:28; Tit 2:13; 2 Pet 1:1) to his contention that Ignatius's use of 'God' or 'our God' statements (i.e. in reference to Jesus) are rare until the later second century actually demonstrate just the opposite. Three different authors writing in three different places employing such terminology should be taken, not as exceptions to a rule, but as constituting a pattern that argues against Hübner's contention. The scope of this monograph does not allow additional comments on other more minor points Hübner makes. None alone or in combination make a convincing argument, in my opinion.

[67] P. N. Harrison, *Two Epistles.*

[68] This will be in agreement with the views of Cadoux and Barnard who both accept P. N. Harrison's theory of two epistles but who also reject his date of c. 135 C.E. in favor an earlier date of c. 120 C.E.. C. J. Cadoux, Review of *Polycarp's Two Epistles to the Philippians*, by P. N. Harrison, *JTS* 38 (1937): 267-270; Barnard, *Studies*, 31-39.

Polycarp to the Philippians is actually two letters, written by Polycarp at two different times. The first letter consists of ch. 13 (and possibly 14) which was a cover letter for a collection of Ignatius's letters which the Philippians had requested that Polycarp send. This cover letter would have to be dated within weeks of Ignatius's journey to Rome to face martyrdom, but before definite news of his martyrdom had reached the ears of the Philippians (13.2).

The second letter consists of the main body of our extant letter, chs. 1-12 (and possibly 14). It is Harrison's contention that this letter was written almost twenty years later (c. 135 C.E.) and was directed against the teaching of Marcion whom Polycarp had already encountered in Asia Minor.

The linchpin of Harrison's thesis that we actually have two letters is that ch. 9 lists Ignatius among other martyrs (indicating that they knew he had died), whereas the last sentence of ch. 13 indicates that Ignatius is or may still be alive. Lightfoot, in contrast, (writing before Harrison) argues that the letter is a unity and that it was written at a time "that Polycarp, though he assumes that the saint has suffered martyrdom, is yet without any certain knowledge of the fact."[69] Harrison considers inadequate the explanation that Polycarp did not know that Ignatius was dead but assumed him to be dead.[70]

Harrison also argues that allusions to Ignatius's letters are present in chs. 1-12.[71] Since it would take a certain amount of time for Polycarp to become sufficiently familiar with Ignatius's letters to allude so freely to them, this can be considered an argument in favor of a time later than the few weeks allowed for the writing of ch. 13, and thus an argument for the division into two letters.[72]

An additional argument that the letter is in fact two letters is that 3.1 indicates the purpose of the letter is to respond to a request from the Philippians that Polycarp write about 'righteousness', but ch. 13 indicates the purpose is to respond to the Philippians' request for a collection of Ignatius's letters.[73] It is possible that this is

---

[69] Lightfoot, *The Apostolic Fathers*, part 2, vol. 3, 314.

[70] See also the discussion in Schoedel, *Polycarp*, 37-39.

[71] P. N. Harrison, *Two Epistles*, 163-165.

[72] Schoedel, *Polycarp*, 38 also considers this overstated, since the allusions to Ignatius are not so clear in the first 12 chapters and since there may in fact be allusions to Ignatius in chs. 13-14.

[73] Clayton N. Jefford, *Reading the Apostolic Fathers: An Introduction* (Peabody, Mass.: Hendrickson Publishers, 1996), 74.

a case of dual purposes for one letter, but the two purposes are distinct enough to consider the option of two letters with two distinct purposes to be the stronger in this case.

Barnard adds to Harrison's thesis an argument which, surprisingly, Harrison did not bring forth. Barnard contends that Eusebius (*H.E.* 3.36.14-15) purposely omitted the Greek original of the last sentence of ch. 13 (*Et de ipso Ignatio et de his qui cum eo sunt, quod certius agnoveritis, significate*[74]) because he was trying to cover over the contradiction between ch. 9 (which implies Ignatius had died) and the last sentence of ch. 13 (which implies that Ignatius might still be alive). Eusebius knew he could not quote both without creating a contradiction (even in Greek).[75] This significantly strengthens Harrison's thesis.

Harrison's thesis that we are dealing with two rather than one letter has convinced many scholars and is the position adopted here.

The Date of Polycarp's 'Second Letter'

Assuming that chs. 1-12 (or 1-12+14) is a second letter, written at a different time from ch. 13 (or 13+14), it becomes necessary to inquire into the date of this second letter, which Harrison usually refers to as the 'crisis letter.'[76]

Harrison dates the 'second letter' about 135 C.E. His main arguments for this date are first summarized below. Following their summary they will be critiqued.

1. Harrison claims that 1.1 seems more like an event of the distant past, rather than of the very recent past.[77]

2. The allusions to Ignatius's letters in Polycarp's own letter argue that Polycarp had to have time to absorb them before he could allude to them.[78]

3. Polycarp's use of NT quotations is another of Harrison's arguments. He thinks that Polycarp's extensive use of many NT books presupposes a later date in history.[79]

---

[74] This is only preserved in Latin.

[75] Barnard, *Studies*, 32-33.

[76] The term 'crisis letter' seems an unfortunate term, which overemphasizes the 'crisis' character of the letter.

[77] P. N. Harrison, *Two Epistles*, 155-162.

[78] Ibid., 163-165.

[79] Ibid., 285-310.

4. Polycarp's relationship to Marcion is one of Harrison's key arguments for a later date.[80] Polycarp was writing his letter to combat a form of Marcionism which Polycarp already had encountered in Asia Minor and which had recently arrived in Philippi. The most important phrase in this argument is 'firstborn of Satan' (πρωτότοκος τοῦ σατανᾶ) in 7.1.

Finally, I will add an additional argument for a later date (but will argue against it). If Irenaeus is correct that Polycarp had written other letters besides the one still extant (quoted in Eusebius *H.E.* 5.20) but if Irenaeus only had one in hand (*Adv. Haer.* 3.3.4), then it could be argued that there was good reason that this letter was still available and the others were not. The reason could be that the letter was directed against Marcion and had been used in arguments against the teaching of Marcion extensively, whereas the other letters were more occasional. Thus, the continuing presence of our extant letter and the absence of Polycarp's other letters at the end of the second century could be considered another argument that Polycarp's letter was written to combat Marcionism.

Though this last argument is plausible, I consider it inadequate because it wrongly (I believe) assumes Polycarp's letter to have been written primarily with a polemical purpose. The primarily polemical approach to the letter will be argued against later in this section.

We will look in turn at each of Harrison's arguments, concentrating upon his arguments concerning Polycarp and Marcion. It will be argued that he has misinterpreted the evidence, and that Polycarp's letter should be dated closer to 120 C.E. instead of c. 135 C.E.

Harrison's view of Pol. *Phil.* 1.1 (Συνεχάρην ὑμῖν μεγάλως ἐν τῷ κυρίῳ ἡμῶν Ἰησοῦ Χριστῷ, δεξαμένοις τὰ μιμήματα τῆς ἀληθοῦς ἀγάπης καὶ προπέμψασιν, ὡς ἐπέβαλεν ὑμῖν, τοὺς ἐνειλημένους τοῖς ἁγιοπρεπέσιν δεσμοῖς "I greatly rejoice with you in our Lord Jesus Christ, because you welcomed the representations of the true love and, as was proper for you, helped on their way those men confined by chains suitable for saints") is that it has the tone of one writing about an event of the distant past. In contrast, Cadoux considers the wording of 1.1 to reflect a recent event.[81] Harrison himself almost admits that the other reading is natural, "True, the mere fact that the

---

[80] Ibid., 166-206.
[81] Cadoux, Review of Harrison, 268.

letter opens with a reference to that visit may, at first sight, seem to suggest that the visit had taken place recently. But on further reflection it soon becomes evident that such an inference is by no means necessary."[82] It seems that neither is necessary and that either explanation adequately deals with the sentence found in 1.1.

Schoedel agrees that the event is recent, but argues for it differently, "*Phil.* 1.1 seems to presuppose a relatively recent encounter between the martyrs and the Philippians; thus if *Phil.* 1.1 and *Phil.* 9 are from the same hand, there is less reason to think that Phil. 9 (*sic*) need imply a significant lapse of time between the visit of the martyrs to Philippi and their martyrdom."[83] He bases this upon the suggestion that the text be emended to eliminate the καὶ before the ὅτι in the beginning of 1.2. This emendation would help connect the time of the writing of Pol. *Phil.* more closely to the event described in 1.1.

Schoedel may be correct, but so may Harrison. It seems this question is not immediately resolvable.

Harrison has argued, in a second place, that the allusions to Ignatius's letters in Pol. *Phil.* indicate that some time was needed for Polycarp to absorb the content of Ignatius's letters and thus to allude to them. This has already been mentioned as an argument for Harrison's thesis of two letters. While it may provide some support for the thesis that we are dealing with two letters rather than one, it does not at all argue that twenty years are needed to become familiar with Ignatius's letters. We are arguing that c. 120 C.E. is a more appropriate date, which would still allow enough time for the letters to be collected and somewhat absorbed. Harrison also is probably overstating the degree of dependence Polycarp has on Ignatius, since the allusions to Ignatius's letters are at no point as clear as the numerous quotations from Paul's letters, 1 Peter, and *1 Clement* sprinkled throughout Pol. *Phil.*[84] Moreover, if in fact twenty years had passed, we would rather expect a clear quotation from Ignatius (as with 'Clement') rather than a handful of debatable allusions.

Harrison argues, in a third place, that Polycarp's extensive use of

---

[82] P. N. Harrison, *Two Epistles*, 158.
[83] William R. Schoedel, 'Polycarp's Witness to Ignatius of Antioch,' *VC* 41 (1987): 2.
[84] Schoedel, *Polycarp*, 38.

the NT implies a late date. All are not convinced. Cadoux comments, "The facts which Dr Harrison adduces regarding the quotations from the New Testament are quite consistent with a date about A.D. 120 for cc. i-xii. No books are quoted which Polycarp could not perfectly well have been able to quote at that date."[85]

This third argument largely depends upon which books one considers Polycarp to have drawn upon (the consideration of which itself somewhat depends upon one's judgment of the books Polycarp could have drawn upon). Chapter 2 will argue that at various points Polycarp probably had literary contact with the Psalms, Proverbs, Isaiah, Jeremiah, Tobit, Matthew, Luke, Acts, Romans, 1 and 2 Corinthians, Galatians, Ephesians, Philippians, 2 Thessalonians, 1 and 2 Timothy, 1 Peter, 1 John, and *1 Clement*. Dependence upon Ezekiel, Sirach, Mark, Hebrews, and the letters of Ignatius is also possible.

Most of those listed here had been in circulation for some time by 120 C.E. One of the key considerations is Polycarp's relationship (or lack of relationship) to the four gospels. Though it is disputed, there is good reason to believe that the four gospels were circulating by 120 C.E.. Though there is no clear evidence of the four gospels circulating as a group before Tatian's *Diatessaron* (c. 150-160), Ignatius probably quoted Matthew and John (c. 117),[86] Papias (writing c. 120[87]) knew of Matthew, Mark, and John,[88] and Marcion himself not much later was using a truncated version of Luke's gospel.

Polycarp evidently wrote in a period when both written documents and the oral tradition were valued. Chapter 2 will argue that Polycarp in fact did draw upon Matthew and Luke but may have still been influenced in some cases by forms of the sayings of the Lord which were passed down orally. But for Polycarp himself, this

---

[85] Cadoux, Review of Harrison, 269. Metzger comments, "While this theory has gained approval from a number of scholars, there is, however, no compelling reason for dating the second epistle as late as 135; a year or so after the first epistle would satisfy the internal evidence of the text." Bruce M. Metzger, *The Canon of the New Testament: Its Origin, Development, and Significance* (Oxford: Clarendon Press, 1987), 60.

[86] Oxford Society of Historical Theology, *The New Testament in the Apostolic Fathers* (Oxford: The Clarendon Press, 1905), 137-138.

[87] Goodspeed, *A History*, 90.

[88] Lightfoot, Harmer and Holmes, *The Apostolic Fathers: Greek Texts*, 556.

would probably have been almost equally as true in 135 as in 120.[89]

Harrison's most important argument for the date of c. 135 C.E. may be his connection of Marcion with the phrase 'first-born of Satan' (πρωτότοκος τοῦ σατανᾶ) in Polycarp's denunciation in 7.1. Irenaeus indicates that Polycarp at a later stage did refer to Marcion as 'first-born of Satan' (*Adv. Haer.* 3.3.4). There are, nonetheless, a number of considerations that militate against the identification of this phrase in 7.1 with Marcion.

The definite article is missing where we might have expected it had Polycarp's denunciation been against a particular person. It is also reasonable to assume that Polycarp called others besides Marcion 'first-born of Satan'.[90] Dahl has argued that the phrase 'first-born of Satan' comes from Jewish sources and that it first referred to Cain.[91] Thus, it is likely that this phrase was not unique to Polycarp's interactions with Marcion, but may have been part of common anti-heretical rhetoric in use among Jewish Christians and subsequently among non-Jewish Christians like Polycarp.

Pol. *Phil.* 7.1 itself argues against the idea that Polycarp's polemic is directed specifically against the teaching of Marcion, because of the phrase "and claims that there is neither resurrection nor judgment" (λέγῃ μήτε ἀνάστασιν μήτε κρίσιν) in connection with the phrase 'the first-born of Satan'. Barnard comments, "Neither did Marcion deny judgement – in fact he held as firmly as any Catholic that men would be rewarded or punished hereafter according to their deeds in this life, although it was the Demiurge who would be their judge."[92] There is also no attempt by Polycarp to denounce Marcion's view of the OT, which was certainly a central characteristic of his teaching.[93] Lightfoot suggests that the line "to suit his own sinful desires" (πρὸς τὰς ἰδίας ἐπιθυμίας) in 7.1 was inapplicable

[89] Papias, writing in the same period (c. 120 C.E.), helps us remember that "oral tradition was often more highly valued than written materials in a cultural setting that relied upon and trusted memory far more than is customary today." Barnard, *Studies*, 35.

[90] Walter Bauer, *Die apostolischen Väter II: Die Briefe des Ignatius von Antiochia und der Polykarpbrief* (Tübingen: J. C. B. Mohr [Paul Siebeck], 1920), 291-292.

[91] Nils Alstrup Dahl, 'Der Erstgeborene Satans und der Vater des Teufels (Polyk. 7₁ und Joh 8₄₄),' in *Apophoreta: Festschrift für Ernst Haenchen* (Berlin: Verlag Alfred Töpelmann, 1964), 70-84.

[92] Barnard, *Studies*, 34.

[93] Cadoux, Review of Harrison, 268.

to Marcion whose moral character was 'unimpeachable'.[94]

Harrison is forced to argue that the Marcion Polycarp was arguing against had different views on some points from those he came to hold after going to Rome and encountering Cerdo.[95] There is not a shred of evidence for this except Harrison's desire to harmonize with his own thesis. Harnack is more likely correct when he says, "It is very probable that Marcion had fixed the ground features of his doctrine, and had laboured for its propagation, even before he came to Rome."[96]

Nielsen, like Harrison, argues that Polycarp may in fact be attacking Marcion in 7.1. But his argument is different from Harrison's. Nielsen suggests that Polycarp's focus upon Pauline quotations, to the near exclusion of OT references, and in greater measure than other NT references, may indicate that Polycarp accepted the same canon as Marcion when he wrote his letter.[97] Nielsen summarizes,

> If Marcion were the false teacher of *Philippians*, we could expect Polycarp to attack Docetism and stress the marriage relationship against Marcion's asceticism (4,2). Moreover, we would expect Polycarp to make it plain that he shares his opponent's high view of Paul, both as *the* apostle and as the author of Scripture. Finally, we would expect Polycarp to refrain from an obvious onslaught against Marcion's thinking on the OT simply because the two were not that far apart. Are not all of these expectations fulfilled in Polycarp's letter?[98]

Nielsen has perhaps made an important point about the similarities between Polycarp and Marcion on their respective emphases on Paul. But Polycarp (unlike Marcion) also drew extensively upon 1 Peter. Finally, why would we 'expect' Polycarp to make clear that he shares Marcion's view of Paul or to stay away from attacking his views on the OT? Though Polycarp does not use the OT extensively, he never disparages it, speaks of a different god of the OT, or avoids it when there is occasion to use it. Rather, it seems Polycarp's

---

[94] Lightfoot, *The Apostolic Fathers*, part 2, vol. 1, 586.

[95] P. N. Harrison, *Two Epistles*, 183-206.

[96] Adolf von Harnack, *History of Dogma*, vol. 1, trans. Neil Buchanan (London: Williams & Norgate, 1905), 267, n. 1.

[97] Nielsen, 'Polycarp and Marcion,' 298-299. This is in line with Nielsen's view that Polycarp considered Paul's writings to be Scripture (Nielsen, 'Polycarp, Paul,' 199-216), but against the opinions of others (such as Schoedel who says, "There is no evidence that any of the New Testament books are regarded as Scripture." Schoedel, *Polycarp*, 5).

[98] Nielsen, 'Polycarp and Marcion,' 299.

emphasis upon Paul may have more to do with the occasion of his letter, directed as it was to one of Paul's churches, Philippi. Nielsen's thesis, like that of Harrison, also suffers under the assumption that the whole letter somehow polemically addresses Marcionism. Lindemann comments about Polycarp's lack of polemical intent even though he clearly esteems Paul, "Dabei gibt es für die These, hinter dieser Wertschätzung des Paulus stehe eine polemische Absicht, überhaupt kein Indiz."[99]

Nielsen's argument can also be turned on its head. If Polycarp had indeed been arguing against Marcion, would not he have used less of Paul rather than more as later writers contending with Marcionism tended to do?[100]

An argument that the date of the letter is closer to 120 C.E. than to 135 C.E. may be found in the theology of the letter (see the discussion of eschatology in ch. 5). Bovon-Thurneysen has located the eschatology of Polycarp *between* the NT and 2 Clement.[101] This, though not conclusive in any sense, is a supporting argument that an earlier rather than a later date is preferable.

In summary, I have dealt with Harrison's thesis at length in order to determine a date for Pol. *Phil.* Harrison's view that Polycarp's letter is actually two letters rather than one appears to be the stronger position. But Harrison's view that the second letter (chs. 1-12) was written in c. 135 seems not to be as strong as an earlier date closer to 120 C.E.. Pol. *Phil.* 1.1 does not clearly argue either for a recent event or an event long past unless Schoedel's emendation is correct – in which case an earlier date is more likely. Allusions to Ignatius's letters, though probably present, are not as clear as other quotations in the letter, and certainly do not necessitate twenty years to be mentally assimilated. The NT quotations and allusions do not necessitate a later date, since most of the books cited would have been accessible to Polycarp in 120 C.E. Even though Polycarp would later refer to Marcion as 'first-born of Satan' there are reasons to believe Marcion is not addressed in Pol. *Phil.* 7.1, including immediate contextual considerations and the lack of doctrines which set

---

[99] Lindemann, *Paulus im ältesten Christentum*, 91.

[100] "Notwithstanding these attempts to save Paul for the church, he was largely silenced by the apologists, and this neglect lasted practically until the time of Augustine." J. Christiaan Beker, *Heirs of Paul: Paul's Legacy in the New Testament and in the Church Today* (Minneapolis: Fortress Press, 1991), 28.

[101] Bovon-Thurneysen, 'Ethik,' 256.

Marcion apart from other docetists. Neither do Polycarp's many quotations from Paul support the idea that his use is somehow related to Marcion's dependence on Paul.

Thus, the majority (chs. 1-12 or possibly 1-12+14) of Pol. *Phil.* was probably not written in c. 135 C.E. as Harrison suggests, but rather nearer to 120 C.E.

Genre and Purpose

Since the question of imitation is so intricately intertwined with the question of genre, a more lengthy discussion will be deferred until that question is opened in ch. 3. In general, I agree with Holmes's summary of the genre of Pol. *Phil.*:

> Polycarp's letter is a complex hortatory letter that (1) combines elements of at least three common letter types (paraenesis, advice and admonition), and (2) employs in portions of the letter a sermonic or homiletical style of discourse, the word of exhortation. While its structure owes more to the word of exhortation model than to either Hellenistic epistolary conventions or rhetorical theory, awareness of the latter two is evident throughout the letter.[102]

The primary purpose of Pol. *Phil.* is disputed. If Harrison's thesis is not correct and Pol. *Phil.* is a single letter, then the primary impetus for its writing was as a cover letter for the collection of the letters of Ignatius. In this construction, the letter(s) which Polycarp received from the Philippians included both a correspondence about the letters of Ignatius (Pol. *Phil.* 13.1) and a request that Polycarp write to them about 'righteousness' (Pol. *Phil.* 3.1). It may also have included a discussion of the problem of the greed of Valens (11.1), but this is not known.

If Harrison is correct, then the question of the purpose of Polycarp's second letter (chs. 1-12 and perhaps 14) is not that of a cover letter.

---

[102] Holmes, 'Polycarp of Smyrna,' 935. For further study on ancient epistolography, see Heikki Koskenniemi, *Studien zur Idee und Phraseologie des griechischen Briefes bis 400 n. Chr.* Soumalaisen Tiedekatemian Toimituksia; Annales Academiae Scientarium Fennicae 102.2 (Helsinki: Akateeminen Kirjakauppa, 1952); John L. White, 'New Testament Epistolary Literature in the Framework of Ancient Epistolography,' in *Aufstieg und Niedergang der Römischen Welt*, ed. H. Temporini and W. Haase, 1730-1756 (Berlin: Walter de Gruyter, 1984); Franz Schnider and Werner Stenger, *Studien zum neutestamentlichen Briefformular.* New Testament Testament Tools and Studies, XI (Leiden: E. J. Brill, 1987).

What then was Polycarp's compositional purpose if a single purpose is detectable?

The first suggestion is that Polycarp is writing to counteract Marcionism[103] or at least some form of docetism. There is no doubt that Polycarp does oppose some form(s) of docetism in Pol. *Phil.* 7.1 but there should be considerable doubt about whether this functions as his overarching purpose. Harrison and Bauer[104] both emphasize the *crisis* nature of the letter and use 7.1 as the fulcrum for their contention. In contrast, Jefford comments, "Neither the theme of *docetism* nor of abuse of power figures prominently."[105] The letter deals with such varied subjects as general Christian virtues, the responsibilities of wives and widows, the qualities of deacons, warnings to younger men and women, the responsibilities of presbyters, false teaching, temptation, suffering, self-control, and the monetary abuse of a former presbyter named Valens. Making the anti-docetic comments in Pol. *Phil.* 7.1 the main *purpose* of the letter does not account for all the data in the book. The contention of a crisis tone also does not fit what we encounter when we read the letter as a whole.[106] Irenaeus more accurately reflects the pastoral tone of Polycarp's letter when he advises believers to read it because they "can learn both the character of his faith and the message of truth" (*Adv. Haer.* 3.3.4).

A second suggestion is that Polycarp is writing primarily to deal

---

[103] P. N. Harrison, *Two Epistles*, 166-206.

[104] Walter Bauer, *Orthodoxy and Heresy in Earliest Christianity*, 2d German ed., with added appendices, by Georg Strecker, trans by a team from the Philadelphia Seminar on Christian Origins, ed. Robert A. Kraft and Gerhard Krodel (Philadelphia: Fortress Press, 1971; repr., Mifflintown, Pa.: Sigler Press, 1996), 72 posited that Polycarp wrote to a small minority of 'ecclesiastically oriented people' in an otherwise heterodox Philippi making much of Polycarp's encouragement in 7.2: "...abandon the foolishness of the great majority and the false teachings, and let us return to the word which was transmitted to us from the beginning." Thus, for Bauer, it is the majority that rejects the ecclesiastical faith, which created a significant crisis for Polycarp.

[105] Jefford, *Reading*, 78.

[106] Harrison overemphasizes the crisis tone of the letter as the following melodramatic sentence (about 7.1) indicates, "The really appalling circumstance, that shocks even Polycarp out of his native tolerance and strains almost to breaking-point even his Christian forbearance, and causes him now to shrink back with horror, and now to lash out with a severity, more than that, a ferocity of denunciation...the really devilish thing, as Polycarp sees it, is the spread of certain false teachings, nominally and hypocritically Christian, but essentially Satanic." Harrison, *Two Epistles*, 169.

with the problems in the Philippian church created by the sin of Valens.[107] Maier has developed this theme in a sociological direction and argues that Polycarp was particularly trying to maintain community boundaries in the wake of the social confusion caused by the greed of Valens.[108] Though the incident of Valens' greed obviously was substantial for Polycarp, since he denounced greed repeatedly throughout his letter,[109] it is not the primary purpose of his letter. It does not adequately account for Polycarp's stated purpose (Pol. *Phil.* 3.1) nor the variety of subjects addressed in the letter.

It seems, instead, that the primary purpose of the letter is found in Polycarp's statement of purpose (Pol. *Phil.* 3.1). He is responding to the Philippians' request that he write to them about the problem of righteousness.[110] The theme of righteousness is repeated throughout the letter (2.3; 3.1, 3; 4.1; 5.2; 8.1; 9.1). His manner throughout is both 'hortatory and admonitory'.[111] Since righteousness for Polycarp includes fidelity to 'the word delivered to us from the beginning' (7.2) and centers on ethics, including greed, the anti-docetic theme and the issue of greed should be considered sub-themes under the greater discussion of 'righteousness'.

Can we delimit the nature of the request posed to Polycarp by the Philippian church? Though any reconstruction is tentative, I wish to suggest that the request made to Polycarp may have read something like this: "Please write us a letter about righteousness *as Paul did*." There is, of course, no way of proving that their request was framed in such a way. But this suggestion helps explain certain

---

[107] Adolf von Harnack, *Miscellen zu den apostolischen Vätern, den Acta Pauli, Apelles, dem Muratorischen Fragment, den pseudocyprianischen Schriften und Claudianus Marmertus*, TU 2-20/3b (Leipzig: J. C. Hinrichs, 1900), 86-93. Peter Steinmetz, 'Polykarp von Smyrna über die Gerechtigkeit,' *Hermes* 100 (1972): 63-75.

[108] Harry O. Maier, 'Purity and Danger in Polycarp's Epistle to the Philippians: The Sin of Valens in Social Perspective,' *JECS* 1 (1993): 229-247. On p. 238 he comments, "We offer the tentative appraisal that the link between idolatry and avarice in Phil. 11.1-2 is best interpreted by placing it in a social setting in which well-to-do presbyters continue to enjoy and secure prosperity by retaining socio-economic links within pagan society. On this view, Polycarp's reference to Valens' avarice is that the presbyter has strayed too close to the world." It should be noted that this scenario makes adequate sense of the text (as a sub-theme), but so do other scenarios such as a situation where Valens pilfered the community purse.

[109] Lightfoot, *The Apostolic Fathers*, part 2, vol. 3, 314.

[110] Lindemann, 'Paul in...Apostolic Fathers,' 43.

[111] David K. Rensberger, 'As the Apostle Teaches: The Development of the Use of Paul's Letters in Second-Century Christianity' (Ph.D. diss., Yale University, 1981), 119.

peculiarities of Pol. *Phil.*. It explains why Polycarp composed his letter in a style which was modeled after Paul's own letters (see ch. 3). It explains why he so frequently quoted Paul, why he mentioned Paul at three different points in his letter and yet why he explicitly stated that "neither I nor anyone like me can keep pace with the wisdom of the blessed and glorious Paul." (Pol. *Phil.* 3.1). If Polycarp received such a request, however, it is relatively clear in light of his response that he understood the request to focus upon 'righteousness' as *righteous living* (with an ethical impulse) rather than as a fundamental theological concept (see ch. 5). This reconstruction cannot be proven, but it fits the evidence of the text very comfortably.

Methodology

In ch. 2, each possible citation or allusion to earlier (especially Christian) writings found in Pol. *Phil.* will be analyzed. In this section I will try to make plain the assumptions, categories and procedures used in this analysis. Since much work on Pol. *Phil.* has been engaged without a discussion of method, the reader is often at a loss to know why a particular scholar considered a particular phrase to be an almost certain allusion when another scholar does not even mention it.

Difficulties in assessing the relationship of a given patristic author to a NT (or any other) text have been mentioned by Suggs:[112]

1. The patristic text has a transmission history of its own.
2. The patristic author may be quoting from memory instead of consulting a text.
3. The patristic author may not be intending to quote at all; he may in fact simply be reflecting biblical language because of constant use.
4. The patristic author may have altered the passage to fit the theological point he is trying to make.
5. The patristic author may be trying to improve upon the style of the biblical passage or harmonize it with the syntax of his own sentence.[113]

---

[112] See comments in Suggs, 'Patristic Evidence,' esp. 140-142.
[113] For a level-headed analysis of the use of patristic citations in text-criticism,

Additional difficulties in assessing whether and how one of the Apostolic Fathers is citing an earlier writing are described by Hernando:

> The task is made more difficult for two reasons: 1) Seldom is the corresponding material sufficient length to provide certainty that the author is quoting; 2) Very often the corresponding material varies in verbal content, form, or both. In regards to the second difficulty, there are a number of possible explanations: 1) The author is citing a New Testament writing from memory; 2) The author is using a New Testament text, but adapting or modifying it for his own purpose; 3) The author is using an independent source of tradition, either oral or written, that preserves a different form of the material.[114]

Certain assumptions undergird this study:

1. If somewhere in Pol. *Phil.* is found a clear quotation from a given writing, the likelihood that Pol. *Phil.* is dependent upon the same source in the case of a less clear example increases. It is very difficult to take a lone allusion to a source as secure when it appears to be the only reference to that source.

2. If there is found in the immediate context of a quotation, allusion or reminiscence one or two apparent additional allusions or reminiscences to the same source, the likelihood of direct dependence in the first case increases significantly. This is particularly significant for Polycarp, who sometimes clusters quotations and allusions from a single writer together.[115] In this light, allusions to the same author in a near context in Polycarp, when such a case exists,

---

see Bruce M. Metzger, 'Patristic Evidence and the Textual Criticism of the New Testament,' *NTS* 18 (1971-1972): 379-400. Note that whereas his concerns as a text critic are narrower than our concerns in this study ("It goes without saying that reminiscences and allusions are of less value to the critic than specific citations of the very words of the scriptural passage" p. 379), his suggestions are still helpful. See also M. -E. Boismard, 'Critique Textuelle et Citations Patristiques,' *RB* 57 (1950): 388-408 for discussion about the importance of citations in patristic writings. Also note Gordon D. Fee, 'The Use of Greek Patristic Citations in New Testament Textual Criticism: The State of the Question,' in *Studies in the Theory and Method of New Testament Textual Criticism*, by Eldon Jay Epp and Gordon D. Fee (Grand Rapids: William B. Eerdmans Publishing Company, 1993) as well as his critique of Boismard's optimism concerning the value of patristic quotations in text criticism in Gordon D. Fee, 'The Text of John in *The Jerusalem Bible*: A Critique of the Use of Patristic Citations in New Testament Textual Criticism,' *JBL* 90 (1971): 163-173.

[114] James Daniel Hernando, 'Irenaeus and the Apostolic Fathers: An Inquiry into the development of the New Testament Canon' (Ph.D. diss., Drew University, 1990), 132-133.

[115] See argument of ch. 4.

are considered supporting evidence of dependence on that author.[116]

3. If there is a distinctive word or phrase in the allusion it is considered more secure.[117]

4. We should assume dependence on a known source rather than an unknown source when a source is known to have existed, particularly when it was likely to have been available to Polycarp.[118]

5. It is my conviction that all the NT writings could have been written and available to Polycarp before the time Polycarp penned his letter (c. 120 C.E.). Thus, decisions based upon a negative assessment of what sources Polycarp could have known (at least in the case of the writings now in our canonical NT) are not given weight in the discussion which follows.[119]

Other methodological concerns include the following:

1. Probabilities rather than certainties form the basis upon which this study proceeds. Nevertheless, there is a considerable cumulative value in knowing the likelihood of dependence upon an earlier source.

2. We must distinguish between the concept of trying to *transmit* a direct quotation of Jesus or an apostle from the *use* of a tradition. In

---

[116] Schoedel, *Polycarp*, 37 following Helmut Koester, *Synoptische Überlieferung bei den apostolischen Vätern* (Berlin: Akadamie-Verlag, 1957), 119-120 argues as such in 12.3, "Direct dependence on Matthew (with contamination from Luke) in this passage is indicated by the fact that the connection of themes in Matt. 5:44 and 5:48 has the marks of a Matthean construction." Lovering argues that though one might consider 1 Tim 6:10 in 4.1 to be a general maxim and not dependent on 1 Timothy if standing alone, "the proximity of the reflection [to the quote of 1 Tim 6:7]...makes the dependence a virtual certainty." Eugene Harrison Lovering, 'The Collection, redaction, and early circulation of the corpus Paulinum' (Ph.D. diss., Southern Methodist University, 1988), 229.

[117] See, for example, the discussion of the quotation of Gal 6:7 in Pol. *Phil.* 5.1, "God is not *mocked*." The word μυκτηρίζω is so colorful that it makes dependence upon Gal 6:7 almost certain.

[118] "A basic premise we hold to in the following study [in Hagner's case on *1 Clement*] is that when a known source is readily available, it is difficult to argue probable dependence in another direction without the strongest of evidence." He adds, "At the same time, although this is a basic conviction underlying the present work, it is not followed blindly or absolutely..." Donald Alfred Hagner, *The Use of the Old and New Testaments in Clement of Rome* (Leiden: E.J. Brill, 1973), 15.

[119] Hagner, Use, 280, n. 1 criticizes Koester, *Synoptische Überlieferung*, 121f. for doing precisely this. He points out that Koester affirms a knowledge of both Matthew and Luke by Polycarp, but not by Ignatius where, in Hagner's opinion, the textual evidence by itself is just as strong. Koester has affirmed use by Polycarp and not by Ignatius, according to Hagner, because he dates Polycarp's writing activity a couple decades after Ignatius wrote.

general, what we find in Pol. *Phil.* is Polycarp's use of a tradition for his particular purposes.[120]

3. A study such as the one undertaken here requires that we try to determine whether Polycarp ever relied upon a manuscript for any of his quotations.[121] Since our general conclusion on this matter informs the particulars of the study, it will be anticipated here. Polycarp quotes from memory. There is no indication that he is reading from a manuscript at any point. The rule of thumb that longer passages indicate reliance on a manuscript[122] has no bearing in Polycarp since he never quotes at length.

4. We must bear in mind that it is possible that in some cases Polycarp was dependent upon phraseology and terminology represented in literature with which he was familiar but which he had no conscious intention of citing. Such dependence would be a result of his immersion into early Christian culture and discussion. Sorting out intention is excessively difficult in most situations.[123]

5. We should beware of the possible influence of circular reasoning upon decisions concerning possible dependence upon earlier literature. By way of example, P. N. Harrison has a vested interest in being optimistic about NT citations and allusions in Pol. *Phil.* He is arguing for a later date (c. 135 C.E.) for the writing of the 'crisis letter' and is trying to use the breadth of Polycarp's knowledge of Christian writings to argue that the composition of this letter is later. But at the same time, the assumption (and desire to prove) that Polycarp is writing later apparently influences him to be optimistic about which sources Polycarp *could* have used. There is reason to believe that he would not have been so optimistic if he had thought the letter were dated earlier.[124]

---

[120] Birger Gerhardsson, *Memory and Manuscript: Oral Tradition and Written Transmission in Rabbinic Judaism and Early Christianity*, trans. Eric J. Sharpe (Uppsala: Almqvist & Wiksells, 1961), 198.

[121] See general comments in Fee, 'The Text of John,' 163.

[122] Metzger, 'Patristic Evidence,' 379.

[123] Thus, the use of such expressions in this study as 'Polycarp added' or 'eliminated' or 'changed' a certain source does not imply that he was *consciously* making these changes, though that is probably true in some instances.

[124] Harrison's interest in being optimistic about the breadth of Polycarp's dependence on earlier texts is seen in the way he begins ch. 20 entitled 'Polycarp and the New Testament.' His first line in the chapter is: "A further indication that our Crisis Letter was written towards the end of Hadrian's reign, rather than under Trajan, is afforded by the extraordinary number of quotations and echoes from a long list of Christian books..." P. N. Harrison, *Two Epistles*, 285. This also shows

6. It should be remembered that text critics tend to be quite conservative in their allowance of literary dependence because their goals require it. But our concern is to study any possible literary relationship, regardless of whether a given allusion has any value for reconstructing the text. Sometimes frequent short allusions to a given text provide insight into a writer's purposes, as will be argued concerning Polycarp's dependence upon Paul's letter to the Philippians.

One of the most difficult, but necessary decisions in a study of a patristic author like Polycarp is to delineate terms and categories within which to work. My working categories are as follows:[125]

1. 'Citation' (or 'quotation' – the same is meant by both). "Those places where a Father is consciously trying to cite, either from memory or by copying, the very words of the biblical text."[126] The key is the intention of the author to quote a text.

1a. A 'true citation' may show any or all (but not necessarily all) of the following: 1) It is extremely close in wording to the original text; 2) It is preceded by an introductory formula; 3) It communicates the entire original thought, "even if it breaks the flow of the patristic writer's argument."[127]

1b. A 'loose citation' is also an intentional citing of a particular writer/text but is often adapted to the context of the patristic writer (particularly at the beginning or ending of the reference). It shows a little more flexibility on the form of the citation than would be the case in a 'true citation'.[128]

1c. A 'compressed citation' is like an exact citation in that it is a citation of the very words of its source and only differs from its source in eliminating certain parts of the citation.[129]

2. An 'allusion' is a short phrase (usually no more than three or four words) which appears to have originated in a distinctively simi-

---

that his motivation in the composition of this chapter was not primarily to study the quotations and allusions to earlier writings in their own right.

[125] See in particular discussions in Fee, 'The Text of John,' 169-170; Hernando, 'Irenaeus,' 147-152; Stephen S. Taylor, 'One Way to Categorize Patristic Citations,' Unpublished paper, 1998. I am following more closely the pattern suggested by S. Taylor.

[126] Fee, 'The Text of John,' 170.

[127] S. Taylor, 'One Way.'

[128] This might be closer to Fee's 'adaptation.' Fee, 'The Text of John,' 169-170. Note that Fee is using J. N. Birdsall's terminology.

[129] Two clear examples are the citation of 1 Cor 6:9-10 in Pol. *Phil.* 5.3 and the citation of 1 John 4:2-3 in Pol. *Phil.* 7.1.

lar phrase found in an earlier writer. Because of the brevity of allusions, it is not always clear whether the patristic writer is consciously or unconsciously using the phrase that he employs. Nevertheless, the most likely explanation in such cases is that the phrase and the form of the phrase was directly influenced by the earlier writer. There is no introductory formula.

3. A 'reminiscence', like an allusion, seems to be dependent upon an earlier source (whether the patristic writer has consciously made the connection or whether the connection has been made because of constant reading/recitation of his sources). The connection with an earlier source often lacks direct verbal correspondences (though a distinctive word may make the connection more secure) but rather is marked by a conjunction of ideas or subject matter.

The term 'reference' will often be used in a general sense to refer to any of the above when needed in the context.

Since we are working with probabilities rather than with certainties, the following terms will be used in descending order:

1. 'almost certain'/ 'virtually certain'/ 'beyond any reasonable doubt'
2. 'probable'/ 'very likely'/ 'most likely'
3. 'possible'/ 'might'/ 'perhaps'/ 'may'
4. 'unlikely'

In the study that follows, I will not (indeed, cannot) mention every possible parallel and reminiscence. Many phrases are too obscure or commonplace to allow one to establish the possibility of dependence. But, where there is at least a possibility, I have tried to mention it, even if briefly.

CHAPTER TWO

AN ANALYSIS OF POLYCARP'S CITATIONS, ALLUSIONS, AND REMINISCENCES

Polycarp demonstrates throughout his letter a thoroughgoing indebtedness to Jewish and especially early Christian writers as well as to the teaching of Jesus. Each possible citation of, allusion to, or reminiscence of earlier writings found in Pol. *Phil.* will be analyzed in this chapter.[1] The analysis which follows is not a commentary on Pol. *Phil.* even though it follows the order of the book. It is an attempt to determine Polycarp's literary dependencies. The reasoning processes behind each decision will be briefly laid out so that later students of Pol. *Phil.* will have a basis upon which to agree or disagree with the decisions made here.[2]

A summary of each 'almost certain,' 'probable,' or 'possible' citation, allusion or reminiscence will be given at the end of each subsection. Cumulative results appear in the appendix. There exists an almost endless number of possible allusions and reminiscences to earlier writings. Those evaluated in this section are clauses, phrases or expressions which for some reason truly point toward a possibility of literary dependence.

Salutation

Πολύκαρπος καὶ οἱ σὺν αὐτῷ πρεσβύτεροι τῇ ἐκκλησίᾳ τοῦ θεοῦ τῇ παροικούσῃ Φιλίππους· ἔλεος ὑμῖν καὶ εἰρήνη παρὰ θεοῦ παντοκράτορος καὶ Ἰησοῦ Χριστοῦ τοῦ σωτῆρος ἡμῶν πληθυνθείη.

Polycarp and the presbyters with him to the church of God that sojourns at Philippi: may mercy and peace from God Almighty and Jesus Christ our Savior be yours in abundance.[3]

---

[1] In a previous article ('Polycarp of Smyrna's View of the Authorship of 1 and 2 Timothy' *VC* 53 [1999]: 349-360) I drew up a list of 'probable' and 'also possible' citations and allusions (see pp. 353-355). Note that my goal in that article was to draw up a list which would, as far as possible, represent the *conservative consensus* among scholars who had drawn up their own lists. In contrast, the decisions in this chapter represent *my own judgments*. This accounts for the differences between the list found in that article and the decisions found here.

[2] Most scholars cited in this chapter have not revealed their reasoning processes; they have simply reported their decisions. Exceptions to this general situation do exist.

[3] I have often simply adopted the excellent English translation of J. B. Lightfoot, J.

The problem of dependence upon earlier sources faces us immediately in the salutation of the letter. Polycarp's greeting is standard Christian fare. Therein lies the problem. Some of the expressions (but not
all) are found in *1 Clement*, Ign. *Phil.*, 1 Timothy, 2 Timothy, Titus, 1
Peter and 2 Peter. The substitution of ἔλεος ('mercy') for χάρις in the
typical Pauline 'grace and peace' could have (but not necessarily) been
inspired by Jude 2,[4] 1 Tim 1:2 or 2 Tim 1:2. The optative verb
πληθυνθείη ('be multiplied') in the salutation is similar to such usage in
the salutations of 1 Peter, 2 Peter, Jude, *1 Clement*, and *Mart. Pol.*[5] But
these observations really only suggest generic similarities, not dependence.

1 Clement provides the strongest parallel,[6] particularly since the phrase
τῇ ἐκκλησίᾳ τοῦ θεοῦ τῇ παροικούσῃ... ('to the church of God that sojourns...') is verbally identical. This suggestion is strengthened by the
use of παρὰ θεοῦ παντοκράτορος ('from God Almighty') which in
1 Clement is ἀπὸ παντοκράτορος θεοῦ and the presence of πληθυνθείη, as
has just been mentioned. Still, the idea of sojourning (the only distinctive word in the salutation) may be based upon similar ideas in 1 Pet 1:1
and 2:11, and could have influenced both *1 Clement* and Polycarp. Influence from 1 Peter would not be a surprise since there is a regular
dependence upon 1 Peter throughout Pol. *Phil.*

Even though similarities such as those listed above exist, the combination of expressions wholly belongs to Polycarp. Therefore, though
he is dependent in a general sense upon conventional Christian practice in the way he forms his greeting, and though he may have been

---

R. Harmer and Michael W. Holmes, trans. and eds., *The Apostolic Fathers: Greek Texts and
English Translations of Their Writings*, 2d ed. (Grand Rapids: Baker Book House, 1992),
though I have at some points modified that translation when I have needed to make the
argument clearer. Where possible I have tried to include an English equivalent to aid
those who are less comfortable in the languages being discussed.

[4] P. N. Harrison, *Polycarp's Two Epistles to the Philippians* (Cambridge: Cambridge
University Press, 1936), 301 suggests Jude 2.

[5] David E. Aune, *The New Testament in its Literary Environment* (Philadelphia: The
Westminster Press, 1987): 185.

[6] William R. Schoedel, *Polycarp, Martyrdom of Polycarp, Fragments of Papias*, vol. 5 of
The Apostolic Fathers: A New Translation and Commentary, ed. Robert M. Grant (Camden,
N.J.: Thomas Nelson & Sons, 1967), 1. Note, however, that Schoedel is in general more
optimistic about dependence upon *1 Clement* by Polycarp throughout the letter than are
other scholars. He comments on p. 5, "Polycarp seems to have been particularly familiar with 1 Clement." This general optimism seems occasionally to influence particulars.

unconsciously influenced by particular expressions found in certain greetings, there is not enough evidence to posit direct dependence upon any particular text, even as regards the salutation of *1 Clement*.

Summary of Salutation: No dependence can be demonstrated.

Pol. Phil. *1.1*

Συνεχάρην ὑμῖν μεγάλως ἐν τῷ κυρίῳ ἡμῶν Ἰησοῦ Χριστῷ, δεξαμένοις τὰ μιμήματα τῆς ἀληθοῦς ἀγάπης καὶ προπέμψασιν, ὡς ἐπέβαλεν ὑμῖν, τοὺς ἐνειλημένους τοῖς ἁγιοπρεπέσιν δεσμοῖς, ἅτινά ἐστιν διαδήματα τῶν ἀληθῶς ὑπὸ θεοῦ καὶ τοῦ κυρίου ἡμῶν ἐκλελεγμένων·

I greatly rejoice with you in our Lord Jesus Christ, because you welcomed the representations of the true love and, as was proper for you, helped on their way those men confined by chains suitable for saints, which are the diadems of those who are truly chosen by God and our Lord;

The phrase Συνεχάρην ὑμῖν μεγάλως ἐν τῷ κυρίῳ ἡμῶν Ἰησοῦ Χριστῷ ('I greatly rejoice with you in our Lord Jesus Christ') appears to allude to similar expressions in Paul's letter to the Philippians.[7] The closest expression is found in the canonical[8] Phil 4:10, Ἐχάρην δὲ ἐν κυρίῳ μεγάλως ὅτι... ('But I rejoiced in the Lord greatly...'). The contexts of both expressions are also similar. Paul is praising/thanking the

---

[7] Many scholars suggest a connection of some sort with Phil 4:10 and 2:17 but many add 'perhaps' or call this 'an echo' of the canonical Philippians. See J. B. Lightfoot, *The Apostolic Fathers: Clement, Ignatius and Polycarp*, 2d ed., part 2, vol. 3 (London: Macmillan and Co., 1890; repr., Peabody, Mass.: Hendrickson Publishers, 1989), 322; P. N. Harrison, *Two Epistles*, 291; James A. Kleist, *The Didache, the Epistle of Barnabas, the Epistles and the Martyrdom of St. Polycarp, the Fragments of Papias, the Epistle to Diognetus*, vol. 6, Ancient Christian Writers, ed. Johannes Quasten and Joseph C. Plumpe (Westminster, Md.: The Newman Press, 1948), 186, n. 5; Walter Bauer, *Die apostolischen Väter II: Die Briefe des Ignatius von Antiochia und der Polykarpbrief* (Tübingen: J.C.B. Mohr [Paul Siebeck], 1920), 285. Barnett comments, "The verbal correspondence between the passages is considerable when Phil. 2:17 and 4:10 are taken together." Albert E. Barnett, *Paul Becomes a Literary Influence* (Chicago: The University of Chicago Press, 1941), 171-172. Robert M. Grant, *The Formation of the New Testament* (New York: Harper & Row, 1965), 103 only mentions 4:10. Édouard Massaux, *The Influence of the Gospel of Saint Matthew on Christian Literature before Saint Irenaeus. Book 2: The Later Christian Writings*, trans. Norman J. Belval and Suzanne Hecht, ed. Arthur J. Bellinzoni (Macon, Ga.: Mercer University Press, 1990), 38 also only mentions 4:10 but considers the dependence probable.

[8] I sometimes employ the term 'canonical' with the letter Paul wrote to the Philippians to distinguish it from the letter Polycarp is writing to the Philippians. It does not mean that Polycarp himself considered Philippians to be 'canonical' in the narrower sense used in the post-Irenaeus period.

Philippians for the renewal of their concern for him and their substantial (financial) help for him during his imprisonment. Polycarp similarly uses this expression to praise/thank the Philippians for their concern and substantial care for the saints (Ignatius and his company) who were in chains on their way to Rome. A contention of dependence is strengthened when we observe that the canonical Phil 2:17 also contains the expression Χαίρω καὶ συγχαίρω πᾶσιν ὑμῖν ('I rejoice and share my joy with you all') followed by Paul's exhortation in 2:18 τὸ δὲ αὐτὸ καὶ ὑμεῖς χαίρετε καὶ συγχαίρετέ μοι ('And you too, rejoice in the same way and share your joy with me'). Paul wants the Philippians not simply to rejoice (χαίρω) but to rejoice together (συγχαίρω) with him. Again, the context is that of sharing in Paul's sufferings. The earlier part of 2:18 makes this clear, "But even if I am being poured out as a drink offering upon the sacrifice and service of your faith..."

This is the first in a long series of loose allusions and reminiscences to Paul's letter to the Philippians. Polycarp, in this letter, does not generally *quote* Paul's Philippians. Nevertheless, perhaps more than with any other letter, a general atmosphere of dependence upon the canonical Philippians seems to be fairly strong when taken as a whole. Grant comments that here Polycarp has begun his letter with a reference "to the particular Pauline epistle which he believes his correspondents value most highly."[9]

There may be a reminiscence of Johannine language in the expression τῆς ἀληθοῦς ἀγάπης ('of the true love'). Both the issues of truth and of love are important for John, both in his gospel and in his letters, as his repetition of related words demonstrates.[10] Nevertheless, the language used by Polycarp is too general and verbal correspondence is lacking. A general dependence upon the language of John is possible but direct dependence cannot be demonstrated. Both Bardsley and Stuckwisch suggest that in general the commendation of the Philippians for welcoming these prisoners is reminiscent of the commendation found in 3 John 5-8 for those who welcomed travelling Christians (probably evangelists).[11] Nevertheless, apart from the concepts of truth and love, there is nothing verbal to connect the passages, and the specific situa-

[9] Grant, *Formation*, 103.
[10] Lightfoot notes John 14:6; 1 John 4:8, 16. Lightfoot, *The Apostolic Fathers*, part 2, vol. 3, 322.
[11] H. J. Bardsley, 'The Testimony of Ignatius and Polycarp to the Writings of St John,' *JTS* 14 (1913): 218; D. Richard Stuckwisch, 'Saint Polycarp of Smyrna: Johannine or Pauline Figure?,' *CTQ* 61 (1997): 120.

tions being addressed are distinct enough that we should probably conclude that a reminiscence of 3 John 5-8 is not present. Again, this does not preclude the possibility of a general influence of Johannine language.

ἁγιοπρεπέσιν δεσμοῖς ('by chains suitable for saints') may be reminiscent of Ign. *Smyrn.* 11:1 θεοπρεπεστάτοις δεσμοῖς ('God-pleasing chains') and perhaps Ign. *Eph.* 11:2 where Ignatius refers to his chains as πνευματικοὺς μαργαρίτας ('spiritual pearls').[12] The connection is strengthened when one considers what Polycarp is discussing in general. He is commending the Philippians for welcoming those in chains – almost certainly a reference to Ignatius and company as they passed through Philippi on their way to martyrdom.[13] The general context supports the suggestion that Polycarp is borrowing his concept from Ignatius. The similarity, though, is primarily conceptual rather than verbal.

The most distinctive word in 1.1 is διαδήματα ('diadems') a word that appears nowhere else in the Apostolic Fathers or in the NT apart from Rev 19:12.[14] The context of Rev 19:12 (where Christ is pictured as sitting on a white horse with diadems on his head) is radically different than Pol. *Phil.* 1.1 (where the chains are the diadems of the martyrs). Literary dependence is unlikely.

Summary of 1.1: A possible allusion to Phil 4:10 and 2:17. Possible dependence upon Johannine language in general. A possible reminiscence of Ign. *Smyrn.* 11:1 and Ign. *Eph.* 11:2.

Pol. Phil. *1.2*

καὶ ὅτι ἡ βεβαία τῆς πίστεως ὑμῶν ῥίζα, ἐξ ἀρχαίων καταγγελλομένη χρόνων, μέχρι νῦν διαμένει καὶ καρποφορεῖ εἰς τὸν κύριον ἡμῶν Ἰησοῦν Χριστόν, ὃς ὑπέμεινεν ὑπὲρ τῶν ἁμαρτιῶν ἡμῶν ἕως θανάτου καταντῆσαι, ὃν ἤγειρεν ὁ θεός λύσας τὰς ὠδῖνας τοῦ ᾅδου.

and because your firmly rooted faith, renowned from the earliest times, still perseveres and bears fruit to our Lord Jesus Christ, who endured for our sins, facing even death, whom God raised up, having loosed the pangs of Hades.

---

[12] Schoedel, *Polycarp*, 8, 10.
[13] Note that Ignatius is mentioned in this connection in 9.1 making this interpretation almost certain.
[14] P. N. Harrison, *Two Epistles*, 305.

Polycarp continues to praise the Philippian church. It is possible that he had some of the Pauline commendations in mind, but such similarities do not demonstrate dependence. Paul commends the Philippian church (4:15) for their faithfulness (unique among the churches) of sharing financially in his work.[15] In Rom 1:8 Paul commends the Romans with the words "because your faith is being proclaimed throughout the whole world."[16] The only conceptual connection with Rom 1:8 is with the word καταγγελλομένη ('renowned'/ 'announced'). Harnack suggests that the commendation here is derived from the description of the spread of the gospel from Thessalonica in 1 Thess 1:7-8.[17] Polycarp, in Harnack's understanding, could apply the description of one Macedonian Christian community to another.[18] Even if we assume Harnack is correct, it is difficult to know how the commendation in Pol. *Phil.* is drawing upon 1 Thess 1:7-8 (even conceptually) apart from the obvious fact that they are both commendations. A final possibility is that the phrase ἐξ ἀρχαίων καταγγελλομένη χρόνων ('renowned from the earliest times') reflects similar language in Acts 15:7 ἀφ᾽ ἡμερῶν ἀρχαίων ('from the early days') or Acts 15:21 ἐκ γενεῶν ἀρχαίων ('from ancient generations').[19] Still, with such a short phrase and since a closer verbal parallel is lacking, dependence is unlikely.

The metaphor of bearing fruit (here, καρποφορεῖ) was widespread by the time of Polycarp, particularly since Jesus used the figure in his parable of the soils (Matt 13:23; Luke 8:15). The same concept is found in Rom 7:4 and Col 1:6.[20] There is no way to demonstrate whether Polycarp had any of these passages in mind. Grant says that "...his mention of their firmly rooted faith (1:2) is probably another echo of

---

[15] Barnett, *Paul*, 172.

[16] P. N. Harrison, *Two Epistles*, 292.

[17] Adolf von Harnack, *Miscellen zu den apostolischen Vätern, den Acta Pauli, Apelles, dem Muratorischen Fragment, den pseudocyprianischen Schriften und Claudianus Marmertus*, TU 2-20/3b (Leipzig: J. C. Hinrichs, 1900), 86-93.

[18] See the discussions of 3.2 and the plural 'letters' and the discussion of 11.3.

[19] Schoedel, *Polycarp*, 8.

[20] Johannes Bapt. Bauer, *Die Polykarpbriefe* (Göttingen: Vandenhoeck & Ruprecht, 1995), 41; Lightfoot comments, "See Col. i.6, which passage Polycarp perhaps had in his mind." Lightfoot, *The Apostolic Fathers*, part 2, vol. 3, 323. Oxford Society of Historical Theology, *The New Testament in the Apostolic Fathers* (Oxford: The Clarendon Press, 1905), 101 notes about Col 1:5-6, "These passages are parallel in thought, but except for the one word καρπφορεῖ there is no verbal connexion between them" and gives it their lowest rating. A dependence here upon Colossians is particularly unlikely in light of the absence of other references to Colossians in Pol. *Phil.*

Philippians 4:15-17."[21] Without any verbal similarities, there is no way to sustain such a suggestion, though it should be admitted that Polycarp is trying to commend the Philippians using much Pauline language throughout and so may have in a general sense alluded to Paul's commendations of the Philippians here.

Christ who endured (ὃς ὑπέμεινεν) suffering and death in this passage, is also the one who endured (ὃς...ὑπέμεινεν) in Heb 12:2.[22] The only verbal connection between the two passages, however, is ὑπέμεινεν preceded by the relative pronoun. Though the terminology of endurance may sound distinctive to our ears, it was not for Polycarp. It was a natural way for him to describe the godly response to suffering (see 8.1, 2; 9.1; 12:2; 13.2). It is not distinctive enough to posit dependence.

The final phrase of the verse ὃν ἤγειρεν ὁ θεός λύσας τὰς ὠδῖνας τοῦ ᾅδου ("whom God raised up, having loosed the pangs of Hades") seems clearly to have been dependent upon Acts 2:24 ὃν ὁ θεὸς ἀνέστησεν λύσας τὰς ὠδῖνας τοῦ θανάτου ("whom God raised up again, having loosed the pangs of death"), though not all agree.[23] The verbal similarities are obvious. The main difference is that Polycarp used the synonym ἤγειρεν for ἀνέστησεν. Note that Acts 3:15 and 4:10 both use ἤγειρεν[24] and it was common to use this verb in reference to God raising Jesus from the dead.

The quotation in Pol. *Phil.* 1.2 from Acts 2:24 follows the Western readings of Acts 2:24 (Codex Bezae, the Latin of Codex Bezae, Coptic

---

[21] Grant, *Formation*, 103.

[22] P. N. Harrison considers this a possible echo. P. N. Harrison, *Two Epistles*, 295-296.

[23] P. N. Harrison, *Two Epistles*, 288-289; Robert M. Grant, 'Polycarp of Smyrna,' *ATR* 28 (1948): 142-143; J. B. Bauer, *Die Polykarpbriefe*, 41; and Lightfoot, *The Apostolic Fathers*, part 2, vol. 3, 323 all agree that this is a quotation of Acts 2:24. Hagner thinks it is inconclusive. Donald Alfred Hagner, 'The Sayings of Jesus in the Apostolic Fathers and Justin Martyr,' in *Gospel Perspectives: The Jesus Tradition Outside the Gospels*, vol. 5, ed. David Wenham (Sheffield: JSOT Press, 1984), 240, 263 n. 38. The Oxford Committee relegates it to a class 'C' which seems overly pessimistic. Knox does not think that Polycarp is at all dependent upon Acts 2:24, citing rather the Oxford Committee's suggestion (Oxford Committee, 98) that the dependence could be on a source for Acts rather than for Acts itself. John Knox, *Marcion and the New Testament: An Essay in the Early History of the Canon* (Chicago: The University of Chicago Press, 1942), 127. Some special pleading is evident, however, since he is trying to argue that Luke-Acts in part was written as a response to Marcionism. Knox's special pleading is seen in the following quote from p. 127: "In view of the fact that this is the one instance of clear connection between Acts and other Christian literature down to Irenaeus (even Justin cannot be proved to have known Acts), I prefer to follow the Oxford Committee in believing that the connection is of this kind."

[24] P. N. Harrison, *Two Epistles*, 288-289.

[Bohairic], Syriac, the Vulgate, Irenaeus 3.12.2) which contain ᾅδου instead of the more common θανάτου.[25]

In Peter's speech in Acts 2 this phrase is followed by a lengthy quotation from David (Acts 2:25-28; Ps 16:8-11) in which appears the phrase ὅτι οὐκ ἐγκαταλείφεις τὴν ψυχήν μου εἰς ᾅδην ("because you will not abandon my soul to Hades," Acts 2:27). A few verses later in Acts 2:31 appears the quotation of Ps 16:10 οὔτε ἐγκατελείφθη εἰς ᾅδην ("nor was he abandoned to Hades"). It seems that in the Western textual tradition, the θανάτου of Acts 2:24 has been harmonized to these later verses resulting in ᾅδου instead of θανάτου. The likelihood that this is what occurred is increased when one remembers that in Ps 18:5 (MT 18:6; LXX 17:6) appears the phrase חבלי־שאול = ὠδῖνες ᾅδου ('the cords of Sheol/Hades') whereas the previous verse had חבלי־מות = ὠδῖνες θανάτου and could have been an additional influence upon a copyist of Acts 2.[26]

Assuming then from internal considerations that θανάτου rather than ᾅδου is original, and in light of Polycarp's early date, the question must be asked whether Polycarp was influenced by an early Western reading of Acts 2:24 or whether Polycarp himself might have been responsible for the harmonization of this verse with the later verses (and thus brought about the change from θανάτου to ᾅδου, thereby influencing the Western textual tradition). Either is possible, though we should probably prefer the first; in general it is safer to assume that someone would transmit an error than to assume that they are the original source of the error. It only takes one person to contaminate an entire manuscript tradition, whereas many persons will carry such an error forward when they copy it.

That Polycarp is actually dependent upon Peter's speech in Acts 2 is supported by the juxtaposition of this phrase with the quotation from 1 Pet 1:8 that follows immediately.[27] It seems quite likely that Polycarp is bringing together phrases that he considers to belong together since in his thinking the source of both is Peter.

Finally, it will be argued later that Polycarp follows Luke rather than

---

[25] UBS 4th rev. ed. categorizes θανάτου in Acts 2:24 as an 'A' reading – almost certain.

[26] See comments in Schoedel, *Polycarp*, 8. Note, in addition to Ps 18, Ps 116:3 and 2 Sam 22:6. Lightfoot comments that in the LXX "ὠδῖνες being a mistranslation of the ambiguous Hebrew חבלי, which differently vocalized means 'pains' or 'fetters'." Lightfoot, *The Apostolic Fathers*, part 2, vol. 3, 323.

[27] J. B. Bauer, *Die Polykarpbriefe*, 41; Schoedel, *Polycarp*, 8.

Matthew in some instances. The use of Luke by Polycarp supports the contention that Polycarp is dependent upon Acts here.

If Polycarp is in fact dependent upon Acts 2:24, the fact that he is using Acts is really quite remarkable. In this case, he not only knows and uses Acts, but knows it from a variant textual tradition. If Polycarp wrote c. 120 C.E., the date for the composition of Acts would have to be early enough both for Polycarp to use it and for him to use it from a variant textual tradition.

Summary of 1.2: A possible reminiscence of Paul's many commendations to the Philippian church. An almost certain loose citation of Acts 2:24 from the Western textual tradition.

Pol. Phil. *1.3*

εἰς ὃν οὐκ ἰδόντες πιστεύετε χαρᾷ ἀνεκλαλήτῳ καὶ δεδοξασμένῃ εἰς ἣν πολλοὶ ἐπιθυμοῦσιν εἰσελθεῖν, εἰδότες ὅτι χάριτί ἐστε σεσωσμένοι, οὐκ ἐξ ἔργων, ἀλλὰ θελήματι θεοῦ διὰ Ἰησοῦ Χριστοῦ.

Though you have not seen him, you believe in him with an inexpressible and glorious joy (which many desire to experience), knowing that by grace you have been saved, not because of works, but by the will of God through Jesus Christ.

The first phrase εἰς ὃν οὐκ ἰδόντες πιστεύετε χαρᾷ ἀνεκλαλήτῳ καὶ δεδοξασμένῃ (lit. "into whom not seeing you believe with inexpressible and glorious joy") is clearly a citation of 1 Pet 1:8 ὃν οὐκ ἰδόντες ἀγαπᾶτε, εἰς ὃν ἄρτι μὴ ὁρῶντες πιστεύοντες δὲ ἀγαλλιᾶσθε χαρᾷ ἀνεκλαλήτῳ καὶ δεδοξασμένῃ (lit. "whom not seeing you love, in whom not seeing now but believing you rejoice with inexpressible and glorious joy"). Massaux comments, "The literary contact is definite: the idea is absolutely similar, the terms are practically identical; Polycarp simply omitted a few."[28] Polycarp is almost certainly dependent upon 1 Peter here .

The second phrase εἰς ἣν πολλοὶ ἐπιθυμοῦσιν εἰσελθεῖν (lit. "into which many desire to enter") is probably drawn again from 1 Peter where only a few verses later Peter writes εἰς ἃ ἐπιθυμοῦσιν ἄγγελοι παρακύψαι ("into which angels desire to look," 1 Pet 1:12). This is not nearly so exact as the quotation from 1 Pet 1:8 just preceding. Nevertheless, it is probable that Polycarp is alluding to 1 Pet 1:12, at least for

---

[28] Massaux, *Influence*, 42.

the *form* of the quotation.[29] It follows immediately on the heals of an almost certain quotation of 1 Pet 1:8 which follows immediately the almost certain quotation of Peter's speech in Acts 2:24. In addition, the near proximity of 1 Pet 1:12 to 1 Pet 1:8 argues that the phrase Polycarp uses here (at least in form) is influenced by the progression in 1 Peter.

Nevertheless, the *content* of the phrase is reminiscent of sayings of Jesus. The 'desire' (found both in Pol. *Phil.* 1.3 and 1 Pet 1:12) 'to see' (found only in 1 Pet 1:12) by 'many' (found only in Pol. *Phil.* 1.3) could have been suggested by Jesus' teaching that many ('righteous men' Matt 13:17, 'prophets and kings' Luke 10:2) desired to see (and hear) what the listeners of Jesus saw (and heard) but did not have the opportunity.[30] Equally likely is the suggestion that the 'enter' and the 'into the joy' (the referent of the relative pronoun in Pol. *Phil.* 1.3 is χαρᾷ) and the general suggestion of desire to enter is reminiscent of the phrase found in Matt 25:21, 23, "Well done, good and faithful slave...enter into the joy of your master."[31]

There is no evidence of Polycarp working from a tcxt here (or anywhere in his letter). He evinces a thorough familiarity with the teaching of the Lord, though there is no clear evidence in this case whether it has been mediated through the oral tradition or through written documents. The form of the phrase is from 1 Pet 1:12 but the content of the phrase represents the teaching of the Lord.

Finally, we come to a quite clear adapted citation from Eph 2 εἰδότες ὅτι χάριτί ἐστε σεσῳσμένοι, οὐκ ἐξ ἔργων, ἀλλὰ θελήματι θεοῦ διὰ Ἰησοῦ Χριστοῦ ("knowing that by grace you have been saved, not because of works, but by the will of God through our Lord Jesus Christ.") It is introduced by the formula εἰδότες ὅτι. This citation formula appears here (1.3) and again in Pol. *Phil.* 4.1 and 5.1 before quotations of phrases found in our NT. It also appears in 6.1, though the source of that quotation is not clear.

The first line of the quotation found here parallels exactly Eph 2:5b χάριτί ἐστε σεσῳσμένοι ("by grace you have been saved") and Eph 2:8 τῇ γὰρ χάριτί ἐστε σεσῳσμένοι ("for by grace you have been saved").

---

[29] "Structurally an adaptation of 1 Pet 1:12, but the content is reminiscent of Matt. 25:21, 23." Schoedel, *Polycarp*, 9. Also Massaux, *Influence*, 42.

[30] "It would be suggested by Matt. xiii.17, Luke x.24." Lightfoot, *The Apostolic Fathers*, part 2, vol. 3, 323. The Oxford Society seems overly cautious, "There is no reason to suppose that the parallel here is more than accidental." Oxford Society, 103.

[31] Schoedel, *Polycarp*, 9. J. B. Bauer suggests the possible influence of 1 Pet 1:12, Matt 25:21, 23 and Matt 13:17 and comments, "...dem Verfasser analoge Texte im Gedächtnis zussamenfließen." J. B. Bauer *Die Polykarpbriefe*, 41-42.

The second line of the quotation continues with the context of Eph 2:8-9 which reads τῇ γὰρ χάριτί ἐστε σεσωσμένοι διὰ πίστεως· καὶ τοῦτο οὐκ ἐξ ὑμῶν, θεοῦ τὸ δῶρον· οὐκ ἐξ ἔργων, ἵνα μή τις καυχήσηται ("for by grace you have been saved through faith, and this not of yourselves, it is a gift of God, not of works that no one should boast"). Though Polycarp skips two of the middle phrases in Eph 2:8 (καὶ τοῦτο οὐκ ἐξ ὑμῶν, θεοῦ τὸ δῶρον "and this not of yourselves, it is a gift of God"), the following phrase οὐκ ἐξ ἔργων ("not of works") is exactly parallel to the same expression in Eph 2:9. Not only are these phrases identical to those found in Eph 2:5, 8, 9 but they function adequately as a summary of the intent of Paul's thought. That Polycarp is dependent upon Ephesians directly rather than upon an oral tradition originating with Paul[32] is supported by Polycarp's probable dependence on Eph 4:26 in Pol. *Phil.* 12.1.

Rensberger notes that even though the general idea of salvation by grace is already found in Jewish texts such as Dan 9:18, the verbal resemblance is such that it is highly likely that Polycarp is directly influenced by Ephesians 2.[33]

The final phrase of 1.3 ἀλλὰ θελήματι θεοῦ διὰ Ἰησοῦ Χριστοῦ ("but by the will of God through Jesus Christ") should probably be accounted for by looking at the general context of Ephesians 2 even though outside parallels exist. Almost the same expression (ἐν τῷ θελήματι τοῦ θεοῦ) appears in Rom 1:10.[34] The identical phrase ἀλλὰ θελήματι θεοῦ appears in 1 Pet 4:2. But this expression is such a stock phrase that the connection with Rom 1:10 or 1 Pet 4:2 probably should not be made.[35] Barnett notes, "All that he [Polycarp] says can be accounted for from the Ephesian passage."[36]

---

[32] Lindemann says it is possible that 1.3 does not cite Paul directly but draws on an oral tradition which was understood to have come from Paul. Andreas Lindemann, 'Paul in the Writings of the Apostolic Fathers,' in *Paul and the Legacies of Paul*, ed. William S. Babcock (Dallas: Southern Methodist University Press, 1990), 43. The support of dependence upon Ephesians 2 is very strong including (but not limited to) Grant, 'Polycarp of Smyrna,' 143; Massaux, *Influence*, 35; Hans von Campenhausen, 'Polykarp von Smyrna und die Pastoralbriefe,' chap. in *Aus der Frühzeit des Christentums: Studien zur Kirchengeschichte des ersten und zweiten Jahrhunderts* (Tübingen: J. C. B. Mohr [Paul Siebeck], 1963), 242 (though I do not agree with his negative assessment in the same sentence of Polycarp's dependence upon the Pastoral Epistles); Lightfoot, *The Apostolic Fathers*, part 2, vol. 3, 324.

[33] David K. Rensberger, 'As the Apostle Teaches: The Development of the Use of Paul's Letters in Second-Century Christianity,' (Ph.D. diss., Yale University, 1981), 115.

[34] P. N. Harrison, *Two Epistles*, 292.

[35] J. B. Bauer, *Die Polykarpbriefe*, 42, 44.

[36] Barnett, *Paul*, 173.

Summary of 1.3: An almost certain loose citation of 1 Pet 1:8. A probable allusion to 1 Pet 1:12 in form but influenced in content from the sayings of the Lord (as represented by Matt 13:17; Luke 10:2 and Matt 25:21, 23). An almost certain true (though compressed) citation of Eph 2:5, 8, 9.

Pol. Phil. *2.1*

Διὸ ἀναζωσάμενοι τὰς ὀσφύας δουλεύσατε τῷ θεῷ ἐν φόβῳ καὶ ἀληθείᾳ, ἀπολιπόντες τὴν κενὴν ματαιολογίαν καὶ τὴν τῶν πολλῶν πλάνην, πιστεύσαντες εἰς τὸν ἐγείραντα τὸν κύριον ἡμῶν Ἰησοῦν Χριστὸν ἐκ νεκρῶν καὶ δόντα αὐτῷ δόξαν καὶ θρόνον ἐκ δεξιῶν αὐτοῦ· ᾧ ὑπετάγη τὰ πάντα ἐπουράνια καὶ ἐπίγεια, ᾧ πᾶσα πνοὴ λατρεύει, ὃς ἔρχεται κριτὴς ζώντων καὶ νεκρῶν, οὗ τὸ αἷμα ἐκζητήσει ὁ θεὸς ἀπὸ τῶν ἀπειθούντων αὐτῷ.

Therefore prepare for action and serve God in fear and truth, leaving behind the empty and meaningless talk and the error of the crowd, and believing in him who raised our Lord Jesus Christ from the dead and gave him glory and a throne at his right hand; to whom all things in heaven and on earth were subjected, whom every breathing creature serves, who is coming as Judge of the living and the dead, for whose blood God will hold responsible those who disobey him.

Hanson sees in 2.1 a string of phrases which represented early Christian creedal teaching, at least in content if not also in form.[37] This section at the least provides a small window into some of the elements in the doctrinal system of at least some Christian groups in the early part of the second century.

The first phrase Διὸ ἀναζωσάμενοι τὰς ὀσφύας ("Therefore, girding up the loins") is in wording and form exactly the same as the clause in 1 Pet 1:13. That it is probably dependent upon 1 Peter is supported by the following considerations. It includes the conjunction διό along with the rest of the clause instead of another conjunction. In Pol. *Phil.* it follows soon after a phrase which has earlier been argued is in form dependent upon 1 Pet 1:12 and which itself follows a quite clear citation of 1 Pet 1:8. In 1 Pet 1:13 the phrase Διὸ ἀναζωσάμενοι τὰς ὀσφύας ("Therefore girding up the loins") is followed by τῆς διανοίας ὑμῶν ("of your mind"). 1 Peter's additional phrase is best explained as being unneeded by Polycarp who assumes that his readers are familiar with this commonplace expression and know the rest of the verse. The connec-

_____
[37] R. P. C. Hanson, *Tradition in the Early Church* (Philadelphia: The Westminster Press, 1962), 54-55.

tion with the return of the Lord is found particularly in 1 Pet 1:13. Finally, it will be argued below that it is followed only a few phrases later by a quotation from 1 Pet 1:21.

Another possibility is Eph 6:14 which contains the expression περιζωσάμενοι τὴν ὀσφὺν ὑμῶν ἐν ἀληθείᾳ ("having girded your loins with truth").[38] Though verbally not as exact as the expression in 1 Pet 1:13, Eph 6:14 has the advantage of combining the concept of girding up loins with the word ἀληθείᾳ, which is found in the same sentence in Pol. *Phil.* 2.1. It should also be noted that Ephesians has just been cited (Eph 2:5, 8, 9) and is as much on Polycarp's mind as is 1 Peter. Thus, though the form is probably dependent upon 1 Pet 1:13, an allusion to Eph 6:14 is also possible.

The rest of the same sentence contains the phrase δουλεύσατε τῷ θεῷ ἐν φόβῳ καὶ ἀληθείᾳ ("serve God in fear and truth"). It may be dependent upon Ps 2:11 (δουλεύσατε τῷ κυρίῳ ἐν φόβῳ "serve the Lord in fear," cf. עבדו את־יהוה ביראה).[39] It is verbally parallel to the form of the phrase in the Greek of Ps 2:11 except for the use of θεῷ by Polycarp instead of κυρίῳ. It has been suggested that Polycarp's use of Ps 2:11 is mediated through *1 Clem.* 19:1.[40] The difficulty is that it is not easy to argue that *1 Clement*'s brief expression ἐν φόβῳ καὶ ἀληθείᾳ ("in fear and truth") which has no other verbal or conceptual connection to Ps 2:11 is dependent upon Ps 2:11. A better solution for Pol. *Phil.* 2.1 is that Polycarp is drawing directly upon the phrase in Ps 2:11 and adding καὶ ἀληθείᾳ because of the conceptual connection to Eph 6:14 as has just been argued. Polycarp's dependence upon Ps 2:11 should not only be judged possible, but probable in light of what appears to be an additional employment of the same passage by Polycarp in 6.3.[41]

The next phrase ἀπολιπόντες τὴν κενὴν ματαιολογίαν καὶ τὴν τῶν πολλῶν πλάνην ("leaving behind the empty and meaningless talk and the error of the crowd") contains the distinctive word ματαιολογίαν. Since it only occurs in that form in 1 Tim 1:6 (cf. Tit 1:10) among the writings of the NT and the Apostolic Fathers, one might be tempted to posit some sort of connection. Still, unless a word is highly unusual, it is

---

[38] The phrase in Eph 6:14 may very well have been dependent upon Isa 11:5.

[39] Lightfoot, *The Apostolic Fathers*, part 2, vol. 3, 324; W. Bauer, *Die apostolischen Väter II*, 286; W. Sanday, *The Gospels in the Second Century* (London: Macmillan and Co., 1876), 36; Charles William McNatt, 'An Investigation of Old Testament Usage in the Pastoral Epistles and Selected Apostolic Fathers,' (Ph.D. diss., Southwestern Baptist Theological Seminary, 1972), 141-144.

[40] P. N. Harrison, *Two Epistles*, 329; McNatt, 'Old Testament Usage,' 142.

[41] Lightfoot, *The Apostolic Fathers*, part 2, vol. 3, 333.

precarious to posit dependence based upon a single word.[42]

The following phrases πιστεύσαντες εἰς τὸν ἐγείραντα τὸν κύριον ἡμῶν Ἰησοῦν Χριστὸν ἐκ νεκρῶν καὶ δόντα αὐτῷ δόξαν καὶ θρόνον ἐκ δεξιῶν αὐτοῦ ("believing in the one who raised our Lord Jesus Christ from the dead and gave him glory and a throne at his right hand") appears to contain a loose citation of 1 Pet 1:21. 1 Pet 1:21 reads τοὺς δι᾽ αὐτοῦ πιστοὺς εἰς θεὸν τὸν ἐγείραντα αὐτὸν ἐκ νεκρῶν καὶ δόξαν αὐτῷ δόντα, ὥστε τὴν πίστιν ὑμῶν καὶ ἐλπίδα εἶναι εἰς θεόν ("who through him are believers in God, who raised him from the dead and gave him glory, so that your faith and hope are in God"). In Pol. *Phil.* 2.1 the phrase as it is found in 1 Peter has been modified to the context and syntax of Polycarp's sentence. Thus, instead of 1 Peter's noun πιστοὺς Polycarp uses the aorist participle πιστεύσαντες. Instead of 1 Peter's pronoun αὐτὸν Polycarp writes τὸν κύριον ἡμῶν Ἰησοῦν Χριστὸν. Polycarp needs to make these changes to preserve the flow and clarity of the text. Otherwise the phrases εἰς τὸν ἐγείραντα and ἐκ νεκρῶν καὶ δόντα αὐτῷ δόξαν are verbally the same. If one might be tempted to attribute the earlier parts of this sentence to conventional Christian usage, the inclusion of καὶ δόντα αὐτῷ δόξαν makes it difficult to imagine that Polycarp's phraseology is drawn from anywhere but 1 Pet 1:21.[43]

Concerning καὶ θρόνον Lightfoot writes, "The addition καὶ θρόνον is perhaps suggested by Clem. Rom 59 (65) δόξα...θρόνος αἰώνιος."[44] There is no way to demonstrate this. The view that this addition is Polycarp's own seems preferable.

The concept of right hand is derived primarily in Christian thought from Ps 110:1 which is frequently referred to in the NT. By the time of Polycarp, the terminology and concept was so wide-spread that a direct reminiscence of that passage should not be assumed.

Next in Pol. *Phil.* 2.1 is the clause ᾧ ὑπετάγη τὰ πάντα ἐπουράνια καὶ ἐπίγεια ("to whom all things in heaven and on earth were subjected"). Though there is a slightly closer parallel in the form of 1 Cor 15:28

---

[42] Lightfoot comments, "The word occurs in I Tim. i.6, and the corresponding adjective ματαιολόγος in Tit. i.10. It is not improbable that Polycarp is here quoting Clem. Rom. 9 ἀπολιπόντες τὴν ματαιοπονίαν κ.τ.λ.... If so we should perhaps read ματαιοπονίαν here." Lightfoot, *The Apostolic Fathers*, part 2, vol. 3, 324. If Lightfoot is arguing that we should read Polycarp's text based upon the form in *1 Clement* it seems like a precarious suggestion. His suggestion that Polycarp is in some sense quoting *1 Clement* is possible but seems impossible to demonstrate.

[43] Massaux, *Influence*, 43; Kleist, *The Didache...*, 187, n. 16; Schoedel, *Polycarp*, 10; Oxford Society, 87-88.

[44] Lightfoot, *The Apostolic Fathers*, part 2, vol. 3, 324.

ὅταν δὲ ὑποταγῇ αὐτῷ τὰ πάντα ("but when all things are subjected to him") there is reason to think that an allusion to Paul's letter to the Philippians may be present. The canonical Phil 3:21 κατὰ τὴν ἐνέργειαν τοῦ δύνασθαι αὐτὸν καὶ ὑποταξαι αὐτῷ τὰ πάντα ("by the exertion of his power even to subject all things to himself") contains the subjection of everything to Christ. This, combined with the presence of ἐπουρανίων καὶ ἐπιγείων ("of those in heaven and on earth") in Phil 2:10 (ἵνα ἐν τῷ ὀνόματι Ἰησοῦ πᾶν γόνυ κάμψῃ ἐπουρανίων καὶ ἐπιγείων καὶ καταχθονίων, "that at the name of Jesus every knee should bow, of those in heaven and on earth and under the earth") points toward possible dependence upon the canonical Philippians by Polycarp rather than dependence upon 1 Cor 15:28. Dependence upon Philippians is supported by the regular allusions and reminiscences to that letter throughout Pol. *Phil.* Polycarp's phrase also looks at the subjection of everything to Christ from the perspective of an accomplished fact, a perspective more closely paralleled by Philippians than by 1 Cor 15:28. One could argue that both 1 Cor 15:28 *and* Phil 3:21 and 2:10 lie behind Polycarp's clause,[45] but dependence upon Philippians alone seems more likely.

In the phrase ᾧ πᾶσα πνοὴ λατρεύει ("whom every breathing thing serves") there may be allusions to 1 Kings 15:29, Ps 150:6(5) and/or Isa 57:16[46] but these are inconclusive.

The phrase ὃς ἔρχεται κριτὴς ζώντων καὶ νεκρῶν ("who is coming as judge of the living and the dead") is verbally and conceptually parallel to Acts 10:42 οὗτός ἐστιν ὁ ὡρισμένος ὑπὸ τοῦ θεοῦ κριτὴς ζώντων καὶ νεκρῶν ("this is the one who has been appointed by God as judge of the living and the dead"). The phrase κριτὴς ζώντων καὶ νεκρῶν is identical in both. Nevertheless, because this phrase is such a conventional phrase,[47] the likelihood that it is directly influenced by Acts 10:42 cannot be judged as being any more than possible.[48]

---

[45] Most who accept dependence consider this a conflation of 1 Cor 15:28, Phil 2:10 and Phil 3:21. See for example Barnett, *Paul*, 173; Lightfoot, *The Apostolic Fathers*, part 2, vol. 3, 325; P. N. Harrison, *Two Epistles*, 292. Oxford Society seems overly cautious according the possibility of dependence on 1 Cor 15:28 an A,d rating (A=knowledge of 1 Corinthians is certain, d=dependence on 1 Cor 15:28 very unlikely) and on Phil 2:10; 3:21 a B,c rating (B=knowledge of Philippians is probable, c=dependence on Phil 2:10; 3:21 is unlikely) but adds the comment, "As the context in Polycarp shows clearly that the passage refers to Christ, it is likely that he is dependent on Philippians." So why did this passage get a 'c' rating if is 'is likely'?
[46] Kleist, *The Didache...* 187 n. 18; Lightfoot, *The Apostolic Fathers*, part 2, vol. 3, 325.
[47] Note similar phrases in 2 Tim 4:1; 1 Pet 4:5 and *2 Clem* 1.1.
[48] Many scholars agree with this assessment, for example Hagner, 'The Sayings of

The final phrase of Pol. *Phil.* 2.1 οὗ τὸ αἷμα ἐκζητήσει ὁ θεὸς ἀπὸ τῶν ἀπειθούντων αὐτῷ ("for whose blood God will hold responsible those who disobey him") contains no part which demonstrably can be linked with an earlier text. Similar wording and the concept of God holding someone responsible for another's 'blood' are common. Note in this regard Ezek 3:18, 20; 33:6, 8; Gen 42:22; 2 Sam 4:11; Luke 11:50, 51. Polycarp is probably in a general sense dependent upon biblical phraseology, though no particular text can be shown to have given rise to his use of the concept here.[49]

Summary of 2.1: A probable allusion to 1 Pet 1:13 combined with a possible allusion to Eph 6:14. A probable allusion to Ps 2:11. A probable loose citation of 1 Pet 1:21. A possible allusion to Phil 3:21 and 2:10. A possible allusion to Acts 10:42.

Pol. Phil. 2.2

ὁ δὲ ἐγείρας αὐτὸν ἐκ νεκρῶν καὶ ἡμᾶς ἐγερεῖ, ἐὰν ποιῶμεν αὐτοῦ τὸ θέλημα καὶ πορευώμεθα ἐν ταῖς ἐντολαῖς αὐτοῦ καὶ ἀγαπῶμεν ἃ ἠγάπησεν, ἀπεχόμενοι πάσης ἀδικίας, πλεονεξίας, φιλαργυρίας, καταλαλιᾶς, ψευδομαρτυρίας· μὴ ἀποδιδόντες κακὸν ἀντὶ κακοῦ ἢ λοιδορίαν ἀντὶ λοιδορίας ἢ γρόνθον ἀντὶ γρόνθου ἢ κατάραν ἀντὶ κατάρας.

But he who raised him from the dead will raise us also, if we do his will and follow his commandments and love the things he loved, while avoiding every kind of unrighteousness, greed, love of money, slander and false testimony; not repaying evil for evil or insult for insult or blow for blow or curse for curse.

The first clause of 2.2 ὁ δὲ ἐγείρας αὐτὸν ἐκ νεκρῶν καὶ ἡμᾶς ἐγερεῖ ("but he who raised him from the dead also will raise us") is possibly a loose citation of 2 Cor 4:14 εἰδότες ὅτι ὁ ἐγείρας τὸν κύριον Ἰησοῦν καὶ ἡμᾶς σὺν Ἰησοῦ ἐγερεῖ... ("knowing that he who raised the Lord Jesus will raise us also with Jesus..."). Though some would argue dependence upon 2 Cor 4:14 is probable,[50] it seems difficult to argue for more than

---

Jesus,' 240, 263 n. 38; Massaux, *Influence*, 35; Schoedel, *Polycarp*, 11. Lightfoot considers it a quotation. Lightfoot, *The Apostolic Fathers*, part 2, vol. 3, 325.

[49] McNatt is convinced that dependence upon the LXX form of Ezek 3:18 is present, but provides no rationale. McNatt, 'Old Testament Usage,' 142-143.

[50] Some scholars are fairly confident that a loose citation exists, for example: Barnett, *Paul*, 173; Oxford Society, 91; Massaux, *Influence*, 35-36; Schoedel, *Polycarp*, 11; Lightfoot, *The Apostolic Fathers*, part 2, vol. 3, 325. Others like me seem less certain, W. Bauer, *Die apostolischen Väter II*, 286; Kleist, *The Didache...*, 187 n. 20. Grant also is unsure and thinks that perhaps it is derived from the oral tradition, Grant, 'Polycarp of Smyrna,' 143.

possible dependence for the following reasons: 1) If Polycarp has adapted 2 Cor 4:14, he has not included Paul's εἰδότες ὅτι ('knowing that') even though it is an introductory formula Polycarp likes to use (1.3; 4.1; 5.1; 6.1). Certainly there are differences between the two passages (Paul is giving a reason, whereas Polycarp uses it in a conditional sentence), but Polycarp could have incorporated it. 2) Paul employs τὸν κύριον Ἰησοῦν as the object of the participle whereas Polycarp employs the pronoun αὐτὸν. 3) Polycarp's form includes the prepositional phrase ἐκ νεκρῶν. 4) Paul's σὺν Ἰησοῦ is not present in Polycarp. 5) Moreover, the idea is paralleled by such passages as 1 Cor 6:14 and Rom 8:11. In light of these considerations and since the content is conventional, no more than possible dependence on 2 Cor 4:14 can be suggested. The best argument for literary dependence on 2 Cor 4:14 is the somewhat striking repetition by Polycarp of καὶ ἡμᾶς.[51]

The middle section of 2.2 has a conditional clause which includes Christian virtues and vices ἐὰν ποιῶμεν αὐτοῦ τὸ θέλημα καὶ πορευώμεθα ἐν ταῖς ἐντολαῖς αὐτοῦ καὶ ἀγαπῶμεν ἃ ἠγάπησεν, ἀπεχόμενοι πάσης ἀδικίας, πλεονεξίας, φιλαργυρίας, καταλαλιᾶς, ψευδομαρτυρίας ("if we do his will and follow his commandments and love the things he loved, while avoiding every kind of unrighteousness, greed, love of money, slander and false testimony"). The structure of these and the following phrases is rhythmic, at times even rhyming when the five genitive feminine singular nouns are listed together. This suggests either that Polycarp received this in a form suitable for memorization or organized it himself into such a form. Direct dependence of any particular word or phrase cannot be demonstrated.

Bardsley, following Stanton, has suggested that "if we do his will and follow his commandments and love the things he loved" is generally dependent upon Johannine language.[52] This suggestion may be correct but is impossible to demonstrate. There may be enough resemblance to Johannine language here, though, to call into question a contention that Polycarp shows *no* evidence of contact with the Johannine tradition.

Schoedel has suggested that the vice list found here is reminiscent of *1 Clem.* 35:5.[53] That they are both vice lists no one will deny. That

---

[51] Massaux, *Influence*, 35-36.
[52] Bardsley, 'Testimony,' 218. "Do his will" (John 7:17, also 1 John 2:17); "If you love me, keep my commandments" (John 14:15); "Walk as he walked" (1 John 2:6).
[53] Schoedel, *Polycarp*, 12.

Polycarp's list is reminiscent of that particular vice list, which is considerably longer and has only occasional similarities, is not at all obvious.

Polycarp's use of ἀπεχόμενοι makes one think of Job, who is repeatedly described as abstaining from evil (Job 1:1, 8 and 2:3, with the singular ἀπεχόμενος). But one word usually is not strong enough evidence for a literary connection.[54]

The final clause of 2.2 is μὴ ἀποδιδόντες κακὸν ἀντὶ κακοῦ ἢ λοιδορίαν ἀντὶ λοιδορίας ἢ γρόνθον ἀντὶ γρόνθου ἢ κατάραν ἀντὶ κατάρας ("not repaying evil for evil or insult for insult or blow for blow or curse for curse"). The first part of this is an almost certain true citation of 1 Pet 3:9 which reads μὴ ἀποδιδόντες κακὸν ἀντὶ κακοῦ ἢ λοιδορίαν ἀντὶ λοιδορίας.[55] This phrase is identical in Pol. *Phil.* 2.2 and in 1 Pet 3:9.

Harrison suggests that perhaps the following 'blow' (γρόνθος) was drawn from Aquila's Greek version of Exod 21:18.[56] Harrison, it appears, was searching to find another argument for a later date for the composition of Pol. *Phil.* (namely, the fourth decade of the second century). If dependence upon Aquila's version could be demonstrated, it would support his case for a later date. Unfortunately, a single word does not a dependence make, particularly in light of Schoedel's suggestion. Schoedel suggests that it is more likely that Polycarp adapts into 'daily speech' the teaching found in Matt 5:39 and Luke 6:28-29, and considers direct dependence upon the Lukan version a serious possibility.[57] Jesus teaches that if someone hits you (τύπτω in Luke 6:29; ῥαπίζω in Matt 5:39, both verbally dissimilar to Pol. *Phil.* 2.2) on the cheek, you should turn to him the other. The previous verse in the Lukan account (6:28), however, says "bless those who curse you" (καταράομαι, as in Polycarp's second addition ἢ κατάραν ἀντὶ κατάρας), and "pray for those who mistreat you." That a reminiscence of the Lord's teaching is present here is supported by Polycarp's immediate move to the teaching of the

---

[54] Polycarp's repetition of the encouragement to abstain from all evil (2.2; 5.3; 6.1, 3) is understood by Harrison to perhaps be dependent upon 1 Thess 4:3 and 5:22, though he knows this is tentative. P. N. Harrison, *Two Epistles*, 293. This is particularly a problem in light of the lack of other supporting references to 1 Thessalonians in Pol. *Phil.*

[55] That this is a quotation of 1 Peter has gained almost universal support, for example, J. B. Bauer, *Die Polykarpbriefe*, 44; Lightfoot, *The Apostolic Fathers*, part 2, vol. 3, 325; Schoedel, *Polycarp*, 12; Oxford Society, 88, though the Oxford Society comments after giving it an A, b rating, "This is almost certainly a quotation from I Peter, but the possibility cannot be excluded that both Polycarp and I Peter are quoting a proverb in the part common to them."

[56] P. N. Harrison, *Two Epistles*, 171.

[57] Schoedel, *Polycarp*, 13.

Lord in the next sentence. There is no way to tell from this particular phrase whether this reminiscence of the Lord's teaching is mediated through a written gospel (such as Luke) or through the oral tradition. The juxtaposition of the striking-on-the-cheek saying with the blessing-those-who-curse-you saying in Luke does not necessarily argue for dependence upon Luke since the two sayings were likely preserved together at some points in the oral tradition. Nevertheless, that a probable dependence upon the teaching of the Lord is present is more likely than that these additions were "of his [Polycarp's] own invention."[58]

Summary of 2.2: A possible loose citation of 2 Cor 4:14. An almost certain true citation of 1 Pet 3:9. A probable reminiscence of the Lord's teaching such as is found in Luke 6:28-29 and Matt 5:39, but whether through an oral or written medium is unclear.

Excursus: Written Gospels and Oral Tradition

The question of dependence on the sayings of the Lord came to the surface in our discussion of 2.2. In 2.3 Polycarp refers to the teachings of the Lord explicitly and then lists quite a few. Before an analysis of that section, a brief discussion of the nature of the Dominical oral tradition in the early parts of the second century seems appropriate.

Polycarp seems to have lived in a period of transition. He lived in a time when the oral tradition was still highly regarded.[59] Much of the evidence from antiquity has shown that in most ancient societies the oral word was often more highly valued than written documents.[60] That this attitude was displayed at many points in the developing church should not be a surprise. At the same time, the written gospels were becoming more and more influential, though regional differences surely existed.

Helmut Koester is usually associated with the view that knowledge

---

[58] Massaux, *Influence*, 43.

[59] The example of Papias's preference for the 'abiding voice' has already been given (Eusebius, *H.E.* 3.39). Stonehouse has shown that although Papias did in fact have this high regard for the oral traditions, it does *not* mean that he depreciated written gospels. It is not a necessary inference. N. B. Stonehouse, 'The Authority of the New Testament,' in *The Infallible Word*, ed. N. B. Stonehouse and Paul Wooley (Philadelphia: Presbyterian and Reformed Publishing Company, 1946), 130-132.

[60] There was, in Gerhardsson's words, "an attitude of scepticism to the written word." Birger Gerhardsson, *Memory and Manuscript: Oral Tradition and Written Transmission in Rabbinic Judaism and Early Christianity*, trans. Eric J. Sharpe (Uppsala: Almqvist & Wiksells, 1961), 196-197.

of the written Gospels cannot be proven in the Apostolic Fathers; rather, the words of Jesus are often mediated orally.[61] He has been followed by many scholars.[62] Koester also argues for the independence of many of the sayings of Jesus in the Apostolic Fathers (i.e. 'agrapha'). Nevertheless, even Koester thinks that in Polycarp's letter there is evidence of the influence of the written gospels (in particular Matthew and Luke) during a period when orality was still important.[63] Still, we must constantly remind ourselves that the emergence of written gospels did not immediately supplant the value placed upon the tradition passed down in oral form. Thus, it is often difficult to know whether a written gospel or a saying mediated orally (if not both) is being used by a writer in Polycarp's time in a given instance.[64]

This does not mean that the oral tradition was unstable (a common assumption).[65] Kenneth Bailey has presented a model that argues both that the oral traditions were handed down informally *and* that they were still quite stable. His model is formed out of comparisons with modern oral traditions as they are passed around pre-literate cultures in the Middle East today.[66] His view is that some oral traditions in such cultures are *controlled* (i.e. quickly receiving a fixed form) but that they are also often *informal* (i.e. protected more by shared consensus than even by an authoritative body assigned to protect the tradition).[67] He gives a number of telling examples of how traditions become quickly fixed and are protected by unwritten rules governing such traditions in oral cultures. This can be contrasted to form-critical approaches which view the oral traditions as *informal* but largely *uncontrolled*. It can also be contrasted to the view of Birger Gerhardsson who understands them to be

---

[61] Helmut Koester (Köster), *Synoptische Überlieferung bei den apostolischen Vätern* (Berlin: Akademie-Verlag, 1957).

[62] See comments in William R. Schoedel, 'The Apostolic Fathers,' in *The New Testament and Its Modern Interpreters*, ed. Eldon Jay Epp and George W. MacRae (Philadelphia: Fortress Press and Atlanta: Scholars Press, 1989), 459.

[63] My agreement that Polycarp is in fact depending upon Matthew and Luke at some points for the *form* of his sayings of the Lord in 2.2-3 (see discussion on following pages) is why I do not think Polycarp's sayings should be viewed as independent 'agrapha' in the narrow sense of the term (an area of almost unabated study since the time of Resch).

[64] See discussion in Hagner, 'The Sayings of Jesus,' 250-252.

[65] Contra the findings and assumptions of form criticism.

[66] Kenneth E. Bailey, 'Informal Controlled Oral Tradition and the Synoptic Gospels,' *Asia Journal of Theology* 5 (1991): 34-54.

[67] Bailey also acknowledges the existence of formal controlled traditions and uncontrolled oral material.

controlled and *formal*.[68] Bailey's approach accounts for the emphasis upon and confidence in orality found in the early second century.[69] Because the traditions had a basic stability to them, those who inherited them still had a basic trust in them.[70]

Pol. Phil. *2.3*

μνημονεύοντες δὲ ὧν εἶπεν ὁ κύριος διδάσκων· Μὴ κρίνετε, ἵνα μὴ κριθῆτε· ἀφίετε, καὶ ἀφεθήσεται ὑμῖν· ἐλεᾶτε, ἵνα ἐλεηθῆτε· ᾧ μέτρῳ μετρεῖτε, ἀντιμετρηθήσεται ὑμῖν· καὶ ὅτι μακάριοι οἱ πτωχοὶ καὶ οἱ διωκόμενοι ἕνεκεν δικαιοσύνης, ὅτι αὐτῶν ἐστιν ἡ βασιλεία τοῦ θεοῦ.

but instead remembering what the Lord said as he taught: 'Do not judge, that you may not be judged, forgive, and you will be forgiven, show mercy, that you may be shown mercy, with the measure you use, it will be measured back to you'; and 'blessed are the poor and those who are persecuted for righteousness' sake, for theirs is the kingdom of God.'

Polycarp uses the introductory formula μνημονεύοντες δὲ ὧν εἶπεν ὁ κύριος διδάσκων ("but remembering what the Lord said when he taught..."). Hagner thinks that this formula points to an oral source for these sayings.[71] He notes that appearances of formulae similar to the one found here seem also to refer to sayings from the oral tradition

---

[68] Gerhardsson, *Memory and Manuscript*.

[69] Sanday suggests, in light of the allusions to the gospels in Polycarp and elsewhere in the Apostolic Fathers, that if non-extant writings were drawn upon instead of the canonical gospels those documents were "writings so closely resembling our Gospels and so nearly akin to them that their existence only proves the essential unity and homogeneity of the evangelical tradition." Sanday, *The Gospels*, 87. While I agree that the 'evangelical tradition' (as Sanday calls it) was essentially united during the period of the Apostolic Fathers, Sanday has not proven that such a unity presupposes only written documents. It seems rather that he has made the assumption of much of scholarship that a tradition must be written to be stable. But at this point the work of Kenneth Bailey (and Gerhardsson) demonstrate that an oral history can also be quite stable.

[70] This does not mean that there were not those who intentionally changed (or 'twisted' Pol. *Phil.* 7.1) the sayings of the Lord. The eventual preference for written gospels probably had more to do with perceived threats of the 'heretics' (Gnostics, Marcionites, etc.) who used the words of Jesus in their own way, and perhaps the missiological need (given the church's explosive growth), than with a breakdown in passing on the tradition.

[71] Hagner, *Use*, 306-307. Hagner's study of the earlier *1 Clement* may have influenced him toward a disposition to see primary dependence upon the oral traditions in these following statements.

(note particularly Acts 20:30; *1 Clem.* 13:1; 46:7).[72] But, as Gerhardsson points out, the use of formulae to introduce a quote from the Jesus tradition do not in themselves indicate whether it is from a written or an oral tradition.[73] Based upon the argument below, this seems to have been the case with Polycarp's formula – they do not automatically point toward an oral source or a written source. It will be argued below that Polycarp's four maxims were influenced (not primarily in form) by a similar list of seven maxims in *1 Clem.* 13.2 (though rearranged by Polycarp and corrected toward Matthew and Luke). Thus, the presence of this formula in Pol. *Phil.* 2.3 is best explained by noting that 'Clement' also heads his list with a formula in 13.1, μάλιστα μεμνημένοι τῶν λόγων τοῦ κυρίου Ἰησοῦ, οὓς ἐλάλησεν διδάσκων ἐπιείκειαν καὶ μακροθυμίαν. Οὕτως γὰρ εἶπεν· ("Rather, remembering the words of the Lord Jesus who spoke, teaching gentleness and patience. For he said this:"). Polycarp, then, is following the lead of 'Clement,' not mainly for the *form* of the formula, but in the *fact* that 'Clement' also headed his list of maxims with a formula. In other words, Polycarp uses a formula here because 'Clement''s letter also has one.

But we still have not answered the question of whether Polycarp depends upon *1 Clem.* 13.1-2 when he employs the sayings of the Lord, so we turn to that question now. Polycarp uses four sayings of the Lord followed by one more. We will deal with the last saying separately from the first four because Polycarp himself separates it from the first four with a καὶ ὅτι. In addition, the last saying has no parallels with *1 Clement* and so needs to be evaluated separately. Polycarp's first four maxims are:

1. Μὴ κρίνετε, ἵνα μὴ κριθῆτε·
2. ἀφίετε, καὶ ἀφεθήσεται ὑμῖν·
3. ἐλεᾶτε, ἵνα ἐλεηθῆτε·
4. ᾧ μέτρῳ μετρεῖτε, ἀντιμετρηθήσεται ὑμῖν·

Note the rhythm and rhyme of these sayings. Line 1 and 3 both have a ἵνα followed by a verb ending in -θῆτε. Lines 2 and 4 both end in -θήσεται ὑμῖν.[74] This may indicate that these sayings were arranged to

---

[72] Ibid., 141-147, 258, 273.
[73] Gerhardsson, *Memory and Manuscript*, 197-198. The same holds true for references to the gospel (τὸ εὐαγγέλιον). Dehandschutter, 'Polycarp's Epistle,' 285, in agreement with these general comments by Gerhardsson notes that though Polycarp uses the expression τὰ λόγια τοῦ κυρίου in reference to those who twist the sayings of the Lord in 7.1 he never uses it "*in connection with a quotation*".
[74] Massaux, *Influence*, 29.

be memorized. The same could be said of the sayings found in *1 Clement*.[75] 'Clement' has seven sayings.

1. Ἐλεᾶτε ἵνα ἐλεηθῆτε, (#3 in Pol. *Phil.*)
2. ἀφίετε ἵνα ἀφεθῇ ὑμῖν· (#2 in Pol. *Phil.*)
3. ὡς ποιεῖτε, οὕτω ποιηθήσεται ὑμῖν· (not in Pol. *Phil.*)
4. ὡς δίδοτε, οὕτως δοθήσεται ὑμῖν· (not in Pol. *Phil.*)
5. ὡς κρίνετε, οὕτως κριθήσεσθε· (#1 in Pol. *Phil.*)
6. ὡς χρηστεύεσθε, οὕτως χρηστευθήσεται ὑμῖν· (not in Pol. *Phil.*).
7. ᾧ μέτρῳ μετρεῖτε, ἐν αὐτῷ μετρηθήσεται ὑμῖν. (#4 in Pol. *Phil.*)

It is highly probable that Polycarp is aware of 'Clement''s list when he makes his own. The fact that they are congregated in a similar fashion in his letter argues such, as does Polycarp's regular use of *1 Clement* elsewhere. Moreover, the way Polycarp separates out the final saying from the four maxims found also in *1 Clement* argues for treating these as a group and thus probably for dependence upon *1 Clement*.[76] Many scholars accept dependence upon *1 Clement* in this instance[77] but conjecture that the differences are caused by Polycarp citing *1 Clement* by memory. A more satisfactory accounting of the evidence is that Polycarp's relationship to *1 Clement* in this case is primarily in the *fact* that 'Clement' has such a list and less on the *form* of each individual saying. In other words, Polycarp may have been influenced by 'Clement' to employ such maxims in his own exhortation.

The first evidence for this assertion lies in the differences between the two lists. Differences in such a case speak more loudly than do similarities. If Polycarp is drawing upon *1 Clement* directly, how is it that the order is so significantly different? If the changes are (supposedly) due to a lapse in memory, how does Polycarp make it rhyme so nicely? If Polycarp's primary source for the form of these sayings is *1 Clement*, why are there differences in wording (again toward a more stylized form in Pol. *Phil.*)? Polycarp's wording is different in three out of the four sayings from the wording used by *1 Clement*. Finally, if Polycarp is depending directly on *1 Clement* (apart from the simple *fact* that 'Clement'

---

[75] Donald Alfred Hagner, *The Use of the Old and New Testaments in Clement of Rome* (Leiden: E. J. Brill, 1973), 306. Hagner notes on 306-307 n. 5, "This holds true even if Polycarp is dependent upon Clement," which he thinks is probably *not* so.

[76] Unless there was a catechism or some other written document with these sayings in them from which both Polycarp and 'Clement' drew.

[77] For example, Koester, *Synoptische Überlieferung*, 114-20 and against his statements in Helmut Koester, *Ancient Christian Gospels: Their History and Development* (London: SCM Press Ltd and Philadelphia: Trinity Press International, 1990), 19-20

uses such sayings) why does he leave out three of the sayings preserved by 'Clement'?[78]

It seems more likely that Polycarp is aware of *1 Clement* and perhaps encouraged by 'Clement' to include such a list in his own letter but corrects the *form* of the text toward the written gospels.[79] An argument for this is that he excises the two sayings found in *1 Clement* that are *not* found in any of the synoptic writers.[80] All four of Polycarp's maxims are found in the synoptic gospels.

The first maxim, Μὴ κρίνετε, ἵνα μὴ κριθῆτε, is identical in form to that found in Matt 7:1 and closer (than *1 Clement*) in form to Luke 6:37.[81] *1 Clement*, in contrast, reads ὡς κρίνετε, οὕτως κριθήσεσθε. It looks like Polycarp prefers to use the *form* of Matt 7:1 rather than the form employed in *1 Clement*.[82] That he is correcting toward Matthew is supported by the 'peculiarly Matthean elements' in the quotation which follows the four maxims.[83]

Polycarp's second maxim, ἀφίετε, καὶ ἀφεθήσεται ὑμῖν, is not in form directly dependent upon any saying found in the synoptic writers. Still, Polycarp uses a different form from that found in *1 Clement* (ἀφίετε ἵνα ἀφεθῇ ὑμῖν). In so doing he may be correcting 'Clement''s form toward a form which he knows from somewhere else. The meaning, of course, is the same. It may be supposed that Polycarp, like 'Clement', uses an abbreviated form of the teaching found in Matt 6:14, "For if you forgive men their transgressions, your heavenly father will also forgive you."[84] Since both 'Clement' and Polycarp have abbreviated forms of

---

[78] Hagner has used many of the arguments of this paragraph to argue that Polycarp is not depending at all upon *1 Clement* in this passage. He bases his argument upon 1) wording, 2) order, 3) similarity and differences of introductory formulae, 4) the stylized nature of the sayings. Hagner, 'The Sayings of Jesus,' 236.

[79] Harrison comments, "But Polycarp...substitutes again and again for Clement's loose wording the exact terms now of Matthew, now of Luke, and now a combination of the two, adding at the same time matter contained in them for which Clement offers no equivalent, and omitting matter contained in Clement for which neither Gospel has any equivalent." P. N. Harrison, *Two Epistles*, 286.

[80] Koester, *Synoptische Überlieferung*, 117; P. N. Harrison, *Two Epistles*, 286.

[81] Hernando prefers dependence upon Matt 7:1-2, calling it both a 'verbal' and a 'conceptual' allusion. James Daniel Hernando, 'Irenaeus and the Apostolic Fathers: An Inquiry into the development of the New Testament Canon,' (Ph.D. diss., Drew University, 1990), 193.

[82] Koester, *Synoptische Überlieferung*, 117.

[83] Schoedel, *Polycarp*, 12.

[84] Bruce M. Metzger, *The Canon of the New Testament: Its Origin, Development, and Significance* (Oxford: Clarendon Press, 1987), 61 notes that though Matthew and Luke do seem to be combined in these four maxims there are some parts which are not in the canonical gospels.

this teaching (though they are slightly different in form), it is likely that such abbreviations were found among the oral traditions which both Polycarp and 'Clement' would have known. This seems somewhat more likely than that either 'Clement' or Polycarp themselves abbreviated it.

Polycarp's third maxim, ἐλεᾶτε, ἵνα ἐλεηθῆτε, is identical in form to 'Clement''s first maxim. Polycarp evidently has no reason to correct it. It is not found in this form in the synoptic gospels. It may be considered a short form of Matt 5:7, μακάριοι οἱ ἐλεήμονες, ὅτι αὐτοὶ ἐλεηθήσονται ("blessed are the merciful, for they shall be shown mercy"). Both 'Clement' and Polycarp probably know it from an oral source, though it need not be assumed that Polycarp draws upon such a source without awareness that 'Clement' did the same. In the absence of extant written documents, it seems best to argue that both maxim #2 and maxim #3 are mediated through an oral source rather than through some unknown written document, though an early document cannot be ruled out.

The fourth maxim ᾧ μέτρῳ μετρεῖτε, ἀντιμετρηθήσεται ὑμῖν argues for correction of *1 Clement* in the direction of Luke 6:38. That he is correcting 'Clement' is seen in his excising 'Clement''s ἐν αὐτῷ which appears nowhere in the synoptic tradition.[85] He has chosen the complex verb form ἀντιμετρηθήσεται against the simpler form μετρηθήσεται which is found in *1 Clement*, Matthew (7:2) and Mark (4:24). Only Luke 6:38 uses the form ἀντιμετρηθήσεται. And apart from the γάρ conjunction in Luke, the form is identical to that of Polycarp. Correction toward Luke in this instance is not certain, but apart from positive evidence to the contrary, it seems to best account for the evidence as it stands.

Some scholars argue for Polycarp's dependence upon the oral tradition of the sayings of the Lord in these four maxims and not upon the written gospels or upon *1 Clement*.[86] Some consider dependence upon *1 Clement* to be clear but not dependence upon the gospels.[87] Sanday notes how difficult it is to find a hypothesis that accounts for all the evidence and posits the existence of a written gospel separate from the canonical

---

[85] Koester, *Synoptische Überlieferung*, 117.

[86] Hagner, *Use*, 141-147, 258, 273; also Hagner, 'The Sayings of Jesus,' 236; Knox, *Marcion*, 143; Philip Carrington, *The Early Christian Church*, vol. 1 (Cambridge: Cambridge University Press, 1957), 459; Barnett, *Paul*, 171; Edgar J. Goodspeed, *The Formation of the New Testament* (Chicago: The University of Chicago Press, 1926), 37.

[87] J. B. Bauer, *Die Polykarpbriefe*, 44-45. Massaux suggests a primitive catechism which has been derived from the Matthean Sermon on the Mount, though he posits dependence upon Matthew for the quotation following these four maxims. Massaux, *Influence*, 30-31.

gospels to which Polycarp had access.[88] Grant thinks it is impossible to tell.[89] General dependence upon *1 Clement* with correction in *form* toward the synoptic writers Matthew and Luke or toward the oral tradition (as in Maxim #2) is the option preferred here.

The final reference to the words of Jesus in Pol. *Phil.* 2.3 is καὶ ὅτι μακάριοι οἱ πτωχοὶ καὶ οἱ διωκόμενοι ἕνεκεν δικαιοσύνης, ὅτι αὐτῶν ἐστὶν ἡ βασιλεία τοῦ θεοῦ. ("and 'blessed are the poor and those who are persecuted for righteousness' sake, for theirs is the kingdom of God'"). This saying is set apart from the four maxims which precede it by καὶ ὅτι, probably because these sayings are not found among those in *1 Clement* 13.2. Dependence upon the Sermon on the Mount is clear. I have just argued that Polycarp corrects 'Clement' toward Matthew in maxim #1 and toward Luke in maxim #4. This contention is supported by this last quotation which appears to be a conflation of Luke 6:20 (cf. Matt 5:3) with Matt 5:10.

Luke 6:20 reads Μακάριοι οἱ πτωχοί, ὅτι ὑμετέρα ἐστὶν ἡ βασιλεία τοῦ θεοῦ ("Blessed [are you] poor, because yours is the kingdom of God.") Polycarp's first phrase μακάριοι οἱ πτωχοὶ and his last ὅτι αὐτῶν ἐστὶν ἡ βασιλεία τοῦ θεου (if we ignore for the moment the middle phrase καὶ οἱ διωκόμενοι ἕνεκεν δικαιοσύνης) are, apart from Polycarp's αὐτῶν where Luke has ὑμετέρα, identical to Luke's form. Matt 5:3, on the other hand, reads Μακάριοι οἱ πτωχοὶ τῷ πνεύματι, ὅτι αὐτῶν ἐστὶν ἡ βασιλεία τῶν οὐρανῶν ("Blessed are the poor in spirit, for theirs is the kingdom of heaven."). Matthew has the well-known addition to οἱ πτωχοὶ of τῷ πνεύματι, whereas Luke has only οἱ πτωχοὶ. Polycarp chooses Luke's form. Moreover, Polycarp depends upon Luke's ἡ βασιλεία τοῦ θεοῦ instead of Matthew's ἡ βασιλεία τῶν οὐρανῶν.[90]

Nevertheless, two considerations make it highly likely that the Matthean beatitudes are also directly influencing Polycarp. Polycarp inserts in the middle of this quote καὶ οἱ διωκόμενοι ἕνεκεν δικαιοσύνης

[88] Sanday, *The Gospels*, 86.
[89] Robert Grant, *An Introduction*, vol. 1, The Apostolic Fathers: A New Translation and Commentary, ed. Robert M. Grant (New York: Thomas Nelson & Sons, 1964), 66. Oxford Society 101-102 is noncommittal.
[90] Massaux thinks that dependence upon Matthew is an adequate explanation and that Luke just dropped τῷ πνεύματι (and presumably the change from Matthew's τῶν οὐρανῶν to τῶν θεοῦ which is also found in Luke?) Massaux, *Influence*, 30-31. I wish to suggest that the nature of Massaux's study may have influenced him to be sensitive to appearances of Matthew and less inclined to look for influence from Luke even where it seems evident.

which is apart from the tense of the participle identical in form to Matt 5:10 (μακάριοι) οἱ δεδιωγμένοι ἕνεκεν δικαιοσύνης ("blessed [are] those who have been persecuted on account of righteousness"). He has probably added it because he is about to introduce his discussion of 'righteousness' in 3.1.[91] Koester considers this virtual proof that Polycarp is dependent upon Matthew.[92] Supporting this is the αὐτῶν found in both Matt 5:10 (as well as in Matt 5:3) which could have influenced Polycarp toward the αὐτῶν instead of Luke's ὑμετέρα (though Luke influenced the form ἡ βασιλεία τοῦ θεου).

Admittedly, Polycarp could have been dependent upon the oral tradition for his changes. But the evidence in this final quotation of Jesus points toward dependence on Luke and Matthew via a conflation of Luke 6:20 (cf. Matt 5:3) and Matt 5:10.[93] The mere probability that Polycarp is choosing in one case Matthew and in another Luke, shows us that it is the words of Jesus more than the text of Matthew and Luke that hold authority for Polycarp. At the same time, the fact that he has just previously corrected *1 Clement* toward the texts of Matthew in one case and Luke in another shows that he considers Matthew and Luke to be accurate representations of the words of the Lord.

Summary of 2.3: Probable general dependence upon *1 Clem.* 13.1-2 for the *fact* but less for the *form* of the introductory formula and the four maxims. Possible correction toward Matt 7:1 in maxim #1 and toward Luke 6:38 in maxim #4. Possible influence also from the oral tradition. Probable citation (conflation) of Luke 6:20 (cf. Matt 5:3) with Matt 5:10.

Pol. Phil. *3.1*

Ταῦτα, ἀδελφοί, οὐκ ἐμαυτῷ ἐπιτρέψας γράφω ὑμῖν περὶ τῆς δικαιοσύνης ἀλλ᾽ ἐπεὶ ὑμεῖς προεπεκαλέσασθέ με.

I am writing you these things about righteousness, brothers, not on my own initiative but because you invited me.

---

[91] Boudewijn Dehandschutter, 'Polycarp's Epistle to the Philippians: An Early Example of "Reception"', in *The New Testament in Early Christianity: La réception des écrits néotestamentarios dans le christianisme primitif*, ed. Jean-Marie Sevrin (Leuven: Leuven University Press, 1989), 288.

[92] Koester, *Synoptische Überlieferung*, 118.

[93] So also Lightfoot, *The Apostolic Fathers*, part 2, vol. 3, 326; Kleist, *The Didache...*, 188 n. 24.

In Pol. *Phil.* 3.1 is found Polycarp's purpose statement. Schoedel suggests that Polycarp is responding to a request from the Philippians "to discuss the meaning of the (Pauline) term righteousness (vs. 1)."[94] On the contrary, I think it far less likely that the Philippians asked for an explanation of the term – as though they did not understand it – than that they desired exhortation (motivation) and practical instruction in how to live rightly as Christians. They had received such exhortation and instruction when Paul had written to their parents and grandparents and desired Polycarp to do something similar. I have already suggested in the introduction that the nature of their request was that Polycarp write to them about righteousness 'as Paul did.' The nature of Polycarp's response makes it unlikely that they had asked him to explain the meaning of Paul's use of the term righteousness.[95]

Summary of 3.1: There are no allusions to earlier writings in 3.1.

Pol. Phil. *3.2*

οὔτε γὰρ ἐγὼ οὔτε ἄλλος ὅμοιος ἐμοὶ δύναται κατακολουθῆσαι τῇ σοφίᾳ τοῦ μακαρίου καὶ ἐνδόξου Παύλου, ὃς γενόμενος ἐν ὑμῖν κατὰ πρόσωπον τῶν τότε ἀνθρώπων, ἐδίδαξεν ἀκριβῶς καὶ βεβαίως τὸν περὶ ἀληθείας λόγον, ὃς καὶ ἀπὼν ὑμῖν ἔγραψεν ἐπιστολάς· εἰς ἃς ἐὰν ἐγκύπτητε, δυνηθήσεσθε οἰκοδομεῖσθαι εἰς τὴν δοθεῖσαν ὑμῖν πίστιν,

For neither I nor anyone like me can keep pace with the wisdom of the blessed and glorious Paul, who, when he was among you in the presence of the men of that time, accurately and reliably taught the word concerning the truth. And when he was absent he wrote you letters, if you study them carefully, you will be able to build yourselves up in the faith that has been given to you...

Polycarp's insistence that he cannot keep pace with Paul whom he calls 'blessed' and 'glorious' itself argues that the Philippians had asked Polycarp to write to them a letter like Paul's.

The way Polycarp describes Paul's wisdom reminds one of 2 Pet 3:15, though it is not necessary to posit literary dependence either direction.

---

[94] Schoedel, *Polycarp*, 13.

[95] On the term δικαιοσύνη, Kleist's warning will suffice until our discussion in ch. 5, "The word δικαιοσύνη (here rendered 'the practice of holy living'), which abounds in shades of meaning varying with the context, has unfortunately, through centuries of repetition, been forced into the straight jackets of 'justice' and 'righteousness.'" Kleist, *The Didache...*, 188 n. 25.

In *1 Clem.* 47.1, Paul's first letter to the Corinthians is also μακαρίου Παύλου ('of the blessed Paul'). A reminiscence of *1 Clement* 47 may be present, and not primarily because of the reference to the 'glorious Paul.' 'Clement' refers to the letter (1 Corinthians) that Paul had written to the Corinthians when 'Clement' himself wrote to Corinth with hopes of motivating the Corinthians to avoid factions. So also Polycarp may have taken a cue from 'Clement' and mentioned Paul's letter-writing activity to the Philippians, again with paraenetic intent.

The language of 'face to face' (κατὰ πρόσωπον) and 'when absent' (ἀπὼν) as applied to Paul contains the same expressions found in 2 Cor 10:1 (cf. also 10:11), though other parallels are absent. The sentence structure and application of the expressions are different.[96] More likely is the connection of Paul's presence and absence (again ἀπὼν) with his letter-writing activity to the Philippians in Phil 1:27. A reminiscence of Phil 1:27 may be supported by similar expressions in Phil 2:12 (though there he uses παρουσίᾳ and ἀπουσίᾳ).

Polycarp says that when Paul was with them (i.e. in Philippi with their spiritual parents and grandparents) he accurately and reliably taught them τὸν περὶ ἀληθείας λόγον ("the word concerning truth"). It should not surprise us that Polycarp uses an expression that is probably Pauline in a general sense, though Polycarp employs περὶ).[97] Apart from Paul, the only other time in the NT that λόγος plus the genitive ἀληθείας is used is James 1:18. In the letters of Paul,[98] on the other hand, are four examples of similar expressions. In 2 Cor 6:7 one of the ways Paul commends himself as a servant of God is ἐν λόγῳ ἀληθείας ("by the word of truth"). In Eph 1:13 the recipients are told that after they had heard τὸν λόγον τῆς ἀληθείας ("the word of truth"), which is equivalent to the gospel in which they believed, they were sealed by the promised Holy Spirit. The parallel passage in Col 1:5 has the expression ἐν τῷ λόγῳ τῆς ἀληθείας τοῦ εὐαγγελίου ("by the word of truth which is the gospel").[99] Finally, the challenge of 2 Tim 2:15 contains the phrase ὀρθοτομοῦντα τὸν λόγον τῆς ἀληθείας ("handling accurately the word

---

[96] The Oxford Society comments, "No stress can be laid on the very slight resemblance of this passage to 2 Cor. 10¹." Oxford Society, 91.

[97] Does this, perhaps, signal a slight drift from Paul's meaning? Paul spread 'the word' which was equivalent to 'the gospel.' Polycarp speaks of Paul accurately and reliably teaching the word (doctrine?) 'concerning the truth.'

[98] Polycarp considered all the letters of Paul from which he quoted to be Pauline. See especially the argument of ch. 4.

[99] Note, however, that no clear allusion to Colossians is found anywhere else in Pol. *Phil.*

of truth").[100] In light of the large number of allusions to Paul's writings
in Pol. *Phil.*, one would expect that at this particular point in his letter
the expression used would be Pauline, and this appears to be the case.[101]
The most, however, that can be said about this expression is that an
allusion to a Pauline expression (such as is found in 2 Cor 6:7, Eph
1:13, Col 1:5 and 2 Tim 2:15) is probable, though it is less likely that
Polycarp had a specific text in mind.[102]

Summary of 3.2: A possible reminiscence of *1 Clem.* 47.1. A possible
reminiscence of Phil 1:27. A probable allusion to a Pauline expression
("the word of truth") though no specific text is identifiable.

Excursus: The Plural ἐπιστολάς

Polycarp's plural 'letters' (ἐπιστολάς) has generated an extensive debate, particularly in light of the fact that only one Pauline letter to the
Philippians is extant. A short summary of possible explanations follows:

1. Polycarp is mistaken.
2   Polycarp knows of more than one letter to the Philippians.[103]
    The other letters have either been:
    a. Lost, or
    b. Merged together in our canonical Philippians.
3. It is possible to represent a single letter by the plural. Polycarp
    is doing just that in this case.[104]

---

[100] Grant comments, "Polycarp's 'word of truth' looks like an allusion to 2 Timothy (2:15, 18)..." Grant, *Formation*, 103.

[101] Note also the conceptual parallel to 2 Cor 4:2 μὴ περιπατοῦντες ἐν πανουργίᾳ
μηδὲ δολοῦντες τὸν λόγον τοῦ θεοῦ ἀλλὰ τῇ φανερώσει τῆς ἀληθείας συνιστάνοντες
ἑαυτοὺς πρὸς πᾶσαν συνείδησιν ἀνθρώπων ἐνώπιον τοῦ θεοῦ ("not walking in crafti-
ness or adulterating the word of God, but by the manifestation of truth commending
ourselves to every man's conscience in the sight of God.")

[102] The addition of περί by Polycarp may be simply an improvement in the style
away from Paul's Hebrew genitive.

[103] Grammatically, of course, this is the simplest explanation. W. Bauer, *Die
apostolischen Väter II*, 287. Bauer bases this upon current usage (*1 Clem* 47.1; Ign. *Eph.*
12.2, *Smyrn.* 11.3, *Pol.* 8.1, and Polycarp's own distinction between singular and plural
in 13.2). He has sympathy to Harnack's position that the plural refers to the letters both
to the Philippians and to the Thessalonians.

[104] Lightfoot, *The Apostolic Fathers*, part 2, vol. 3, 327. Lindemann considers this
suggestion to be embarrassing, Lindemann, *Paulus im ältesten Christentum*, 88. But note
that Greek literature has a number of examples of the plural being used where it is in
fact referring to a single letter. See M. Luther Stirewalt, *Studies in Ancient Greek Epistolography*
(Atlanta: Scholars Press, 1993), 77.

4. Polycarp is simply affirming that any letter Paul has written is useful to every Christian church and thus all his letters are written to the Philippians.[105]

5. In Polycarp's mind, the letters to the Thessalonians (who are Macedonians like the Philippians) are also for the Philippians.[106]

6. Polycarp is exaggerating.[107]

Any of these solutions (or perhaps a combination, since they are not all mutually exclusive) is possible. There does not appear to be enough evidence to resolve this issue.

On a separate issue, it is, as Massaux says 'infinitely probable' from Polycarp's statement here that Polycarp knows the letter Paul wrote to the Philippians.[108] Thus, since we know that Polycarp almost certainly has read and knows the canonical Philippians, we are helped in deciding the likelihood of individual allusions to that letter when we encounter them in Pol. *Phil.*

Pol. Phil. 3.3

ἥτις ἐστὶν μήτηρ πάντων ἡμῶν, ἐπακολουθούσης τῆς ἐλπίδος, προαγούσης τῆς ἀγάπης τῆς εἰς θεὸν καὶ Χριστὸν καὶ εἰς τὸν πλησίον. ἐὰν γάρ τις τούτων ἐντὸς ᾖ, πεπλήρωκεν ἐντολὴν δικαιοσύνης· ὁ γὰρ ἔχων ἀγάπην μακράν ἐστιν πάσης ἁμαρτίας.

...which is the mother of us all, while hope follows and love for God and Christ and for our neighbor leads the way. For if anyone is occupied with these (lit. 'in these'), he has fulfilled the commandment of righteousness, for one who has love is far from all sin.

The end of 3.2 and the beginning of 3.3 are syntactically and logically connected: ...ἐὰν ἐγκύπτητε, δυνηθήσεσθε οἰκοδομεῖσθαι εἰς τὴν δοθεῖσαν ὑμῖν πίστιν, (3) ἥτις ἐστὶν μήτηρ πάντων ἡμῶν, ("...if you study them, you will be able to build yourselves up in the faith which has been given to you, which is the mother of us all.")

---

[105] Andreas Lindemann, *Paulus im ältesten Christentum: Das Bild des Apostels und die Rezeption der paulinischen Theologie in der frühchristlichen Literatur bis Marcion*, BHT 58 (Tübingen: J.C.B. Mohr [Paul Siebeck], 1979), 88-89.

[106] Harnack, *Miscellen*, 86-93. Cf. 1 Thess 1:8.

[107] Note that Polycarp exaggerates elsewhere. In 11.3 he says that Paul boasts about the Philippians in *all* the churches. If all Macedonians are included, though, he may be thinking of such comments as are found in Rom 15:26; 2 Cor 8:1; 11:9; Phil 4:15.

[108] Massaux, *Influence*, 36.

The phrase ἥτις ἐστὶν μήτηρ πάντων ἡμῶν ("which is the mother of us all") in form alludes to Gal 4:26 ἡ δὲ ἄνω Ἰερουσαλὴμ ἐλευθέρα ἐστιν, ἥτις ἐστὶν μήτηρ ἡμῶν ("But the Jerusalem above is free, which is our mother"). Apart from the word πάντων the phrases are identical, but the application in Pol. *Phil.* is to faith (or better, 'the faith').[109] The antecedent of the relative pronoun in Pol. *Phil.* is πίστιν, the last word of 3.2. But this is not the issue in Galatians.[110] In Galatians, 'our mother' is the 'Jerusalem above' which is free. The context is Paul's allegory of Hagar and Sarah. Thus in form, the phrase in Pol. *Phil.* 3.3 is probably taken from Gal 4:26, though Polycarp's application is different from Paul's.

The word πάντων is not found in most of the best manuscripts of Gal 4:26 but is mainly a Byzantine reading. Lightfoot suggests that Polycarp's addition of πάντων was the impetus toward the change in the manuscript tradition rather than vice versa.[111] It is not possible to determine whether the change occurred before Polycarp (even if it could be shown that he is the main influence upon later texts) or whether it originates with Polycarp. A harmonization toward Rom 4:16 at some point before Polycarp (or with Polycarp) seems possible: οὐ τῷ ἐκ τοῦ νόμου μόνον ἀλλὰ καὶ τῷ ἐκ πίστεως Ἀβραάμ, ὅς ἐστιν πατὴρ πάντων ἡμῶν ("not only to those who are of the Law, but also to those who are of the faith of Abraham, who is the father of us all").[112] The form of the phrase in Rom 4:16 is parallel to that found in Polycarp except that in Romans it is 'father' and in Polycarp 'mother.' A connection with Rom 4:16 is further deemed possible when the context in Pol. *Phil.* 3 is considered – a discussion centered on faith. Thus, the phrase found in the beginning of Pol. *Phil.* 3.3 should be considered a probable allusion to Gal 4:26 with possible influence from Rom 4:16.

The next phrase is ἐπακολουθούσης τῆς ἐλπίδος, προαγούσης τῆς ἀγάπης τῆς εἰς θεὸν καὶ Χριστὸν καὶ εἰς τὸν πλησίον ("while hope follows and love for God and Christ and for our neighbor leads the way"). Note that the thought immediately before is about *faith*, and this phrase adds to the triad *hope* and *love*. Polycarp's meaning is somewhat uncertain. The way one understands the function of προαγούσης affects one's

[109] The application in Polycarp reflects the second century belief that faith is the mother of Christians. Grant, 'Polycarp of Smyrna,' 143.

[110] Rensberger, 'As the Apostle Teaches,' 113.

[111] Lightfoot, *The Apostolic Fathers*, part 2, vol. 3, 327. Also, Oxford Committee, 92; Barnett, *Paul*, 174-175.

[112] Schoedel, *Polycarp*, 15 referring to the work of J. C. Plumpe.

understanding of the relationship of these three virtues, which in turn affects the likely source for this triad. It is further complicated when we try to distinguish whether Polycarp has in mind a temporal order (i.e. which happens first), or an order of importance. Is the proper order (and meaning of the passage): 1) love, faith, hope; i.e., hope and faith occur when one first has love; 2) faith, love, hope; i.e., faith leads to hope but love precedes hope (or both hope *and* faith?); 3) faith, hope, love; i.e., they work together, but love is the most important?[113]

If #2 is correct, Polycarp may be drawing upon the same order found in 1 Thess 1:3 or Col 1:4-5.[114] If #3 is correct, the reference is probably to 1 Cor 13:13. In light of the primacy of 1 Cor 13:13, the poetic and memorable form of the chapter as a whole and the fact that 1 Corinthians is often quoted by Polycarp (whereas Colossians and 1 Thessalonians never clearly are), an allusion to 1 Cor 13:13 is probable.[115]

The phrase in Pol. *Phil.* 3.3 about love is followed by another likely reminiscence of Paul: προαγούσης τῆς ἀγάπης τῆς εἰς θεὸν καὶ Χριστὸν καὶ εἰς τὸν πλησίον. ἐὰν γάρ τις τούτων ἐντὸς ᾖ, πεπλήρωκεν ἐντολὴν δικαιοσύνης ("...while love for God and Christ and for our neighbor leads the way. For if anyone is occupied with these, he has fulfilled the commandment of righteousness"). Though the concept of love for God (cf. Matt 22:37-38; Mark 12:29-30 [Luke 10:27]) and neighbor (Matt 22:39; Mark 12:31 [Luke 10:37]) as the two greatest commandments (Matt 22:36; Mark 12:28-29) or as that upon which the entire law depends (Matt 22:40) were widespread in the Jesus tradition, there is little doubt that Polycarp's mention of them in 3.3 is influenced by Paul. Rom 13:8-10 says Μηδενὶ μηδὲν ὀφείλετε εἰ μὴ τὸ ἀλλήλους ἀγαπᾶν· ὁ γὰρ ἀγαπῶν τὸν ἕτερον νόμον πεπλήρωκεν. τὸ γὰρ οὐ μοιχεύσεις, οὐ φονεύσεις, οὐ κλέψεις, οὐκ ἐπιθυμήσεις, καὶ εἴ τις ἑτέρα ἐντολή, ἐν τῷ λόγῳ τούτῳ ἀνακεφαλαιοῦται [ἐν τῷ]· ἀγαπήσεις τὸν πλησίον σου ὡς σεαυτόν. ἡ ἀγάπη τῷ πλησίον κακὸν οὐκ ἐργάζεται· πλήρωμα οὖν νόμου ἡ ἀγάπη. ("Owe nothing to anyone except to love one another; for he

---

[113] Refer to Schoedel, *Polycarp*, 14-15 and his references for a fuller explanation.

[114] Interestingly, these are two letters not supportable elsewhere in Pol. *Phil.* Cf. also 1 Thess 5:8.

[115] Most prefer dependence upon 1 Cor 13:13; Lightfoot, *The Apostolic Fathers*, part 2, vol. 3, 327; Barnett, *Paul*, 175; Lindemann, 'Paul in...Apostolic Fathers,' 43-44 who says that Polycarp's use here is 'deliberate,' 'not merely incidental.' Oxford Society, 85, is overly cautious, giving this passage a 'c' rating (possible) even though 1 Corinthians in general is an 'A' (certain).

who loves his neighbor has fulfilled the law. For this, 'You shall not commit adultery, You shall not murder, You shall not steal, You shall not covet,' and if there is any other commandment, it is summed up in this saying, 'You shall love your neighbor as yourself.' Love does no wrong to a neighbor; love therefore is the fulfillment of the law.") Moreover, Gal 5:14 reads ὁ γὰρ πᾶς νόμος ἐν ἑνὶ λόγῳ πεπλήρωται, ἐν τῷ· ἀγαπήσεις τὸν πλησίον σου ὡς σεαυτόν ("For the whole Law is fulfilled in one word, in the statement, 'You shall love your neighbor as yourself.") and Gal 6:2 reads Ἀλλήλων τὰ βάρη βαστάζετε καὶ οὕτως ἀναπληρώσετε τὸν νόμον τοῦ Χριστοῦ ("Bear one another's burdens, and thus fulfill the law of Christ.") It is the language of fulfillment that creates the verbal link to Paul rather than directly to the Jesus tradition (though I do not doubt that Polycarp knows Paul is depending upon the teaching of Jesus). Though Rom 13:8-10 has the fuller discussion and thus could be considered the primary medium, Gal 4:26 has just been cited and could have provided the impulse which caused Polycarp to think of Gal 5:14 (and perhaps 6:2). Thus, we have a probable reminiscence of Paul's use of the Jesus tradition in Rom 13:8-10 and/or Gal 5:14 (cf. 6:2).[116] Polycarp's expression ἐντολὴν δικαιοσύνης ('command of righteousness') will be analyzed in more detail in ch. 5.

The final phrase of Pol. Phil. 3.3 is ὁ γὰρ ἔχων ἀγάπην μακράν ἐστιν πάσης ἁμαρτίας ("for one who loves is far from all sin"). Schoedel points out that there are similar expressions in Sir 15:8 and Ep Jer 72.[117] The phrase is too short and too common to make any connection sure. 1 Pet 4:8 is also similar in ideas: ὅτι ἀγάπη καλύπτει πλῆθος ἁμαρτιῶν ("because love covers a multitude of sins"). The lack of verbal similarities makes direct dependence on 1 Pet 4:8 unlikely.

Summary of 3.3: A probable allusion to Gal 4:26 with possible influence from Rom 4:16. A probable allusion to 1 Cor 13:13. A probable reminiscence of Paul's use of the Jesus tradition in Rom 13:8-10 and/or Gal 5:14 (cf. 6:2).

---

[116] J. B. Bauer, *Die Polykarpbriefe*, 47. Most scholars have opted for Rom 13:8-10 as the primary (if not sole) source of this reminiscence. For example, Barnett, *Paul*, 175 and Lightfoot, *The Apostolic Fathers*, part 2, vol. 3, 327-328 both consider Romans to be primary but do not rule out Galatians.

[117] Schoedel, *Polycarp*, 15.

Pol. Phil. 4.1

Ἀρχὴ δὲ πάντων χαλεπῶν φιλαργυρία, εἰδότες οὖν ὅτι οὐδὲν εἰσηνέγκαμεν εἰς τὸν κόσμον, ἀλλ᾽ οὐδὲ ἐξενεγκεῖν τι ἔχομεν, ὁπλισώμεθα τοῖς ὅπλοις τῆς δικαιοσύνης καὶ διδάξωμεν ἑαυτοὺς πρῶτον πορεύεσθαι ἐν τῇ ἐντολῇ τοῦ κυρίου·

But the love of money is the beginning of all troubles. Knowing, therefore, that we brought nothing into the world, nor do we have anything to take out, let us arm ourselves with the weapons of righteousness and let us first teach ourselves to follow the commandment of the Lord.

The first two quotations will be dealt with together. Ἀρχὴ δὲ πάντων χαλεπῶν φιλαργυρία, εἰδότες οὖν ὅτι οὐδὲν εἰσηνέγκαμεν εἰς τὸν κόσμον, ἀλλ᾽ οὐδὲ ἐξενεγκεῖν τι ἔχομεν ("But the love of money is the beginning of all troubles. Knowing, therefore, that we brought nothing into the world, nor do we have anything to take out..."). Polycarp seems to be drawing upon 1 Timothy 6 twice here. 1 Tim 6:10 states, ῥίζα γὰρ πάντων τῶν κακῶν ἐστιν ἡ φιλαργυρία ("For the love of money is a root of all sorts of evil"); and 1 Tim 6:7 reads, οὐδὲν γὰρ εἰσηνέγκαμεν εἰς τὸν κόσμον, ὅτι οὐδὲ ἐξενεγκεῖν τι δυνάμεθα· ("For we have brought nothing into the world, so we cannot take anything out of it either.") The reference to 1 Tim 6:10 is not nearly so exact as the reference to 1 Tim 6:7. But the proximity of the two, particularly in light of the formal similarities to 1 Tim 6:7 makes it almost impossible to deny dependence.[118] Though there are numerous examples that can be given of similar sayings concerning money in Greek literature,[119] "the proximity of the reflection...makes the dependence a virtual certainty."[120] The Oxford Society comments, "It is almost impossible to believe that these passages are independent."[121]

The most notable change is Polycarp's use of ἀρχή rather than the more distinctive ῥίζα found in 1 Tim 6:10. It may be noted that Polycarp has already used ῥίζα in 1.2 where he lauds the Philippians for "the firm root of their faith." It cannot be demonstrated but may be conjec-

---

[118] Note that the citation as it appears in 1 Tim 6:7 may have ultimately had its source in Job 1:21, though even that is not certain. Here, the source is primarily influenced by 1 Timothy. McNatt, 'Old Testament Usage,' 144-145; Kleist, *The Didache...*, 189 n. 33.

[119] See discussion in J. B. Bauer, *Die Polykarpbriefe*, 48-50

[120] Eugene Harrison Lovering, 'The Collection, redaction, and early circulation of the corpus Paulinum,' (Ph.D. diss., Southern Methodist University, 1988), 229. Also, Rensberger, 'As the Apostle Teaches,' 114, 124-125; Schoedel, *Polycarp*, 16; Massaux, *Influence*, 36; Lightfoot, *The Apostolic Fathers*, part 2, vol. 3, 328.

[121] Oxford Society, 95-96.

tured that he hesitates to use such a vivid word positively to laud them in ch. 1 and then again use it negatively in reference to the love of money in 4.1.

Polycarp's employment of ἀλλ' οὐδὲ instead of the ὅτι in 1 Tim 6:7 does not argue against dependence; rather it appears to be an improvement over the anomalous ὅτι found between the two clauses.[122]

The formula εἰδότες ὅτι "indicates that he is conscious of quoting and points to the priority of I Timothy."[123]

The only serious way to challenge dependence upon 1 Timothy 6 by Polycarp is to reverse the dependence and make 1 Timothy dependent upon Polycarp as W. Bauer and others have suggested.[124] Campenhausen considers Polycarp himself (or a representative of Polycarp) to be the likely author of the Pastorals.[125] Scholarly opinion now stands against them.[126]

That Pol. *Phil.* 4.1 actually quotes from 1 Timothy is supported by the following *Haustafeln*. Even today it is difficult to discuss the needs of widows without immediately thinking of 1 Timothy 5. A good explanation for Polycarp's move to the *Haustafeln* at this point in his letter is that he has referred twice, back-to-back, to 1 Timothy 6 and this conjured up the context of 1 Timothy 5 in his mind.

Next is the phrase ὁπλισώμεθα τοῖς ὅπλοις τῆς δικαιοσύνης καὶ διδάξωμεν ἑαυτοὺς πρῶτον πορεύεσθαι ἐν τῇ ἐντολῇ τοῦ κυρίου ("...let us arm ourselves with the weapons of righteousness and let us first teach ourselves to follow the commandment of the Lord"). The very distinctive metaphor τοῖς ὅπλοις τῆς δικαιοσύνης ('with the weapons of righteousness') is almost certainly Pauline.[127] It is probably dependent upon 2 Cor 6:7 διὰ τῶν ὅπλων τῆς δικαιοσύνης ('by the weapons of righteousness'), which agrees mostly in form and has a complementary context. But note that the phrases ὅπλα ἀδικίας ('weapons/instruments of

---

[122] Schoedel, *Polycarp*, 16.

[123] Oxford Society, 95-96.

[124] Walter Bauer, *Orthodoxy and Heresy in Earliest Christianity*, 2d German ed., with added appendices, by Georg Strecker, trans. by a team from the Philadelphia Seminary on Christian Origins, ed. Robert A. Kraft and Gerhard Krodel (Philadelphia: Fortress Press, 1971; repr., Mifflintown, Pa.: Sigler Press, 1996), 224.

[125] Campenhausen, 'Polykarp von Smyrna.'

[126] "In fact those who reject the authenticity of the letters have generally abandoned dates very far into the second century for their composition; most locate them at about the turn of the century." Philip H. Towner, *The Goal of our Instruction: The Structure of Theology and Ethics in the Pastoral Epistles*, JSNTSup 34 (Sheffield: Sheffield Academic Press, 1989), 22-23.

[127] Oxford Society, 90.

unrighteousness') and ὅπλα δικαιοσύνης ('weapons/instruments of righteousness') appear in Rom 6:13, though the contexts are not nearly so compatible. The phrase τὰ ὅπλα τοῦ φωτός ('the weapons of light') preceded by the hortatory subjunctive ἐνδυσώμεθα ('let us put on') is parallel in thought but not verbally. Eph 6:13 is the well-known passage where the readers are exhorted to take up the whole armor of God, including the breastplate of righteousness (6:14). All of these could have formed the background to Polycarp's expression and make it almost certain that Polycarp is depending upon Paul, though the connection with 2 Cor 6:7 is more probable than the others.

Summary of 4.1: An almost certain allusion to 1 Tim 6:10 followed by an almost certain loose citation of 1 Tim 6:7. An almost certain allusion to the general Pauline metaphor 'weapons of righteousness' and probably an allusion to 2 Cor 6:7.

Pol. Phil. 4.2

ἔπειτα καὶ τὰς γυναῖκας ὑμῶν ἐν τῇ δοθείσῃ αὐταῖς πίστει καὶ ἀγάπῃ καὶ ἁγνείᾳ, στεργούσας τοὺς ἑαυτῶν ἄνδρας ἐν πάσῃ ἀληθείᾳ καὶ ἀγαπώσας πάντας ἐξ ἴσου ἐν πάσῃ ἐγκρατείᾳ, καὶ τὰ τέκνα παιδεύειν τὴν παιδείαν τοῦ φόβου τοῦ θεοῦ·

Then instruct your wives to continue in the faith delivered to them and in love and purity, cherishing their own husbands in all fidelity and loving all others equally in all chastity, and to instruct the children with instruction that leads to the fear of God.

The *Haustafeln* of Pol. *Phil.* 4.2-6.2 remind one of similar instructions in Eph 5:22-6:9; Col 3:18-4:1; Tit 2:1-10; Ign. *Pol.* 4-5; *Did* 4.9-11 and various places in 1 Timothy and *1 Clement*. 1 Timothy and *1 Clement* in particular appear to have exercized some influence upon Polycarp in this section.[128] A general influence of 1 Timothy is probable throughout Polycarp's own description of household duties in 4.2-6.2, though many particulars will be dependent upon other sources.[129] In the discussions of 4.2-6.2 which follow, parallels to 1 Timothy will be pointed

---

[128] "...the exhortation is formulated in the manner of the household lists (iv-vi)..." Martin Dibelius, *A Fresh Approach to the New Testament and Early Christian Literature* (New York: Charles Scribner's Sons, 1936), 180.

[129] Lindemann, 'Paul in...Apostolic Fathers,' 43; Schoedel, *Polycarp*, 17. Carrington suggests that the references drawn from 1 Tim 6 in Pol. *Phil.* 4.1 lead Polycarp into "an exhortation in the style of that Epistle." Carrington, *The Early Christian Church*, vol. 1, 460. Lovering comments, "The battle imagery which follows and the exhortations to teach oneself and one's household first and then to teach the widows their duties in

out in tandem with the relevant passages as they arise.

In the immediate passage (4.2-3), dependence upon *1 Clement* in particular is strong – ('ganz starke Abhängigkeit'[130]). The first probable allusion is to *1 Clem.* 1.3 στεργούσας καθηκόντως τοὺς ἄνδρας ἑαυτῶν ("cherishing properly their own husbands").[131] This is verbally and conceptually parallel to Polycarp's στεργούσας τοὺς ἑαυτῶν ἄνδρας ("cherishing their own husbands").

The next connection is to *1 Clem.* 21:6-8. Polycarp's exhortation καὶ τὰ τέκνα παιδεύειν τὴν παιδείαν τοῦ φόβου τοῦ θεοῦ ("and to instruct the children with instruction that leads to the fear of God") is very similar to *1 Clem.* 21:6 τοὺς νέους παιδεούσωμεν τὴν παιδείαν τοῦ φόβου τοῦ θεοῦ ("let us instruct our young with instruction that leads to the fear of God") and should be considered a loose citation. There is also instruction about children in *1 Clem.* 21.8 which includes τὰ τέκνα and the concept of the fear of God. These are all set among instructions to wives, which is the same as the setting in Pol. *Phil.* 4.2. Concerning this instruction to wives, a couple additional conceptual parallels can be drawn between Pol. *Phil.* 4.2 and *1 Clem.* 21.6-8, including: 1) the fear of the Lord, and 2) the emphasis on love and purity. These, along with the previous and following connections to *1 Clement* make dependence on *1 Clem.* 21.6-8 probable.

Summary of 4.2: A probable general dependence in Pol. *Phil.* 4.2-6.2 upon the *Haustafeln* of 1 Timothy. A probable allusion to *1 Clem.* 1.3. A probable loose citation of *1 Clem.* 21:6.

Pol. Phil. *4.3*

τὰς χήρας σωφρονούσας περὶ τὴν τοῦ κυρίου πίστιν, ἐντυγχανούσας ἀδιαλείπτως περὶ πάντων, μακρὰν οὔσας πάσης διαβολῆς, καταλαλιᾶς, ψευδομαρτυρίας, φιλαργυρίας, καὶ παντὸς κακοῦ, γινωσκούσας ὅτι εἰσὶ θυσιαστήριον θεοῦ καὶ ὅτι πάντα μωμοσκοπεῖται, καὶ λέληθεν αὐτὸν οὐδὲν οὔτε λογισμῶν οὔτε ἐννοιῶν οὔτε τι τῶν κρυπτῶν τῆς καρδίας.

---

faith and prayer (cf. Pol. *Phil.* 4.3 with 1 Tim 5:5) all relate to the Haustafel of 1 Timothy in ways that would not normally be persuasive evidence of dependence but together add up to nothing less." Lovering, 'Collection,' 229. In contrast, Barnard, who follows Selwyn's general argument, argues that 4.2 is representative of early Christian catechesis. According to Barnard, these phrases should not be viewed as allusions to particular texts. L. W. Barnard, *Studies in the Apostolic Fathers and Their Backgrounds* (Oxford: Basil Blackwell, 1966), 36-37.

[130] J. B. Bauer, *Die Polykarpbriefe*, 50.

[131] Schoedel, *Polycarp*, 16-17; Lightfoot, *The Apostolic Fathers*, part 2, vol. 3, 328.

The widows must think soberly about the faith of the Lord and pray
unceasingly for everyone and stay far away from all malicious talk, slander, false testimony, love of money, and any kind of evil, knowing that
they are God's altar, and that all sacrifices are carefully inspected and
nothing escapes him, whether thoughts or intentions or secrets of the
heart.

The discussion about widows (perhaps the office of widows[132]) is
part of the general dependence upon 1 Timothy continuing throughout these *Haustafeln* in Pol. *Phil.* 4.2-6.2, as has been mentioned above.
In this case, the similarity is presumably with 1 Tim 5:3-6, though specific verbal connections with 1 Timothy are sparse.[133]

Polycarp instructs the widows to ἐντυγχανούσας ἀδιαλείπτως περὶ
πάντων ("pray unceasingly for everyone"). It seems possible that there
is present a reminiscence of the widow Anna in the temple who (cf.
Luke 2:37) after the death of her husband was "a widow to the age of
eighty-four. And she never left the temple, serving night and day with
fastings and prayers." The temple imagery of a widow as θυσιαστήριον
θεοῦ ('God's altar') which Polycarp will shortly mention may help
strengthen the connection with Anna. Moreover, if we assume a general connection with 1 Timothy in this section (which appears to be the
case) 1 Tim 5:5 which describes a widow as one who "continues in
entreaties and prayers night and day" could either be the source of this
reminiscence[134] or the bridge to the reminiscence by Polycarp of the
tradition about Anna in the temple. This, however, cannot be considered more than a possibility.

The widows are exhorted to stay far from whatever is malicious
(διαβολῆς). This is the same term used in 1 Tim 3:11 (μὴ διαβόλους, cf.
Tit 2:3) where 'women' (deaconesses?) are instructed that they should
not be malicious[135] Again, the general connection to 1 Timothy is supported even if a direct correspondence cannot be demonstrated.

There is no direct biblical parallel to Polycarp's figurative use of
θυσιαστήριον ('altar'). Ignatius, however, uses it figuratively repeatedly

---

[132] "It seems clear that Polycarp is here referring to the office or order of widows,
both from the expressions used...and from the position which they occupy immediately
before the deacons and priests." Lightfoot, *The Apostolic Fathers*, part 2, vol. 3, 329.

[133] Raymond Brown, *An Introduction to the New Testament* (New York, Doubleday, 1997),
665.

[134] Lightfoot suggests a possible connection to 1 Tim 5:5. Lightfoot, *The Apostolic
Fathers*, part 2, vol. 3, 329.

[135] W. Bauer, *Die apostolischen Väter II*, 288; Lightfoot, *The Apostolic Fathers*, part 2, vol.
3, 329.

(Ign. *Eph.* 5.2; *Magn.* 7.2; *Trall.* 7.2; *Rom.* 2.2). Ignatius's figurative use
of this word may have influenced Polycarp to also use it figuratively. If
it were not for the intimate intersection of the lives of Ignatius and
Polycarp, this would be speculative, but in light of their relationship, an
influence by Ignatius is possible. At the same time, the idea of a person
or a person's actions being a sacrifice to God is found in the canonical
Phil 2:17 and 4:18. In light of the numerous subtle allusions to Paul's
Philippians in Polycarp's letter, this may provide at least part of the
conceptual background.

Polycarp's statement in 4.3 that "all [sacrifices] are inspected" (πάντα
μωμοσκοπεῖται) may be an allusion to *1 Clem.* 41.2.[136] 'Clement,' who is
describing the sacrifices in Jerusalem mentions μωμοσκοπηθὲν τὸ
προσφερόμενον διὰ τοῦ ἀρχιερέως ("the offering being inspected by the
high priest"). The other allusions to *1 Clement* in this section increase
the probability of dependence here, though the brevity of the allusion
prevents it from being considered any more than possible.

There is reason to consider the clause καὶ λέληθεν αὐτὸν οὐδὲν οὔτε
λογισμῶν οὔτε ἐννοιῶν ("and nothing escapes him, whether thoughts or
intentions") a probable loose citation of *1 Clem.* 21.3. *1 Clem.* 21.3 has
the clause καὶ ὅτι οὐδὲν λέληθεν αὐτὸν τῶν ἐννοιῶν ἡμῶν οὐδὲ τῶν
διαλογισμῶν ὧν ποιούμεθα ("and that nothing escapes him, either of
our thoughts or the plans which we make").[137] The verbal similarities
are evident. Polycarp slightly abbreviates the clause, uses a slightly different order of words and employs the simpler λογισμῶν where 'Clement' uses διαλογισμῶν followed by a relative clause. These differences
are not sufficient to overturn a contention that Polycarp is probably
dependent upon *1 Clem.* 21.3, particularly in light of the other connections to that letter in this section. Polycarp also adds the expression οὔτε
τι τῶν κρυπτῶν τῆς καρδίας ("or any secrets of the heart") which is not
present in *1 Clem.* 21.3. The phrase τὰ κρυπτὰ τῆς καρδίας αὐτοῦ ("the
secrets of his heart"), however, is found in 1 Cor 14:25.[138] The phrases
are verbally similar but not exact. It should be remembered that the
concept that God knows what is secret and hidden in people is a common idea in Jewish and Christian literature.[139] Still, in light of Polycarp's
regular dependence upon phrases found elsewhere in Paul, and in light

---

[136] Schoedel, *Polycarp*, 18-19; Lightfoot, Harmer, and Holmes, *The Apostolic Fathers: Greek Texts*, 211.
[137] Schoedel, *Polycarp*, 19.
[138] cf. 1 Cor 4:5 and Rom 2:15-16 where the concept but not the phrase is found.
[139] For example, Jer 17:10; Heb 4:13.

of the following quotation from Gal 6:7, dependence upon 1 Cor 14:25 should be considered probable and not merely possible.[140]

Summary of 4.3: A possible reminiscence of the widow Anna (cf. Luke 2:37). A possible allusion to Ignatius's figurative use of 'altar' (as in Ign. *Eph.* 5.2; *Magn.* 7.2; *Trall.* 7.2; *Rom.* 2.2) or to Paul's idea in Philippians of a person's actions being a sacrifice to God (Phil 2:17; 4:18). A possible allusion to *1 Clem.* 41.2. A probable loose citation of *1 Clem.* 21.3. A probable allusion to 1 Cor 14:25.

Pol. Phil. *5.1*

Εἰδότες οὖν ὅτι θεὸς οὐ μυκτηρίζεται, ὀφείλομεν ἀξίως τῆς ἐντολῆς αὐτοῦ καὶ δόξης περιπατεῖν.

Knowing, therefore, that God is not mocked, we ought to live in a manner that is worthy of his commandment and glory.

It is almost certain that even though the phrase θεὸς οὐ μυκτηρίζεται ("God is not mocked") is short, we are faced with an exact citation of Gal 6:7.[141] In Gal 6:7 we read Μὴ πλανᾶσθε, θεὸς οὐ μυκτηρίζεται ("Do not be deceived, God is not mocked"). The word μυκτηρίζεται is striking. In fact, in the NT the verb μυκτηρίζω is only found in Gal 6:7. The forms of the two passages are identical. The quotation in Pol. *Phil.* 5.1 is preceded by the introductory formula Εἰδότες...ὅτι.... Literary dependence by Polycarp upon Gal 6:7 is present beyond any reasonable doubt.

The following phrase is ὀφείλομεν ἀξίως τῆς ἐντολῆς αὐτοῦ καὶ δόξης περιπατεῖν ("we ought to walk worthily of his commandment and glory"). The juxtaposition of 'we ought' and the concept of walking (both found in 1 John 2:6) together with 'the commandment' might in a general sense point toward dependence upon Johannine language. But the connection is inconclusive, particularly when it is remembered that the concept of walking worthy is not Johannine.[142]

Summary of 5.1: An almost certain true citation of Gal 6:7.

---

[140] Also Lightfoot, *The Apostolic Fathers*, part 2, vol. 3, 330; Kleist, *The Didache...*, 190 n. 38.
[141] Barnett, *Paul*, 176; Oxford Society, 92; J. B. Bauer, *Die Polykarpbriefe*, 53; W. Bauer, *Die apostolischen Väter II*, 289; Lindemann, 'Paul in...Apostolic Fathers,' 43; P. N. Harrison, *Two Epistles*, 292-293.
[142] Rather, note Eph 4:1; Col 1:10 and 1 Thess 2:12.

Pol. Phil. *5.2*

ὁμοίως διάκονοι ἄμεμπτοι κατενώπιον αὐτοῦ τῆς δικαιοσύνης, ὡς θεοῦ καὶ
Χριστοῦ διάκονοι, καὶ οὐκ ανθρώπων· μὴ διάβολοι, μὴ δίλογοι, ἀφιλάργυροι,
ἐγκρατεῖς περὶ πάντα, εὔσπλαγχνοι, ἐπιμελεῖς, πορευόμενοι κατὰ τὴν
ἀλήθειαν τοῦ κυρίου, ὃς ἐγένετο διάκονος πάντων· ᾧ ἐὰν εὐαρεστήσωμεν ἐν
τῷ νῦν αἰῶνι, ἀποληψόμεθα καὶ τὸν μέλλοντα, καθὼς ὑπέσχετο ἡμῖν ἐγεῖραι
ἡμᾶς ἐκ νεκρῶν καὶ ὅτι, ἐὰν πολιτευσώμεθα ἀξίως αὐτοῦ, καὶ συμβασιλεύσομεν αὐτῷ, εἴγε πιστεύομεν.

Similarly, deacons must be blameless in the presence of his righteousness, as deacons of God and Christ and not of men: not slanderers,
not insincere, not lovers of money, self-controlled in every respect, compassionate, diligent, acting in accordance with the truth of the Lord,
who became a servant of all. If we please him in this present world,
we will receive the world to come as well, inasmuch as he promised to
raise us from the dead and that if we prove to be citizens worthy of
him, we will also reign with him – if, that is, we continue to believe.

Pol. *Phil.* 5.2 begins with instructions to deacons and is a continuation of the probable general dependence upon the *Haustafeln* of 1 Timothy. On the instructions to deacons in particular, Lightfoot comments,
"The instructions here given are suggested by 1 Tim iii.1-13...from which
passage also the words are in part borrowed."[143] Some obvious similarities to 1 Timothy include (but are not limited to): 1) the instructions
to διάκονοι (1 Tim 3:8), 2) μὴ διάβολοι (1 Tim 3:11; cf. Tit 3:2), 3) μὴ
δίλογοι (1 Tim 3:8), 4) ἀφιλάργυροι (1 Tim 3:3), 5) ἐπιμελείω (comp.
ἐπιμελέομαι in 1 Tim 3:5), 6) ἐν τῷ νῦν αἰῶνι (1 Tim 6:17; cf. 2 Tim
4:10; Tit 2:13).[144] But it is the general character and thought of the
passages combined with other similarities in 4.2-6.2 that make a gen-

---

[143] Lightfoot, *The Apostolic Fathers*, part 2, vol. 3, 330-331. Concerning the directions about deacons in chs. 12 and 5 of Pol. *Phil.*, Bernard says, "The directions about
deacons in these two passages are much more closely parallel than even the above
coincidences in language [i.e. 1 Tim 2:1, 2; 4:15; and 3:8f.) would suggest." J. H. Bernard,
The Pastoral Epistles (Cambridge: Cambridge University Press, 1899; repr., Grand Rapids: Baker Book House, 1980), xv.

[144] That there is dependence of some sort on the Pastoral Epistles in the expression
ἐν τῷ νῦν αἰῶνι is supported by the following considerations: 1) The idea expressed by
the phrase is unique to Polycarp and the Pastorals among early Christian writings; 2)
The phrase is used with other expressions unique to the Pastorals (see main text); 3)
The 'faithful saying' found both in 2 Tim 2:11-12 and possibly at the end of Pol. *Phil.*
5.2 'we shall also reign with him' is a probable allusion which literarily ties these documents together in this passage; 4) The use of the expression in Pol. *Phil.* 9.2 which is
almost certainly dependent upon 2 Tim 4:10 is a clear literary connection to this phrase
in particular by Polycarp.

eral dependence upon 1 Timothy probable. Other parallels are possible to make here but are not as fruitful.

The relative clause ὃς ἐγένετο διάκονος πάντων ("who became a servant of all") follows. These last two words are the same as those found in Jesus' instructions to his disciples (cf. Mark 9:35) that if anyone wants to be first he must be πάντων διάκονος. It is difficult to doubt that Polycarp knew Mark when we consider the time in which Polycarp lived. Nevertheless, there is, apart from this two word expression (which is too short for any certainty), no clear example of dependence upon Mark in Pol. *Phil.* This expression could easily have been drawn from an oral saying of Jesus, or it could have been derived from a statement about serving found in a written gospel (cf. Matt 20:28; Mark 10:45; Luke 22:27). In light of the absence of dependence upon Mark elsewhere by Polycarp and the brevity of the expression, a possibility of dependence on Mark 9:35 should be admitted, but not much weight should be given to it.[145]

In the expression καθὼς ὑπέσχετο ἡμῖν ἐγεῖραι ἡμᾶς ἐκ νεκρῶν ("just as he promised to us to raise us from the dead") many commentators have found a reminiscence of the gospel of John (cf. John 5:21, 25; 6:44) since that promise is not found in the synoptic writers.[146] A dependence upon the Johannine tradition seems possible though, as the Oxford Society points out, it is not necessary to connect this statement to the fourth gospel.[147] The possibility should be considered strong enough to stave off critical speculations of why Polycarp did *not* allude to John. Though it is impossible to positively affirm Polycarp's use of the fourth gospel, a negative assessment also is not recommended.

The conditional clause ἐὰν πολιτευσώμεθα ἀξίως αὐτοῦ ("if we live as citizens worthy of him") is probably dependent upon an earlier text

---

[145] Harrison thinks the expression is dependent on Mark 9:35. P. N. Harrison, *Two Epistles*, 288 (though he mistakenly lists this as Pol. *Phil.* 4.1 rather than 5.2). Note that he realizes conclusions from Mark are tentative, but assumes Mark was known, if in fact Matthew and Luke were, which he affirms. Most acknowledge a possible dependence upon Mark 9:35 but feel it cannot be demonstrated. Koester, *Synoptische Überlieferung*, 120, 121; Schoedel, *Polycarp*, 19; Massaux, *Influence*, 32-33; Oxford Society, 101.

[146] E. Jacquier, *Le Nouveau Testament*, vol. 1 (Paris: Libraire Victor Lecoffre, J. Gabalda, 1911), 55. Bardsley, 'Testimony,' 214. Many scholars consider it to be possible but inconclusive, for example, Hagner, 'The Sayings of Jesus,' 240, 263 n. 39; J. N. Sanders, *The Fourth Gospel in the Early Church: Its Origin & Influence on Christian Theology up to Irenaeus* (Cambridge: Cambridge University Press, 1943), 14; Massey Hamilton Shepherd, ed. and trans., 'The Letter of Polycarp, Bishop of Smyrna, to the Philippians,' in *Early Christian Fathers*, ed. Cyril C. Richardson (New York: Collier Books, 1970), 125.

[147] Oxford Society, 103-104. Note that the Oxford Society considers the connection to the Johannine tradition (though not necessarily to the gospel) to be almost certain. I consider the dependence only to be possible.

since the word πολιτευσώμεθα is fairly rare (though the *idea* of spiritual citizenship is not). The verb πολιτεύομαι is found only in the NT in Phil 1:27 and Acts 23:1. It is also found in *1 Clem.* 21.1 and *Herm. Sim.* 5.6.6. The noun πολίτευμα in Phil 3:20 and πολιτεία in *1 Clem.* 2.8 are used in reference to Christian conduct.[148] The nearest parallel in form to the clause as it appears in Pol. *Phil.* 5.2 is the one found in *1 Clem.* 21.1 where 'Clement' discusses what will happen ἐὰν μὴ ἀξίως αὐτοῦ πολιτεούμενοι ("if we do not live as citizens worthily of him"). The phrase, however, is short and it is in a negative context in *1 Clement*. The concept of living as a citizen is weightier than even the form of the phrase and so we should consider a dependence upon Paul's Philippians to be more probable. In Phil 1:27 Paul exhorts Μόνον ἀξίως τοῦ εὐαγγελίου τοῦ Χριστοῦ πολιτεύεσθε ("Only live as citizens worthy of the gospel of Christ"). The vivid πολιτεύομαι is combined with the living 'worthily' (here not just 'of him', that is 'Christ', but 'of the gospel of Christ'). 'Clement' himself is probably influenced by Phil 1:27;[149] Polycarp appears to be, as well. The numerous subtle allusions to Paul's Philippians throughout Pol. *Phil.* supports the probability of dependence there. Still, the possibility that Polycarp was influenced by the form of *1 Clem.* 21.1 should not be ruled out.[150]

It is possible that Polycarp understands the clause καὶ συμβασιλεύσομεν αὐτῷ, εἴγε πιστεύομεν ("we will also reign together with him, provided we believe") to have also been spoken by Christ because of the syntactical connection with 'he promised.'[151] This clause, however, is separated from the clause 'he promised.' The separation alone might allow a move into a quotation of another author without Polycarp even realizing that technically his syntax makes it look like he is quoting a saying of the Lord. This appears to best explain what is occurring here. Polycarp seems to be alluding to 2 Tim 2:12, a passage which itself is quoting or adapting a Christian hymn.[152] Part of that hymn in 2 Tim

---

[148] Hagner, *Use*, 226.

[149] Ibid.

[150] Lightfoot, *The Apostolic Fathers*, part 2, vol. 3, 331 and Schoedel, *Polycarp*, 20 both think the primary dependence is upon *1 Clem.* 21.1. Massaux, *Influence*, 38-39 looks toward Phil 1:27 as the primary influence but cannot rule out influence by *1 Clem.* 21.1 (as I have argued).

[151] Schoedel, *Polycarp*, 20. But he adds, "the verb, 'he promised' cannot be pressed (cf. Justin. *Apol.* 1.10.2)."

[152] Lightfoot, *The Apostolic Fathers*, part 2, vol. 3, 331. Newport J. D. White, *The First and Second Epistles to Timothy and the Epistle to Titus*, The Expositor's Greek Testament IV (New York: George H. Doran Company, 1897; repr., Grand Rapids: Wm. B. Eerdmans Publishing Company, 1974), 78 thinks this *may* be dependent on 2 Tim 2:12.

2:12 says εἰ ὑπομένομεν, καὶ συμβασιλεύσομεν ("if we endure, we shall also reign together"). The operative word in both passages is συμβασιλεύω which appears nowhere else in the Apostolic Fathers. Polycarp adds αὐτῷ. Both are connected with a conditional clause with similar import – continuing in the faith.[153] Influence from 2 Tim 2:12 is probable.[154]

Summary of 5.2: A possible allusion to Mark 9:35. A possible dependence upon the Johannine tradition that Christ promised to raise us from the dead (cf. John 5:21, 25; 6:44). A probable allusion to Phil 1:27 (in form possibly influenced by *1 Clem.* 21.1). A probable allusion to 2 Tim 2:12.

Pol. Phil. *5.3*

Ὁμοίως καὶ νεώτεροι ἄμεμπτοι ἐν πᾶσιν· πρὸ παντὸς προνοοῦντες ἁγνείας καὶ χαλιναγωγοῦντες ἑαυτοὺς ἀπὸ παντὸς κακοῦ. καλὸν γὰρ τὸ ἀνακόπτεσθαι ἀπὸ τῶν ἐπιθυμιῶν ἐν τῷ κόσμῳ, ὅτι πᾶσα ἐπιθυμία κατὰ τοῦ πνεύματος στρατεύεται, καὶ οὔτε πόρνοι οὔτε μαλακοὶ οὔτε ἀρσενοκοῖται βασιλείαν θεοῦ κληρονομήσουσιν, οὔτε οἱ ποιοῦντες τὰ ἄτοπα. διὸ δέον ἀπέχεσθαι ἀπὸ πάντων τούτων, ὑποτασσομένους τοῖς πρεσβυτέροις καὶ διακόνοις ὡς θεῷ καὶ Χριστῷ. τὰς παρθένους ἐν ἀμώμῳ καὶ ἁγνῇ συνειδήσει περιπατεῖν.

Similarly, the younger men must be blameless in all things; they should be concerned about purity above all, reining themselves away from all evil. For it is good to be cut off from the sinful desires in the world, because every sinful desire wages war against the spirit, and neither fornicators nor male prostitutes nor homosexuals will inherit the kingdom of God, nor those who do perverse things. Therefore one must keep away from all these things and be obedient to the presbyters and deacons as to God and Christ. The young women must maintain a pure and blameless conscience.

Once again, we should be reminded that we have argued for a general dependence on 1 Timothy through Pol. *Phil.* 4.2-6.2. To add to our building contention, note that 1 Tim 5:1 contains instructions not to rebuke an older man, clearly an instruction to younger men.[155]

---

[153] "The notion of continuance in the present πιστεύομεν brings it nearer in meaning to ὑπομένομεν than might at first appear, especially when taken in connexion with πολιτευσώμεθα that has preceded." Oxford Society, 97.

[154] It should, however, always be kept in mind that Polycarp *could* have been influenced directly from the same hymn or formula being quoted by the author of 2 Timothy.

[155] Note also instructions to young men in 1 Pet 5:5; Tit 2:6; and *1 Clem.* 1:3.

Polycarp's use of the verb χαλιναγωγέω ('to bridle') could have been
influenced by James 1:26 and 3:2 (also χαλινός in 3:3), the only NT
texts to employ the term. Dependence, however, should be considered
unlikely in light of the very distinctive context of both uses in James
which are specifically about controlling the tongue (i.e. one's speech)
and the lack of clear dependence upon James elsewhere in Pol. *Phil.*

Harrison sees an allusion to the being cut off (ἀνακόπτεσθαι) from
the sinful desires of the world of Pol. *Phil.* 5.3 and the cutting off
(ἀπόκοψον) of an offending hand in Mark 9:43.[156] The relationship can
only be considered conceptual, not literary, and it is tentative at best.

Polycarp then writes ὅτι πᾶσα ἐπιθυμία κατὰ τοῦ πνεύματος
στρατεύεται ("because every desire wages war against the spirit"). 1 Pet
2:11 appears to be the source of this quotation, which reads, Ἀγαπητοί,
παρακαλῶ ὡς παροίκους καὶ παρεπιδήμους ἀπέχεσθαι τῶν σαρκικῶν
ἐπιθυμιῶν αἵτινες στρατεύονται κατὰ τῆς ψυχῆς· ("Beloved, I urge you
as aliens and strangers to abstain from fleshly lusts, which wage war
against the soul"). The combination of ἐπιθυμία with στρατεύω ("a word
of strong colouring"[157]) supports the contention of dependence. A conflation with Gal 5:17 ἡ γὰρ σὰρξ ἐπιθυμεῖ κατὰ τοῦ πνεύματος ("For the
flesh desires against the spirit...") seems to be the most likely source for
Polycarp's κατὰ τοῦ πνεύματος ("against the spirit") instead of 1 Peter's
κατὰ τῆς ψυχῆς ("against the soul"), particularly in light of the similar
application.[158]

A καί separates that quotation from the one which immediately follows: καὶ οὔτε πόρνοι οὔτε μαλακοὶ οὔτε ἀρσενοκοῖται βασιλείαν θεοῦ
κληρονομήσουσιν ("and neither fornicators nor male prostitutes nor
homosexuals will inherit the kingdom of God..."). Polycarp's citation is
a compressed version of 1 Cor 6:9-10: Ἢ οὐκ οἴδατε ὅτι ἄδικοι θεοῦ
βασιλείαν οὐ κληρονομήσουσιν; μὴ πλανᾶσθε· οὔτε πόρνοι οὔτε
εἰδωλολάτραι οὔτε μοιχοὶ οὔτε μαλακοὶ οὔτε ἀρσενοκοῖται οὔτε κλέπται
οὔτε πλεονέκται, οὐ μέθυσοι, οὐ λοίδοροι, οὐχ ἅρπαγες βασιλείαν θεοῦ
κληρονομήσουσιν. ("Or do you not know that the unrighteous shall not

---

Catechetical material could lie behind such passages, though good evidence is lacking.
See Barnard, *Studies*, 37.
[156] P. N. Harrison, *Two Epistles*, 288.
[157] Oxford Society, 88.
[158] Massaux, *Influence*, 43; Oxford Society, 88, 92; Lightfoot, *The Apostolic Fathers*,
part 2, vol. 3, 331; P. N. Harrison, *Two Epistles*, 293. Note also the similarities with
James 4:1 which still seems unlikely to have influenced the quotation.

inherit the kingdom of God? Do not be deceived; neither fornicators, nor idolaters, nor adulterers, nor male prostitutes, nor homosexuals,[159] nor thieves, nor the covetous, nor drunkards, nor revilers, nor swindlers, shall inherit the kingdom of God."). The literary dependence is obvious, and though Polycarp only includes a partial list of sinners (πόρνοι, μαλακοί, ἀρσενοκοῖται), he has drawn each from 1 Cor 6:9-10, employing the first vice πόρνοι as a marker along with the distinctive and identical βασιλείαν θεοῦ κληρονομήσουσιν. He has also maintained the order of the vices. Conscious citing by Polycarp of 1 Cor 6:9-10 is beyond any reasonable doubt.[160]

Polycarp's addition οὔτε οἱ ποιοῦντες τὰ ἄτοπα ("nor those who do perverse things") is not, however, certain. Polycarp could be influenced by 'biblical' language which not uncommonly combined ἄτοπον with ποιεῖν or something similar (i.e. Job 34:12; 26:6; Prov 30:20; 2 Macc 14:23; Luke 23:41)[161] though it is impossible to prove. A better explanation (though not necessarily exclusive of the first) is that Polycarp adds οὔτε οἱ ποιοῦντες τὰ ἄτοπα because he knows he has abbreviated Paul's list of sinners in 1 Cor 6:9-10. He adds a catch-all phrase which would encompass the general way of life being described by Paul.[162] If this is the case, it supports the contention that Polycarp is consciously quoting 1 Cor 6:9-10.[163]

In Polycarp's phrase ὑποτασσομένους τοῖς πρεσβυτέροις καὶ διακόνοις ("being subject to the elders and deacons") may be an allusion to 1 Pet 5:5 Ὁμοίως, νεώτεροι, ὑποτάγητε πρεσβυτέροις ("Likewise, young men, be subject to the elders"). Those being addressed are young men and the words are similar, but dependence cannot be demonstrated. The general dependence on 1 Timothy in 4.2-6.2 does not exclude the possibility of dependence upon 1 Pet 5:5 here, but makes it less likely than

---

[159] On the use of the English word 'homosexuals' to translate ἀρσενοκοῖται refer to the dialogue between D. F. Wright and William L. Petersen. David F. Wright, 'Homosexuals or Prostitutes: The Meaning of ΑΡΣΕΝΟΚΟΙΤΑΙ (1 Cor. 6:9, 1 Tim. 1:10),' *VC* 38 (1984): 125-153. William L. Petersen, 'Can ΑΡΣΕΝΟΚΟΙΤΑΙ be Translated by "Homosexuals"? (1 COR. 6.9; 1 TIM. 1.10)' *VC* 40 (1986): 187-191. David F. Wright, 'Translating ΑΡΣΕΝΟΚΟΙΤΑΙ (1 Cor. 6:9; 1 Tim. 1:10).' *VC* 41 (1987): 396-398.

[160] Massaux, *Influence*, 36-37; Barnett, *Paul*, 176; Oxford Society, 85.

[161] Lightfoot, *The Apostolic Fathers*, part 2, vol. 3, 331. McNatt conjectures that Job 34:12 is the ultimate source of Polycarp's use, though it is probably mediated through something catechetical. McNatt, 'Old Testament Usage,' 146-147.

[162] Barnett, *Paul*, 176; Massaux, *Influence*, 36-37; Oxford Society, 85.

[163] Oxford Society, 85.

it already is. The likelihood of influence from Ignatius (see next paragraph) also makes dependence upon 1 Pet 5:5 less likely.

The idea of being subject to one's leaders ὡς θεῷ καὶ Χριστῷ ("as to
God and Christ") may echo the similar statements of Ignatius (as in
Ign. *Magn.* 2; 6.1; 13.2; *Trall.* 2.2; 3.1; *Smyrn.* 8:1; *Pol.* 6.1).[164] Since this
comparison is so representative of Ignatius's thought, and since Polycarp
is using it in a similar way, influence can be considered possible.

The final sentence in Pol. *Phil.* 5.3 τὰς παρθένους ἐν ἀμώμῳ καὶ ἁγνῇ
συνειδήσει περιπατεῖν ("The young women[165] must maintain a pure
and blameless conscience") is considered by Schoedel to contain a probable quotation of a part of *1 Clem.* 1.3 which reads ...γυναιξίν τε ἐν
ἀμώμῳ καὶ σεμνῇ καὶ ἁγνῇ συνειδήσει πάντα ἐπιτελεῖν παρηγγέλλετε...
("...You instructed the women to perform all their duties with a blameless, reverent, and pure conscience...").[166] The similarities include: 1)
the fact of instruction to women (though different words are used), 2)
ἐν ἀμώμῳ, 3) καὶ ἁγνῇ, and 4) συνειδήσει. The differences include: 1)
the fact that Polycarp's context is hortatory whereas the context of *1
Clement* is descriptive/paraenetic, 2) the use of τὰς παρθένους instead of
γυναιξίν, 3) the absence of καὶ σεμνῇ from Pol. *Phil.*, and 4) the use of
περιπατεῖν instead of 'Clement''s πάντα ἐπιτελεῖν. Polycarp's words are
not distinctive enough to make a dependence any more than possible.
It should also be noted in this context that 1 Timothy repeatedly deals
with the concept of a good or pure conscience (cf. 1 Tim 1:5, 19; 3:9;
4:2).

Summary of 5.3: A probable loose citation of 1 Pet 2:11 (with possible influence from Gal 5:17 for πνεύματος). An almost certain compressed citation of 1 Cor 6:9-10. A possible influence of Ignatius on
the thought of Polycarp that one should submit to one's leaders as to
God and Christ. A possible allusion to *1 Clem.* 1.3.

Pol. Phil. *6.1*

Καὶ οἱ πρεσβύτεροι δὲ εὔσπλαγχνοι, εἰς πάντας ἐλεήμονες, ἐπιστρέφοντες τὰ
ἀποπεπλανημένα, ἐπισκεπτόμενοι πάντας ἀσθενεῖς, μὴ ἀμελοῦντες χήρας ἢ

---

[164] Schoedel, *Polycarp*, 20.
[165] 'Young women' rather than 'virgins' (cf. 1 Cor 7:34) has been employed here
because of the parallel with the generic νεώτεροι in the same verse. The brevity of the
sentence precludes any definite conclusion as to which is the proper translation.
[166] Ibid.

ὀρφανοῦ ἢ πένητος, ἀλλὰ προνοοῦντες ἀεὶ τοῦ καλοῦ ἐνώπιον θεοῦ καὶ ἀνθρώπων, ἀπεχόμενοι πάσης ὀργῆς, προσωποληψίας, κρίσεως ἀδίκου, μακρὰν ὄντες πάσης φιλαργυρίας, μὴ ταχέως πιστεύοντες κατά τινος, μὴ ἀπότομοι ἐν κρίσει, εἰδότες ὅτι πάντες ὀφειλέται ἐσμὲν ἁμαρτίας.

The presbyters, for their part, must be compassionate, merciful to all, turning back those who have gone astray, visiting all the sick, not neglecting a widow, orphan, or poor person, but always aiming at what is honorable in the sight of God and of men, avoiding all anger, partiality, unjust judgment, staying far away from all love of money, not quick to believe things spoken against anyone, nor harsh in judgment, knowing that we are all in debt with respect to sin.

The word εὔσπλαγχνοι ('compassionate'[167]) is common to Pol. *Phil.* 6.1, 1 Pet 3:8 and Eph 4:32 but nothing more can be said except that they all are employing Christian vocabulary.

In the expression ἐπιστρέφοντες τὰ ἀποπεπλανημένα ("turning back those who have gone astray") appears to be an allusion to Ezek 34:4 in the greater context of Ezek 34 (note also esp. 11, 16).[168] Ezek 34:4 (LXX) reads καὶ τὸ πλανώμενον οὐκ ἀπεστρέψατε ("and you have not turned back those who have gone astray"). The neuter object in Pol. *Phil.* 5.1 seems to imply that the metaphor in Polycarp's mind is that of sheep.[169] Lightfoot says that the word πρόβατα ('sheep') "therefore would naturally be supplied by the readers of the letter."[170] Swete has suggested that instead of ἀπεστρέψατε Polycarp read ἐπιστρέψατε, a reading found also in codex A. Though the sheep metaphor is common in both the OT (Ps 23; Isa 53:6), the teaching of Jesus (Matt 18:12-14; Luke 15:4-7), and Christian writers (1 Pet 2:25; *1 Clem.* 59:4) the most probable source of Polycarp's allusion, if it is an allusion, seems to be Ezekiel 34 in which is found an extended use of the sheep metaphor. The common use of ἐπισκέπτομαι by both Polycarp (immediately following) and Ezekiel (34:11) may add additional support to the link. Still, dependence should be judged to be possible and no more.

Brief phrases in lists such as is found here may not be dependent upon earlier literature at all. Massaux suggests a possible 'concrete application' of Matt 25:36, 53 in Polycarp's use of the phrase ἐπισκεπτόμενοι πάντας ἀσθενεῖς ("visiting all the sick").[171] But in light

---

[167] Not 'brave' as in its classical sense.
[168] Schoedel, *Polycarp*, 21; McNatt, 'Old Testament Usage,' 147-151.
[169] Kleist, *The Didache...*, 191 n. 48. Kleist points out that the neuter can denote persons (as in John 6:37).
[170] Lightfoot, *The Apostolic Fathers*, part 2, vol. 3, 332.
[171] Massaux, *Influence*, 33.

of the brevity of the phrase and the use of ἐπισκέπτομαι in Ezek. 34:11 (see above), this should be considered unlikely.[172] Harrison links the exhortation about widows and orphans with James 1:27,[173] but there is no way to demonstrate a link with a subject so widely discussed in the OT.

The phrase ἀλλὰ προνοοῦντες ἀεὶ τοῦ καλοῦ ἐνώπιον θεοῦ καὶ ἀνθρώπων ("but always aiming at what is good before God and men") may be an adaptation of the LXX form of Prov 3:4 which reads καὶ εὑρήσεις χάριν· καὶ προνοοῦ καλὰ ἐνώπιον κυρίου καὶ ἀνθρώπων ("...and you may find grace and aim for good before God and men").[174] The parallels include 1) the use of προνοέω, 2) the use of καλός, 3) the expression ἐνώπιον θεοῦ καὶ ἀνθρώπων (κυρίου instead of θεοῦ[175] in Prov 3:4). Similar expressions are found in Rom 12:17 (προνοούμενοι καλὰ ἐνώπιον πάντων ἀνθρώπων) and 2 Cor 8:21 (προνοοῦμεν γὰρ καλὰ οὐ μόνον ἐνώπιον κυρίου ἀλλὰ καὶ ἐνώπιον ἀνθρώπων) where Paul himself seems to be dependent upon Prov 3:4.[176] In both cases, however, the form of Polycarp's citation points more toward dependence directly upon Prov 3:4 rather than upon his use being mediated through either of the Pauline passages (though probably no one would argue that Polycarp did not know that Paul used similar expressions). Dependence upon Rom 12:17 is unlikely in light of the absence of θεοῦ καὶ in that passage.[177] Dependence on 2 Cor 8:21 should be considered more likely than Rom 12:17, but Polycarp's simpler form points more toward dependence upon Prov 3:4 than upon 2 Cor 8:21 (i.e. Pol. *Phil.*

---

[172] The exhortation to care for the sick in Pol. *Phil.* 6.1 is significant in light of the poor care often given. Giordani comments, "Hospitals are unknown in this period; the condition of the sick is very bad and the assistance given them is rudimentary." Igino Giordani, *The Social Message of the Early Church Fathers*, trans. Alba I. Zizzamia (Patterson, N.M.: St. Anthony Guild Press, 1944), 309.

[173] P. N. Harrison, *Two Epistles*, 301. Harrison is often overly optimistic about literary connections in this letter.

[174] Roman Garrison, *The Graeco-Roman Context of Early Christian Literature*, JSNTsup 127 (Sheffield: Sheffield Academic Press, 1997), 78; Hernando, 'Irenaeus,' 193; Henry Barclay Swete, *An Introduction to the Old Testament in Greek*, rev. Richard Rusden Ottley (Cambridge: Cambridge University Press, 1914; repr. Peabody, Mass.: Hendrickson Publishers, 1989), 414; Lightfoot, Harmer and Holmes, *The Apostolic Fathers: Greek Texts*, 211 (note the change from Lightfoot, *The Apostolic Fathers*, part 2, vol. 3, 333 which listed this as a quotation of 2 Cor 8:21).

[175] It is possible that the change from κυρίου to θεοῦ could have been influenced by NT language such as is found in Luke 2:52, Acts 24:16, Rom 14:18 (cf. Luke 16:15, Acts 5:4, 29, Gal 1:10; 1 Thess 2:4).

[176] Barnett, *Paul*, 181. Note also the conceptual link with Luke 16:15.

[177] Massaux, *Influence*, 39.

6.1 lacks the οὐ μόνον ἀλλὰ ἐνώπιον of 2 Cor 8:21). Still, it must be admitted that Polycarp himself could have used 2 Cor 8:21 and simplified the form himself, a procedure not unfamiliar to Polycarp.

In Polycarp's injunction μὴ ταχέως πιστεύοντες κατά τινος ("not quick to believe things spoken against anyone") is a possible reminiscence of 1 Tim 5:19. In 1 Tim 5:19 the instruction given is to reject an accusation against an elder unless there are two or three witnesses. The numerous conceptual links to 1 Timothy in Pol. *Phil.* 4.2-6.2 supports this possibility. It is also supported by the observation that in Pol. *Phil.* 6.1 the phrase is juxtaposed to another exhortation μακρὰν ὄντες πάσης φιλαργυρίας ("staying far from all love of money"). Since this (along with Polycarp's previous mention of money in 4.1) is preparation for the later discussion of the avarice of Valens (who was probably an elder) the link with 1 Tim 5:19 is strengthened to the level of serious possibility.

The final clause is introduced by the formula εἰδότες ὅτι ("knowing that"). It is the fourth time Polycarp has used it (see 1.3, 4.1, 5.1). In each of the other three instances, it has preceded an almost certain citation from a known source. This is not the case here. The clause πάντες ὀφειλέται ἐσμὲν ἁμαρτίας ("we are all debtors with respect to sin") has no known verbal parallel. Many scholars are content to leave it there, assuming that Polycarp has quoted from a source that is no longer extant.[178] Schoedel (following L. C. Crocket) thinks that this clause is dependent upon Matt 6:12 adding "probably with echoes of Luke 11:4" which links being in debt with the idea of sin.[179] A connection with the Lord's Prayer seems probable for two reasons: 1) Polycarp refers to the section on forgiveness found in the Lord's Prayer in the next line; 2) The concepts of sins and debts are linked by Polycarp. Still, in light of the liturgical nature of the Lord's Prayer (against Schoedel) there is no way to determine whether Polycarp had any literary source in mind.[180] An oral transmission and Polycarp's actualiza-

---

[178] Lightfoot, *The Apostolic Fathers*, part 2, vol. 1, 323-324, 333; Rensberger, 'As the Apostle Teaches,' 114-115 who considers this and the others to have 'the character of proverbs'; Oxford Society, 104.

[179] Schoedel, *Polycarp*, 22.

[180] Hagner, *Use*, 274. Sanday thinks that Polycarp has drawn upon a written gospel but does not know whether Polycarp has drawn upon our present gospel of Matthew (6:14f) or upon another written gospel which was very similar. Sanday, *The Gospels*, 86-87.

tion of the clause from the oral tradition is just as likely.[181] Regardless
of the source, Polycarp's dependence upon the Lord's Prayer could
have been sufficient for Polycarp to have headed the clause with a formula even if he paraphrased a well-known interpretation of the Lord's
Prayer rather than quoting an actual written source. Theologically, an
additional influence on the expression may be seen in Polycarp's use of
the Pauline singular of ἁμαρτία ('sin').[182] We should also keep in mind
that Paul taught in Rom 8:12 "...we are under obligation, not to the
flesh, to live according to the flesh..." in a section on the release from
sin through the work of the Spirit in Christ. Thus, some theological
influence by Paul (and thereby on the form?) is possible.

Summary of 6.1: A possible allusion to Ezek 34:4. A probable loose
citation of Prov 3:4 (possibly mediated through 2 Cor 8:21). A possible
reminiscence of 1 Tim 5:19. A probable allusion to the Lord's Prayer
(mediated orally?) with possible theological indebtedness to Paul.

Pol. Phil. 6.2

εἰ οὖν δεόμεθα τοῦ κυρίου ἵνα ἡμῖν ἀφῇ, ὀφείλομεν καὶ ἡμεῖς ἀφιέναι·
ἀπέναντι γὰρ τῶν τοῦ κυρίου καὶ θεοῦ ἐσμὲν ὀφθαλμῶν, καὶ πάντας δεῖ
παραστῆναι τῷ βήματι τοῦ Χριστοῦ, καὶ ἕκαστον ὑπὲρ ἑαυτοῦ λόγον δοῦναι.

Therefore if we ask the Lord to forgive us, then we ourselves ought to
forgive, for we are in full view of the eyes of the Lord and God, and
we must all stand before the judgment seat of Christ, and each one
must give an account of himself.

The combination of asking God to forgive with the condition that
we should also forgive is not uncommon in the teaching of Jesus (Matt
6:12, 14-15; 18:35; Mark 11:25-26). The inclusion of δεόμεθα points to
an allusion to the Lord's Prayer.[183] But it is not just the Lord's Prayer in
general, but probably the Lord's Prayer as recorded by Matthew.[184]
Only in Matthew is found the juxtaposition of the Lord's Prayer with

---

[181] This is true even though I have argued for dependence upon Matthew 6 in Pol.
Phil. 6.2. Polycarp's thought process could have led him to allude to the Lord's Prayer
(from whatever source) and then when he moved to a more specific appropriation of it
in 6.2, he could have concentrated upon the form found in Matthew.

[182] Lindemann, 'Paul in...Apostolic Fathers,' 43. See discussion in ch. 5.

[183] Massaux, *Influence*, 32; Oxford Society, 102, though the Oxford Society would
not opt for dependence upon Matthew.

[184] Lightfoot, *The Apostolic Fathers*, part 2, vol. 3, 333; Schoedel, *Polycarp*, 22;
Hernando, 'Irenaeus,' 193 calls it a 'conceptual allusion' to Matt 6:12.

the condition that we should also forgive each other to receive forgiveness (6:12; 14-15).[185]

When Polycarp writes πάντας δεῖ παραστῆναι τῷ βήματι τοῦ Χριστοῦ, καὶ ἕκαστον ὑπὲρ ἑαυτοῦ λόγον δοῦναι ("It is for all to stand at the judgment seat of Christ and for each to give an account") he evidently conflates Rom 14:10, 12 with 2 Cor 5:10 (though Rom 14:10, 12 is the primary text). Rom 14:10b reads πάντες γὰρ παραστησόμεθα τῷ βήματι τοῦ θεοῦ ("For we shall all stand at the judgment seat of God") and Rom 14:12 reads ἄρα [οὖν] ἕκαστος ἡμῶν περὶ ἑαυτοῦ λόγον δώσει [τῷ θεῷ] ("So then each one of us shall give account of himself to God"). 2 Cor 5:10 reads τοὺς γὰρ πάντας ἡμᾶς φανερωθῆναι δεῖ ἔμπροσθεν τοῦ βήματος τοῦ Χριστοῦ, ἵνα κομίσηται ἕκαστος τὰ διὰ τοῦ σώματος πρὸς ἃ ἔπραξεν, εἴτε ἀγαθὸν εἴτε φαῦλον ("For we must all appear before the judgment seat of Christ, that each one may be recompensed for his deeds in the body, according to what he has done, whether good or bad"). Rom 14:10, 12 appears to be the primary text though influence from 2 Cor 5:10 seems probable. The primary place of Rom 14:10, 12 is seen in the following: 1) Polycarp's use of παρίστημι rather than φανερόω; 2) The simpler construction τῷ βήματι τοῦ (though the genitive noun is Θεοῦ in Rom 14:10 rather than Χριστοῦ found in 2 Cor 5:10 and Pol. *Phil.* 6.2); 3) The separating of the two clauses by Polycarp by the use of a καὶ whereas there is no separation in 2 Cor 5:10; 4) Polycarp's ἕκαστον ὑπὲρ ἑαυτοῦ λόγον δοῦναι, apart from the infinitive verb and the presence of ἡμῶν is almost identical to Rom 14:12 ἕκαστος ἡμῶν περὶ ἑαυτοῦ λόγον δώσει. Nevertheless, some influence from 2 Cor 5:10 seems probable on the basis of 1) Polycarp's use of δεῖ plus the two infinitival verb forms and the accusative πάντας (whereas Rom 14:10 employs the accusative πάντες plus the verb in the future indicative form); 2) The expression βήματι τοῦ Χριστοῦ (instead of τοῦ Θεοῦ in Rom 14:10).[186]

---

[185] Hagner points out (*Use*, 279 n.5) that Grant (*Formation*, 104) wrongly says that 6.2 is an exact quotation of Matt 13:14-15. Raymond F. Collins, *Introduction to the New Testament* (Garden City, N.Y.: Doubleday & Company, 1983), 19 perpetuates the mistake.

[186] Most scholars are agreed on the conflation of these two passages, including Lightfoot, *The Apostolic Fathers*, part 2, vol. 3, 333; J. B. Bauer, *Die Polykarpbriefe*, 56; Barnett, *Paul*, 176-177; Annegreth Bovon-Thurneysen, 'Ethik und Eschatologie im Philipperbrief des Polykarp von Smyrna,' *TZ* 29 (1973): 244 n.11; Massaux, *Influence*, 37 (though he is less certain about influence from 2 Cor 5:10); Oxford Society, 89-90, 91; Schoedel, *Polycarp*, 22-23; W. Bauer, *Die apostolischen Väter II*, 290; P. N. Harrison, *Two Epistles*, 292. Lindemann, 'Paul in...Apostolic Fathers,' 43 calls it simply 'a quota-

Summary of 6.2: A probable allusion to Matt 6:12, 14-15. An almost certain loose citation of Rom 14:10, 12 with probable influence on the form from 2 Cor 5:10.

Pol. Phil. *6.3*

οὕτως οὖν δουλεύσωμεν αὐτῷ μετὰ φόβου καὶ πάσης εὐλαβείας, καθὼς αὐτὸς ἐνετείλατο καὶ οἱ εὐαγγελισάμενοι ἡμᾶς ἀπόστολοι καὶ οἱ προφῆται οἱ προκηρύξαντες τὴν ἔλευσιν τοῦ κυρίου ἡμῶν, ζηλωταὶ περὶ τὸ καλόν, ἀπεχόμενοι τῶν σκανδάλων καὶ τῶν ψευδαδέλφων καὶ τῶν ἐν ὑποκρίσει φερόντων τὸ ὄνομα τοῦ κυρίου, οἵτινες ἀποπλανῶσι κενοὺς ἀνθρώπους.

So, then, let us serve him with fear and all reverence, just as he himself has commanded, as did the apostles, who preached the gospel to us, and the prophets, who announced in advance the coming of our Lord. Let us be eager with regard to what is good, and avoid those who tempt others to sin and false brothers and those who bear the name of the Lord hypocritically, who lead foolish men astray.

It seems probable, in light of Polycarp's previous use of Ps 2:11 (LXX) in Pol. *Phil.* 2.1 (see discussion of 2.1 above), that Polycarp is again alluding to Ps 2:11 when he says οὕτως οὖν δουλεύσωμεν αὐτῷ μετὰ φόβου καὶ πάσης εὐλαβείας ("so then let us serve him with fear and all reverence").[187] Polycarp's allusion to Ps 2:11 in 2.1 was judged to be probable and the structure of the central phrase was similar. Here the structure of the sentence is different (for the verb is a hortatory subjunctive instead of an imperative, and μετὰ φόβου is used instead of ἐν φόβῳ). But in 6.3 (unlike 2.1) Polycarp adds the words καὶ πάσης εὐλαβείας. Since the LXX of Ps 2:11 reads δουλεύσατε τῷ κυρίῳ ἐν φόβῳ, καὶ ἀγαλλιᾶσθε αὐτῷ ἐν τρόμῳ ("serve the Lord in fear and rejoice in him with trembling") it could be argued that Polycarp's addition of καὶ πάσης εὐλαβείας is a softened form of ἐν τρόμῳ.[188] 'Fear and trembling' is an expression picked up occasionally by NT writers (Eph 6:5; Phil 2:12; 1 Cor 2:3; 2 Cor 7:15; Heb 12:21). Note that this expression may have been softened in Heb 12:28 (but not as much as in

---

tion of 2 Corinthians 5:10.' Certainly Polycarp could have abbreviated 2 Cor 5:10 into the form found in Pol. *Phil.* 6.2, but Polycarp's obvious knowledge of Romans and the similarity in form on a number of points, makes sole dependence on 2 Cor 5:10 unlikely.

[187] Lightfoot, *The Apostolic Fathers*, part 2, vol. 3, 333; McNatt, 'Old Testament Usage,' 151-153.

[188] J. B. Bauer, *Die Polykarpbriefe*, 56.

Pol. *Phil.*) τὸ μετὰ εὐλαβείας καὶ δέους ('with reverence and awe'), which may provide a weak parallel to the softening found in Pol. *Phil.* 6.3.[189] There is not too much that can be made of this addition as an argument for dependence upon Ps 2:11, but it is interesting that the mode of the serving is added both by the Psalmist and by Polycarp, and may add one (albeit tentative) conceptual connection between the two passages. Regardless, the fact that Polycarp seems to allude to Ps 2:11 both in 2.1 and 6.3 mutually reinforces both passages and raises each to the level of probable rather than merely possible.

It fairly may be asked why, if Polycarp is alluding to Ps 2:11, does he follow that allusion with "just as he himself has commanded…" Note, however, that this phrase is also followed by "…as did the apostles, who preached the gospel to us, and the prophets, who announced in advance the coming of our Lord." Polycarp has not used "just as he himself has commanded" as a citation formula. Rather, he apparently is saying that the Lord, the apostles and the prophets all commanded us to serve the Lord in fear and reverence. If this is not the correct reading of the text, then what, syntactically, is it that the apostles and the prophets are commanding us to do? In other words, it is not at all necessary to assume that Polycarp thinks that he is quoting the words of the Lord at this point, merely that he is tying into a teaching affirmed by the Lord along with the prophets and the apostles.

Is there a reminiscence of the language of Acts 7:52 in Polycarp's expression οἱ προφῆται οἱ προκηρύξαντες τὴν ἔλευσιν τοῦ κυρίου ἡμῶν ("and the prophets, who announced in advance the coming of the Lord")? Acts 7:52b reads καὶ ἀπέκτειναν τοὺς προκαταγγείλαντας περὶ τῆς ἐλεύσεως τοῦ δικαίου ("and they killed those who had previously announced the coming of the righteous one"). The concept is the same, but the wording quite different. Particularly telling is that the operative word for Polycarp is the verb προκηρύσσω whereas for the author of Acts it is προκαταγγέλλω. Not only is the form different, the theme of the death of the prophets is absent in Polycarp. In light of these observations, the other lack of verbal parallels, and the conventional concept laying behind the phrase, a reminiscence by Polycarp of Acts 7:52 should be judged unlikely.[190]

---

[189] It cannot be demonstrated that Polycarp's use of εὐλαβεία was influenced by Heb 12:28, though the Oxford Society, 99, tentatively suggests it and Metzger, *Canon*, 61 thinks an echo is likely.

[190] Oxford Committee, 98, considers it unlikely; Hagner, 'The Sayings of Jesus,' 240, 263 n. 38 considers it inconclusive; Lightfoot, *The Apostolic Fathers*, part 2, vol. 3,

Finally, there is no way to establish a solid connection between 6.3 ζηλωταὶ περὶ τὸ καλόν ("zealous for what is good") and the similar phrase ἐὰν τοῦ ἀγαθοῦ ζηλωταὶ γένησθε ("if you become zealous for what is good") in 1 Pet 3:13 or ζηλωτὴν καλῶν ἔργων ("zealous for good works") in Tit 2:14. Neither is striking enough to allow for a contention of dependence.[191]

Summary of 6.3: A probable allusion to Ps 2:11.

Pol. Phil. *7.1*

Πᾶς γάρ ὃς ἂν μὴ ὁμολογῇ Ἰησοῦν Χριστὸν ἐν σαρκὶ ἐληλυθέναι ἀντίχριστός ἐστιν· καὶ ὃς ἂν μὴ ὁμολογῇ τὸ μαρτύριον τοῦ σταυροῦ ἐκ τοῦ διαβόλου ἐστίν· καὶ ὃς ἂν μεθοδεύῃ τὰ λόγια τοῦ κυρίου πρὸς τὰς ἰδίας ἐπιθυμίας καὶ λέγῃ μήτε ἀνάστασιν μήτε κρίσιν, οὗτος πρωτότοκός ἐστι τοῦ σατανᾶ.

For everyone who does not confess that Jesus Christ has come in the flesh is antichrist, and whoever does not acknowledge the testimony of the cross is of the devil, and whoever twists the sayings of the Lord to suit his own sinful desires and claims that there is neither resurrection nor judgment – that person is the first-born of Satan.

The first clause in Pol. *Phil.* 7.1 contains the expression Πᾶς γάρ ὃς ἂν μὴ ὁμολογῇ Ἰησοῦν Χριστὸν ἐν σαρκὶ ἐληλυθέναι ἀντίχριστός ἐστιν ("For everyone who does not confess that Jesus Christ has come in the flesh is antichrist"). This is very evidently a short form of 1 John 4:2-3 πᾶν πνεῦμα ὃ ὁμολογεῖ Ἰησοῦν Χριστὸν ἐν σαρκὶ ἐληλυθότα ἐκ τοῦ θεοῦ ἐστιν, καὶ πᾶν πνεῦμα ὃ μὴ ὁμολογεῖ τὸν Ἰησοῦν ἐκ τοῦ θεοῦ οὐκ ἔστιν· καὶ τοῦτό ἐστιν τὸ τοῦ ἀντιχρίστου, ὃ ἀκηκόατε ὅτι ἔρχεται, καὶ νῦν ἐν τῷ κόσμῳ ἐστὶν ἤδη. ("every spirit that confesses that Jesus Christ has come in the flesh is from God; and every spirit that does not confess Jesus is not from God; and this is the spirit of the antichrist, of which you have heard that it is coming, and now it is already in the world.") 2 John 7 contains a similar expression Ὅτι πολλοὶ πλάνοι ἐξῆλθον εἰς τὸν κόσμον, οἱ μὴ ὁμολογοῦντες Ἰησοῦν Χριστὸν ἐρχόμενον ἐν σαρκί· οὗτός ἐστιν ὁ πλάνος καὶ ὁ ἀντίχριστος. ("For many deceivers have gone out into the world, those who do not acknowledge Jesus Christ as coming in the

---

333, it appears, considers the phrase probably to be dependent upon Acts 7:52, though he does not put it in italics.

[191] J. B. Bauer, *Die Polykarpbriefe*, 56 and Lightfoot, *The Apostolic Fathers*, part 2, vol. 3, 334 suggest a possible allusion.

flesh. This is the deceiver and the antichrist.") Though 2 John 7 is similar both in word and in thought, it is doubtful that Polycarp would have quoted 2 John without having the passage in 1 John in mind, particularly since he accurately reproduces the thought of 1 John, not just the words. What can be affirmed is that the presence of such a verse in 2 John 7 helps to anchor Polycarp's use of the words and concept to the author of the Johannine epistles – of which 1 John is preeminent.

Primary (if not sole) dependence upon 1 John 4:2-3 is supported by the following considerations: 1) The verbal parallels are clear, including πᾶς plus the relative pronoun, the distinctive use of ὁμολογέω, the phrase Ἰησοῦν Χριστὸν ἐν σαρκὶ ἐληλυθέναι, and the link with ἀντίχριστός[192] (a very colorful word) 2) The function is the same in Pol. *Phil.* 7.1 and in 1 John 4:2-3; 3) The following phrase from 1 John 3:8 (ἐκ τοῦ διαβόλου ἐστίν "is of the devil") strengthens the already strong connection to 1 John; 4) Parallel thoughts in 1 John 2:18, 22 make the connection to 1 John strong. Polycarp's general knowledge of 1 John may be reinforced by the fact that Eusebius (*H.E.* 3.39.17) claims that Papias at the same time as Polycarp (and who he said knew Polycarp, *H.E.* 3.39.1) drew testimonies from the first letter of John.[193] Would Papias have known the letter while Polycarp did not?

Most scholars have lined up emphatically to support Polycarp's dependence upon 1 John in Pol. *Phil.* 7.1.[194] This makes the skepticism of the Oxford Society (which gives it a C, c rating) unusual.[195] A few schol-

---

[192] Outside of 1-2 John, Polycarp is the only writer among the authors of the NT or the Apostolic Fathers to use this term in reference to adversaries.

[193] This statement is likely true since Eusebius seems not to have had a very good opinion of Papias.

[194] Bardsley, 'Testimony,' 218 says, "The following passage is as near to I John iv 2-3 as any early citation can be expected to be." Massaux, *Influence*, 34 comments, "A literary contact with these texts is beyond doubt." Metzger, *Canon*, 62 writes that these are "obviously derived from I John iv. 2-3." D. Richard Stuckwisch, 'Saint Polycarp of Smyrna: Johannine or Pauline Figure?' *CTQ* 61 (1997): 120 opines that "The most remarkable 'quotation' of any book of the New Testament in Polycarp's epistle is found in chapter seven." Also J. B. Bauer, *Die Polykarpbriefe*, 57; P. N. Harrison, *Two Epistles*, 300; W. Bauer, *Die apostolischen Väter II*, 290-291; Sanday, *The Gospels*, 276-278; Collins, *Introduction*, 19; Sanders, *The Fourth Gospel*, 14; D. A. Carson, Douglas J. Moo, and Leon Morris, *An Introduction to the New Testament* (Grand Rapids: Zondervan Publishing House, 1992), 446; Dehandschutter, 'Polycarp's Epistle,' 284; Lightfoot, *The Apostolic Fathers*, part 2, vol. 3, 334.

[195] At the same time, if it is so uncertain as to receive a C, c rating, why did they add, "The numerous coincidences of language render it probable that Polycarp either used I John or was personally acquainted with its author"? Oxford Society, 100.

ars express uncertainty.[196] But in light of the verbal and contextual parallels between the two passages, P. N. Harrison is certainly correct when he says, "It seems an excess of caution to doubt that 7.1...is a conscious allusion to I Joh. iv. 2f..."[197] It should be judged to be almost certain, especially in light of the other parallels and possible parallels described below.

The compressed quotation of 1 John 4:2-3 is followed by καὶ ὃς ἂν μὴ ὁμολογῇ τὸ μαρτύριον τοῦ σταυροῦ ἐκ τοῦ διαβόλου ἐστίν ("and whoever does not confess the testimony of the cross is of the devil"). Polycarp's anti-docetic expression τὸ μαρτύριον τοῦ σταυροῦ ("the testimony of the cross"), linked with μαρτυρέω, may be reminiscent of 1 John 5:6-9. 1 John 5:6-9 is likewise anti-docetic and links confession (μαρτυρία) of the cross ('the blood' in 1 John 5:6, 8) with proper belief (though not in the same words). The link to 1 John 5:6-9 becomes plausible when one remembers the quotation from 1 John 4:2-3 which immediately precedes it, the probable allusion to 1 John 3:8 which immediately follows it and the possible link to 1 John 3:12 just after that – all found in Pol. *Phil.* 7.1. Polycarp, as we shall observe later, characteristically clusters phrases and thoughts from a single writer together (though it is not as pronounced here as elsewhere in his letter). But, in the lack of closer verbal links, a reminiscence of 1 John 5:6-9 cannot be considered more than possible.

Whoever does not confess the testimony of the cross ἐκ τοῦ διαβόλου ἐστίν ("is of the devil"), says Polycarp, and in so doing, Polycarp alludes to 1 John 3:8.[198] Polycarp is name-calling, though he does not appear to be creating the three names he uses in 7.1. His use of ἀντίχριστος is drawn from 1 John as discussed above. The third label, πρωτότοκός τοῦ σατανᾶ ("first-born of Satan") is also not original to Polycarp (though often associated with him), nor is it found in biblical texts, but rather

[196] Kleist, *The Didache...*, 192 n. 53; Francis X. Gokey, *The Terminology for the Devil and Evil Spirits in the Apostolic Fathers* (Washington, D.C.: The Catholic University of America Press, 1961), 90-92; Schoedel appears to either change his mind or contradict himself. He puts quotation marks around the references to 1 John in his commentary on ch. 7 indicating that "...Polycarp reflects more or less direct contact with the texts involved..." Schoedel, *Polycarp*, 23-25, 5. But in his later article in *ABD* (William R. Schoedel, 'Polycarp, Epistle of,' *ABD*, vol. 5 [New York: Doubleday, 1992], 391) he says, "But the fact that Polycarp and the First Letter of John have anti-Docetic themes in common (*Phil.* 7) does not necessarily point to a literary relationship between them."
[197] P. N. Harrison, *Two Epistles*, 300.
[198] Dehandschutter, 'Polycarp's Epistle,' 284; Bardsley, 'Testimony,' 218; P. N. Harrison, *Two Epistles*, 300.

probably originates in Jewish sources, and is a label applied to Cain.[199] In the same way, the second of the three labels Polycarp uses is not original to Polycarp. Polycarp says that the one who does not confess the testimony of the cross ἐκ τοῦ διαβόλου ἐστίν ("is of the devil"). This exact clause is found in 1 John 3:8 and, in light of the quotation from 1 John 4:2-3 and the other possible links to 1 John in Pol. *Phil.* 7.1, very probably is drawn from 1 John as well.

It is possible that since Polycarp's first label is drawn from 1 John 4:3 and his second label is probably drawn from 1 John 3:8 that 1 John 3:12 provides the link to his first label. Cain is described in 1 John 3:12 as ἐκ τοῦ πονηροῦ ("of the evil one"). The parallel with ἐκ τοῦ διαβόλου, which Polycarp has just used, and the conceptual link of that phrase with Cain in 1 John 3:12 may have given rise to Polycarp's employment of the third label πρωτότοκός τοῦ σατανᾶ ("first-born of Satan"). This is somewhat tenuous, but a possible reminiscence of 1 John 3:12 may be seen in the expression πρωτότοκός τοῦ σατανᾶ.

Finally, in light of the two citations of the words of the Lord which follow in 7.2, we should probably understand the expression τὰ λόγια τοῦ κυρίου to mean the "sayings of the Lord" (i.e. the sayings which the Lord said) rather than "the sayings about the Lord."[200]

Summary of 7.1: An almost certain compressed citation of 1 John 4:2-3. A possible reminiscence of 1 John 5:6-9. A probable allusion to 1 John 3:8. A possible reminiscence of 1 John 3:12.

Pol. Phil. *7.2*

διὸ ἀπολιπόντες τὴν ματαιότητα τῶν πολλῶν καὶ τὰς ψευδοδιδασκαλίας, ἐπὶ τὸν ἐξ ἀρχῆς ἡμῖν παραδοθέντα λόγον ἐπιστρέψωμεν, νήφοντες πρὸς τὰς εὐχὰς καὶ προσκαρτεροῦντες νηστείαις, δεήσεσιν αἰτούμενοι τὸν παντεπόπτην θεὸν μὴ εἰσενεγκεῖν ἡμᾶς εἰς πειρασμόν, καθὼς εἶπεν ὁ κύριος· Τὸ μὲν πνεῦμα πρόθυμον, ἡ δὲ σὰρξ ἀσθενής.

Therefore let us leave behind the worthless speculation of the crowd and their false teachings, and let us return to the word delivered to us

---

[199] Nils Alstrup Dahl, 'Der Erstgeborene Satans und der Vater des Teufels (Polyk. 7, und Joh 8₄₄),' in *Apophoreta: Festschrift für Ernst Haenchen* (Berlin: Verlag Alfred Töpelmann, 1964), 70-84.

[200] There appears to be a conflict between W. Bauer's two works which address this. In BAGD, 476, it is understood as 'sayings of the Lord.' But in Henning Paulsen, *Die Briefe des Ignatius von Antiochia und der Brief des Polykarp von Smyrna: Zweite, neubearbeitete Auflage der Auslegung von Walter Bauer* (Tübingen: J.C.B. Mohr [Paul Siebeck], 1985), 120 it is understood to mean 'words *about* the Lord.'

from the beginning, let us be self-controlled with respect to prayer and persevere in fasting, earnestly asking the all-seeing God to lead us not into temptation, because, as the Lord said, 'The spirit is willing, but the flesh is weak.'

Polycarp exhorts the Philippians to return to the word delivered to them from the beginning. Similar exhortations are found in Jude 3 and *1 Clem.* 19.2. The rule of faith was to become for the church the primary yardstick for determining what was or was not heretical, which books were or were not acceptable, even which theological interpretation of a given text was correct.[201] It is clear that Polycarp is already working with a yardstick (i.e. the handed-down tradition), though his yardstick is no doubt shorter than that of Irenaeus. Certainly everyone does not share his standard. The docetists, for instance, do not, as Polycarp makes clear in this chapter.

The phrase νήφοντες πρὸς τὰς εὐχάς ("self-controlled in respect to prayers"), though short, is very probably drawn from 1 Pet 4:7 which reads νήψατε εἰς προσευχάς ("be sober for the purpose of prayers").[202] The striking use of νήφω with reference to prayers makes the connection probable. In addition, Polycarp has shown a repeated affinity to the letter of 1 Peter.

Polycarp's use of the word παντεπόπτην ('all-seeing') may have been borrowed from *1 Clement* (cf. 55.6; 64.1).[203] The concept of God seeing everything is so common in the OT and elsewhere (cf. 2 Chr 16:9; Ps 14:2; 53:2; 2 Macc 9:5), it cannot be certain that Polycarp is borrowing from *1 Clement*. The word, however, is distinctive enough and Polycarp seems familiar enough with *1 Clement* to make an allusion possible.

Polycarp enjoins his readers to earnestly ask the all-seeing God μὴ εἰσενεγκεῖν ἡμᾶς εἰς πειρασμόν ("not to lead us into temptation"). The source of the quotation is beyond any reasonable doubt the Lord's Prayer. It is probably taken from Matt 6:13 which reads καὶ μὴ εἰσενέγκῃς ἡμᾶς εἰς πειρασμόν ("and do not lead us into temptation").[204] This is more likely the source than is Luke 11:4 (which is identical in form to Matt 6:13) for the following reasons. The Lord's Prayer has already

---

[201] Rowan A. Greer, 'The Christian Bible and Its Interpretation,' in *Early Biblical Interpretation*, by James L. Kugel and Rowan A. Greer (Philadelphia: The Westminster Press, 1986).

[202] Schoedel, *Polycarp*, 25; Oxford Society, 88; Massaux, *Influence*, 43; Lightfoot, *The Apostolic Fathers*, part 2, vol. 3, 335.

[203] Lightfoot, *The Apostolic Fathers*, part 2, vol. 3, 335.

[204] Massaux, *Influence*, 31-32; Dehandschutter, 'Polycarp's Epistle,' 288; Kleist, *The Didache...*, 192 n. 60;

been referred to in 6.1-2. In discussing that passage, I argued that, though in 6.1 Polycarp *could* have begun his first allusion from an oral or liturgical source, in 6.2 he was probably alluding to the Lord's Prayer via Matt 6:12, 14-15 (and could have depended upon Matthew in both instances). It seems likely that his second reference to the Lord's Prayer also comes from Matthew though it cannot be proven from this passage alone.[205]

This leads us to the following quotation Τὸ μὲν πνεῦμα πρόθυμον, ἡ δὲ σὰρξ ἀσθενής ("The spirit is willing but the flesh is weak"). It is introduced by the formula καθὼς εἶπεν ὁ κύριος[206] ("just as the Lord said"). The form of the citation is exactly the same as is found in Matt 26:41 and Mark 14:38. Matt 26:41, though, is probably the source.[207] Note the following reasons: 1) The former citation of the Lord's Prayer is probably from Matthew; 2) Mark is not clearly enough attested elsewhere in Pol. *Phil.* to support dependence on it here (though we should not conclude Polycarp does not know Mark); 3) The argument against an oral source is suggested by the connection in Matthew (and Mark) itself. Since the quotation we are studying is juxtaposed in Matt 26:41 (and in Mark 14:38) with γρηγορεῖτε καὶ προσεύχεσθε, ἵνα μὴ εἰσέλθητε εἰς πειρασμόν ("watch and pray that you might not enter into temptation"), it can be inferred that even in that passage a connection has already been made between the saying in the garden and the Lord's Prayer – i.e. in ἵνα μὴ εἰσέλθητε εἰς πειρασμόν. Polycarp merely makes explicit the connection which is implicit in Matt 26:41 (and Mark 14:38,

---

[205] It could be argued that the close combination of this quotation with the following quotation Τὸ μὲν πνεῦμα πρόθυμον, ἡ δὲ σὰρξ ἀσθενής ('The spirit is willing but the flesh is weak') which only appears in Matt 26:41 and Mark 14:38 makes it unlikely that Polycarp's source for this part of the Lord's Prayer is either Luke 11:4 or another written or oral source. This argument, however, only works if we assume that Polycarp realized that both texts were from Matthew, which cannot be demonstrated.

[206] Harrison says, "for καθὼς εἶπεν ὁ Κύριος compare Lk. xix. 31f." P. N. Harrison, *Two Epistles*, 287. When, however, we look at Luke 19:31-32 we find a radically different context. The disciples are instructed about how to find a colt and how to go about getting it. The details were specific. When the disciples went, 'they found it just as he told them' (εὗρον καθὼς εἶπεν αὐτοῖς). But it is far more plausible to view this phrase simply as an introductory formula used by Polycarp than to presuppose a parallel for it in the NT. This is one example of many that should warn the reader of Harrison's sometimes radical optimism toward sources upon which Polycarp could have depended.

[207] Koester, *Synoptische Überlieferung*, 114-115; Grant, *Formation*, 104; Lightfoot, *The Apostolic Fathers*, part 2, vol. 3, 335-336; Massaux, *Influence*, 31-32. Barnett, *Paul*, 171 considers this to be dependent upon an oral rather than a written tradition. Knox, *Marcion*, 144 also thinks that the dependence is either on an oral source or more likely should be seen "as a reflection of contemporary liturgical usage."

though Matt 26:41 is probably the source). This makes the link with Matthew's gospel even stronger.

Summary of 7.2: A probable loose citation of 1 Pet 4:7. A possible borrowing of the word παντεπόπτην from *1 Clem.* 55.6; 64.1. An almost certain citation of the Lord's Prayer with Matt 6:13 as its probable source. An almost certain true citation of the words of the Lord with Matt 26:41 its probable source.

Pol. Phil. *8.1*

> Ἀδιαλείπτως οὖν προσκαρτερῶμεν τῇ ἐλπίδι ἡμῶν καὶ τῷ ἀρραβῶνι τῆς δικαιοσύνης ἡμῶν, ὅς ἐστι Χριστὸς Ἰησοῦς, ὃς ἀνήνεγκεν ἡμῶν τὰς ἁμαρτίας τῷ ἰδίῳ σώματι ἐπὶ τὸ ξύλον, ὃς ἁμαρτίαν οὐκ ἐποίησεν, οὐδὲ εὑρέθη δόλος ἐν τῷ στόματι αὐτοῦ· ἀλλὰ δί ἡμᾶς, ἵνα ζήσωμεν ἐν αὐτῷ, πάντα ὑπέμεινεν.

> Let us, therefore, hold steadfastly and unceasingly to our hope and the guarantee of our righteousness, who is Christ Jesus, who bore our sins in his own body upon the tree, who committed no sin, and no deceit was found in his mouth; instead, for our sakes he endured all things, in order that we might live in him.

Polycarp calls Christ Jesus "our hope" and "the guarantee of our righteousness." Both the equating of Christ with hope and the use of the word ἀρραβών are only found in Paul's writings. Paul equates Christ and hope in 1 Tim 1:1[208] and Col 1:27. The only NT appearances of ἀρραβών are 2 Cor 1:22, 2 Cor 5:5, and Eph 1:14, though in each case the Holy Spirit rather than Christ is the referent. In neither the equating of Christ with hope nor in Polycarp's use of ἀρραβών can we demonstrate his dependence upon any of these passages individually. But when taken together, it becomes probable that Polycarp is consciously alluding once again to Paul, even if the particular sources of his allusions cannot be determined.

Polycarp says ὃς ἀνήνεγκεν ἡμῶν τὰς ἁμαρτίας τῷ ἰδίῳ σώματι ἐπὶ τὸ ξύλον ("who carried our sins on his own body on the tree"). This is almost certainly appropriated from 1 Pet 2:24 which reads ὃς τὰς ἁμαρτίας ἡμῶν αὐτὸς ἀνήνεγκεν ἐν τῷ σώματι αὐτοῦ ἐπὶ τὸ ξύλον ("who himself bore our sins in his body upon the tree"). 1 Pet 2:24 itself alludes to Isa 53:4, 12 (having just cited Isa 53:9b) though Polycarp clearly has the 1 Peter text in mind. Polycarp immediately follows this clause

---

[208] Note that the order Χριστὸς Ἰησοῦς is unusual, both for Polycarp and Ignatius, though it is present in 1 Tim 1:1.

with οὐδὲ εὑρέθη δόλος ἐν τῷ στόματι αὐτοῦ ("nor was deceit found in his mouth") which is word-for-word a quotation of 1 Pet 2:22. 1 Peter actually quotes the LXX of Isa 53:9b in this instance. 1 Peter has either followed the LXX exactly (if Ziegler's edition is correct[209]), or has included a εὑρέθη (which is excluded by the best manuscripts of LXX Isaiah – B, ℵ, and L) and subsequently has been followed by Polycarp. The juxtaposition of this clause with the former citation of 1 Pet 2:24 makes dependence upon 1 Pet 2:22 an almost certainty.[210]

Polycarp's employment of ζήσωμεν was probably suggested by its appearance in 1 Pet 2:24. His use of ὑπομένω could have been suggested by its appearance in 1 Pet 2:20.

Summary of 8.1: Probable allusions to Paul's equating of Christ with hope (cf. 1 Tim 1:1; Col 1:27) and Paul's use of the word ἀρραβών (cf. 1 Cor 1:22; 5:5; Eph 1:14), though a specific passage cannot be demonstrated. An almost certain loose citation of 1 Pet 2:24. An almost certain exact citation of 1 Pet 2:22 (which is itself a citation of the LXX of Isa 53:9b).

Pol. Phil. *8.2*

μιμηταὶ οὖν γενώμεθα τῆς ὑπομονῆς [αὐτοῦ], καὶ ἐὰν πάσχωμεν διὰ τὸ ὄνομα αὐτοῦ, δοξάζωμεν αὐτόν. τοῦτον γὰρ ἡμῖν τὸν ὑπογραμμὸν ἔθηκε δι᾿ ἑαυτοῦ, καὶ ἡμεῖς τοῦτο ἐπιστεύσαμεν.

Let us, therefore, become imitators of his patient endurance, and if we should suffer for the sake of his name, let us glorify him. For this is the example he set for us in his own person, and this is what we have believed.

The rest of the paragraph which starts in 8.1 seems to be under the influence of 1 Peter, the letter which at this point has been brought to the forefront by Polycarp's citations of 1 Pet 2:24 and 2:22.[211] The idea of being imitators of Christ, though not uncommon (note, in particular Ign. *Eph.* 10.3), should not be sought outside of the immediate context of 1 Peter 2. It functions as the counterpart to the operative word

---

[209] Joseph Ziegler, ed., *Isaias*, Septuaginta (Göttingen: Vandenhoeck & Ruprecht, 1983), 322.

[210] Oxford Society, 86-87; Lightfoot, *The Apostolic Fathers*, part 2, vol. 3, 336; J. B. Bauer, *Die Polykarpbriefe*, 61; Kleist, *The Didache...*, 193 n. 64; Schoedel, *Polycarp*, 27; Massaux, *Influence*, 43-44.

[211] Lightfoot, *The Apostolic Fathers*, part 2, vol. 3, 336.

ὑπογραμμὸν ('example') which, it seems best to assume, has been incorporated from 1 Pet 2:21 under the influence of the previous quotations from 1 Peter 2. One who follows an example is an imitator of that example.

Concerning Polycarp's use of ὑπογραμμὸν, it should be noted that it is used elsewhere, most notably in *1 Clem.* 5.7; 16.17; 33.8.[212] But 1 Pet 2:21 is its only NT appearance and the word is very colorful. It seems, therefore, highly unlikely that any other text than 1 Pet 2:21 is the source of Polycarp's use of the word ὑπογραμμὸν.

Again, it seems best to locate the source of Polycarp's sentence καὶ ἐὰν πάσχωμεν διὰ τὸ ὄνομα αὐτοῦ δοξάζωμεν αὐτόν ("and if we suffer for the sake of his name let us glorify him") in relationship to 1 Peter rather than outside of that letter.[213] Polycarp's sentence may in a number of ways allude to 1 Pet 4:16 (with influence from 4:14 and 4:15).[214] 1 Pet 4:16 reads εἰ δὲ ὡς Χριστιανός, μὴ αἰσχυνέσθω, δοξαζέτω δὲ τὸν θεὸν ἐν τῷ ὀνόματι τούτῳ ("but if anyone suffers as a Christian, let him not feel ashamed, but in that name let him glorify God"). The following considerations make dependence a serious possibility: 1) The verb πάσχω (which is the implied controlling verb in 1 Pet 4:16 – see 4:15) is present in both contexts; 2) The expression in 1 Pet 4:16 ὡς Χριστιανός is parallel, in the context of 1 Peter 4, with the earlier phrase in 1 Pet 4:14 ἐν ὀνόματι Χριστοῦ ("for the name of Christ"). These may be doing the same work in their contexts as Polycarp's διὰ τὸ ὄνομα αὐτοῦ ("for the sake of his name"). In this regard, the phrase ἐν τῷ ὀνόματι τούτῳ in 1 Pet 4:16 could have aided the link in Polycarp's mind; 3) Polycarp's δοξάζωμεν αὐτόν ("let us glorify him") could be an adapted form of 1 Pet 4:16 δοξαζέτω δὲ τὸν θεὸν ("let him glorify God"). For these reasons, and in light of Polycarp's other uses of 1 Peter in this context, a dependence upon 1 Pet 4:16 should be considered possible.

---

[212] Schoedel, *Polycarp*, 27 suggests these links but prefers dependence upon 1 Pet 2:21.

[213] Because of Polycarp's use of material from the Sermon on the Mount elsewhere, Sanday thinks that a connection to our written gospels (Matt 5:11f) or to a written gospel no longer extant is plausible. Sanday, *The Gospels*, 86-87. But the context of 1 Peter adequately accounts for Polycarp's use – particularly when it is remembered that he can cluster quotations from/allusions to a single author together. Harrison finds a possible connection to Acts 9:16 where it is said concerning Paul, 'for I will show him how much he must suffer for My name's sake.' But it is not exact in form and there is nothing else in the context to confirm this possibility.

[214] Lightfoot, *The Apostolic Fathers*, part 2, vol. 3, 336.

Summary of 8.2: A probable allusion to 1 Pet 2:21. A possible allusion to 1 Pet 4:16.

Pol. Phil. *9.1*

Παρακαλῶ οὖν πάντας ὑμᾶς πειθαρχεῖν τῷ λόγῳ τῆς δικαιοσύνης καὶ ἀσκεῖν πᾶσαν ὑπομονήν, ἣν καὶ εἴδατε κατ᾽ ὀφθαλμοὺς οὐ μόνον ἐν τοῖς μακαρίοις Ἰγνατίῳ καὶ Ζωσίμῳ καὶ Ῥούφῳ ἀλλὰ καὶ ἐν ἄλλοις τοῖς ἐξ ὑμῶν καὶ ἐν αὐτῷ Παύλῳ καὶ τοῖς λοιποῖς ἀποστόλοις·

I urge all of you, therefore, to obey the teaching about righteousness and to exercise unlimited endurance, like that which you saw with your own eyes not only in the blessed Ignatius and Zosimus and Rufus but also in others from your congregation and in Paul himself and the rest of the apostles;

There may be an allusion to Heb 5:13 in Polycarp's phrase τῷ λόγῳ τῆς δικαιοσύνης ("the word of righteousness"). Heb 5:13 reads πᾶς γὰρ ὁ μετέχων γάλακτος ἄπειρος λόγου δικαιοσύνης, νήπιος γάρ ἐστιν· ("For everyone who partakes only of milk is not accustomed to the word of righteousness, for he is an infant"). The λόγου δικαιοσύνης in Heb 5:13 is the only such expression in the NT. Moreover, one almost expects the addition of a demonstrative pronoun by Polycarp. Its absence may point toward an influence of the language of Heb 5:13. Still, the phrase itself is not striking enough to make an influence from Heb 5:13 any more than possible and the context is distinct enough to make one less than certain. Moreover, the mention of Paul by name in the context may indicate the purpose (i.e. to write about righteousness, like Paul) is more on Polycarp's mind than a passage from Hebrews.

It should be noted how strikingly, even out-of-the-ordinary, is Paul's position in this list.[215] This is particularly notable in light of the passing reference to "the rest of the apostles"[216] and the fact that Paul is the only figure from the past mentioned by name.[217] Still, it cannot be demonstrated that this reflects Polycarp's general preference for Paul.[218] It may only reflect his special focus on Paul *in this letter* which is addressed to the Philippian church – a Pauline congregation. Those listed by name

---

[215] Lindemann, *Paulus im ältesten Christentum*, 89.
[216] Campenhausen understood 'the rest of the apostles' to refer to the Twelve. Campenhausen, *Formation*, 180.
[217] Lindemann, 'Paul in...Apostolic Fathers,' 42.
[218] For example, Barnett, *Paul*, 171 says, "Paul stands as the climax in his list of heroes in 9:1."

appear to be ones that the Philippian congregation saw suffer with their own eyes.

The connection of 'Paul himself,' his endurance of suffering, and the experience of it ("you saw with your own eyes") could be another reminiscence to Paul's letter to the Philippians. Phil 1:29-30 reads, "For to you it has been granted for Christ's sake, not only to believe in Him, but also to suffer for His sake, experiencing the same conflict which you saw in me, and now hear to be in me." Many other verses in Paul's Philippians associate Paul's suffering with the experience of it or sharing in it by the Philippians (Phil 1:7; 2:17-18, 30; 3:17; 4:3, 9, 14). None, however, besides Phil 1:29-30 make the connection with what they saw with their own eyes. Thus, Phil 1:29-30 should be considered the most likely location of this reminiscence. This possibility is increased when it is noticed that a short citation of Phil 2:16 immediately follows.

Summary of 9.1: A possible allusion to Heb 5:13. A possible reminiscence of Phil 1:29-30.

Pol. Phil. *9.2*

πεπεισμένους ὅτι οὗτοι πάντες οὐκ εἰς κενὸν ἔδραμον ἀλλ᾽ ἐν πίστει καὶ δικαιοσύνῃ, καὶ ὅτι εἰς τὸν ὀφειλόμενον αὐτοῖς τόπον εἰσὶ παρὰ τῷ κυρίῳ, ᾧ καὶ συνέπαθον. οὐ γὰρ τὸν νῦν ἠγάπησαν αἰῶνα, ἀλλὰ τὸν ὑπὲρ ἡμῶν ἀποθανόντα καὶ δι᾽ ἡμᾶς ὑπὸ τοῦ θεοῦ ἀναστάντα.

be assured that all these did not run in vain but in faith and righteousness, and that they are now in the place due them with the Lord, with whom they also suffered together. For they did not love this present world, but him who died on our behalf and was raised by God for our sakes.

Polycarp says that the aforementioned martyrs οὐκ εἰς κενὸν ἔδραμον ("did not run in vain"). Gal 2:2 has a similar expression, though the context is considerably different. In Gal 2:2, Paul says that he submitted the gospel to the apostles in Jerusalem μή πως εἰς κενὸν τρέχω ἢ ἔδραμον ("lest I might be running or might have run in vain"). A closer passage, both verbally, but especially in context, is Phil 2:16 λόγον ζωῆς ἐπέχοντες, εἰς καύχημα ἐμοὶ εἰς ἡμέραν Χριστοῦ, ὅτι οὐκ εἰς κενὸν ἔδραμον οὐδὲ εἰς κενὸν ἐκοπίασα ("holding fast the word of life, so that in the day of Christ I may have cause to glory because I did not run in vain nor toil in vain"). The phrase ὅτι οὐκ εἰς κενὸν ἔδραμον is contained there and is the likely source of Polycarp's phrase. Gal 2:2 may help confirm that this expression is indeed Pauline, but the source of

Polycarp's employment of this phrase is most probably Phil 2:16.[219] The specific mention of Paul, the eschatological contexts shared both by Polycarp and Phil 2:16 and the Philippians as recipients of Polycarp's letter all argue for influence on Polycarp by Phil 2:16. It is also interesting that the *Epistula Apostolorum* 27 uses Phil 2:16 in a similar way.[220] Assuming an Asian provenance and a date some time in the first half of the second century for the *Epistula Apostolorum*, the parallel use of Phil 2:16 found there provides an indirect confirmation that Polycarp could be appropriating this phrase from Phil 2:16 which, in light of other considerations, we have judged probable.

Polycarp says that these martyrs εἰς τὸν ὀφειλόμενον αὐτοῖς τόπον εἰσὶ παρὰ τῷ κυρίῳ ("are with the Lord in the place due them"). *1 Clem.* 5.4, in a context also extolling the modern martyrs (specifically Peter, but soon after Paul), has a somewhat similar expression. Peter, according to *1 Clem.* 5.4 ἐπορεύθη εἰς τὸν ὀφειλόμενον τόπον τῆς δόξης ("went to the place of glory due him"). The use of ὀφείλω with τόπος by both 'Clement' and Polycarp in contexts which are parallel could suggest contact.[221] It must be admitted, however, that the expression has a ring of conventionality that makes any dependence quite uncertain. Apart from the combination of ὀφείλω with τόπος, the form of the sentences are different (Polycarp uses εἰσὶ, 'Clement' ἐπορεύθη; for Polycarp the place is παρὰ τῷ κυρίῳ, for 'Clement' the place is τῆς δόξης). Literary dependence seems unlikely.

Polycarp's expression ᾧ καὶ συνέπαθον ("with whom they also suffered" – the 'whom' being the Lord) could be a reminiscence of Rom 8:17. The verb συμπάσχω appears only twice in the NT, both times in Paul (Rom 8:17; 1 Cor 12:26) but Rom 8:17 is the only appearance of the word in an eschatological context. Suffering with or dying with Christ, though, is common in Paul (cf. Col 1:24; 2 Cor 1:5; Rom 6:8; 2 Tim 2:12). The importance of Paul in the context of Pol. *Phil.* 9 makes the suggestion that Polycarp is dependent upon Paul's thought for this

---

[219] Barnett, *Paul*, 177; Grant, *Formation*, 103; Oxford Society, 94; Massaux, *Influence*, 39; W. Bauer, *Die apostolischen Väter II*, 293; Lightfoot, *The Apostolic Fathers*, part 2, vol. 3, 337; Schoedel, *Polycarp*, 28; P. N. Harrison, *Two Epistles*, 292 all think dependence on Phil 2:16 is probable. Rensberger, 'As the Apostle Teaches,' 114 is less certain.

[220] See Charles E. Hill, 'The *Epistula Apostolorum*: An Asian Tract from the Time of Polycarp,' *JECS* 7 (1999): 23 and Jacques-Noël Pérès, *L'Épître des apôtres accompagnée du Testament de notre Seigneur et notre Sauveur Jésus-Christ*, Apocryphes, vol. 5 (Turnhout: Brepols, 1994), 86 n. 132.

[221] Possible dependence has been suggested by Lightfoot, *The Apostolic Fathers*, part 2, vol. 3, 338 and Schoedel, *Polycarp*, 29.

clause possible, and his use of the verb συμπάσχω makes Polycarp's most likely source Rom 8:17, particularly in light of the eschatological themes in that passage.

The clause οὐ γὰρ τὸν νῦν ἠγάπησαν αἰῶνα ("for he did not love this present world") is almost certainly an adapted citation of 2 Tim 4:10.[222] In 2 Tim 4:10, Paul says that Demas had deserted him ἀγαπήσας τὸν νῦν αἰῶνα ("having loved this present world"). The following considerations make literary dependence upon 2 Tim 4:10 almost certain: 1) The form in both passages is the same except for the grammatical changes Polycarp employs to adapt it to his context; 2) The contexts of 2 Tim 4:10 and of Pol. *Phil.* 9.2 are both about loyalty during times of trial;[223] 3) The expression ὁ νῦν αἰών in the NT is only found in 1 Tim 6:17; 2 Tim 4:10 and Tit 2:13.[224]

Finally, in ἀλλὰ τὸν ὑπὲρ ἡμῶν ἀποθανόντα καὶ δι' ἡμᾶς ὑπὸ τοῦ θεοῦ ἀναστάντα ("but him who died on our behalf and was raised by God for our sakes") we may find a somewhat fuller quotation of 2 Cor 5:15 ἀλλὰ τῷ ὑπὲρ αὐτῶν ἀποθανόντι καὶ ἐγερθέντι ("but for him who died and rose on their behalf"). If there is dependence, 2 Cor 5:15 is more likely than Ign. *Rom.* 6.1 which only has the phrase τὸν ὑπὲρ ἡμῶν ἀποθανόντα ("who died for us") and says nothing about resurrection.[225] The same is true of 1 Thess 5:10 τοῦ ἀποθανόντος ὑπὲρ ἡμῶν ("who died for us"). Better than 1 Thess 5:10 is Rom 8:34 Χριστὸς [Ἰησοῦς] ὁ ἀποθανών, μᾶλλον δὲ ἐγερθείς, ὃς καί ἐστιν ἐν δεξιᾷ τοῦ θεοῦ, ὃς καὶ ἐντυγχάνει ὑπὲρ ἡμῶν ("Christ [Jesus] is the one who died, rather who was raised, who is at the right hand of God, who also intercedes for us") which has all the conceptual elements in Polycarp's expression, but is verbally somewhat distant. 2 Cor 5:15 is the closest, but can only be judged to be a possibility since the words and expressions are all conventional.

Summary of 9.2: A probable loose citation of Phil 2:16. A possible reminiscence of Rom 8:17. An almost certain loose citation of 2 Tim 4:10. A possible loose citation of 2 Cor 5:15.

---

[222] Oxford Society, 97; Schoedel, *Polycarp*, 29; J. B. Bauer, *Die Polykarpbriefe*, 63; Lightfoot, *The Apostolic Fathers*, part 2, vol. 3, 338.

[223] Oxford Society, 97.

[224] Bernard, *The Pastoral Epistles*, xv, says, "Note that Polycarp generally uses the phrase ὁ αἰὼν οὗτος, not ὁ νῦν αἰών." This is incorrect. Pol. *Phil.* 5.2 reads, ᾧ ἐὰν εὐαρεστήσωμεν ἐν τῷ νῦν αἰῶνι and 9.2 reads, οὐ γὰρ τὸν νῦν ἠγάπησαν αἰῶνα. There is no appearance of ὁ αἰὼν οὗτος in the letter.

[225] Lightfoot, *The Apostolic Fathers*, part 2, vol. 3, 338 implies that he prefers Ign. *Rom.* 6.1 to 2 Cor 5:15 as Polycarp's source. He says, "Comp. 2 Cor v. 15, 1 Thess. v. 10; and especially Ign. *Rom.* 6."

Pol. Phil. *10.1*

In his ergo state et domini exemplar sequimini firmi in fide et immutabiles, fraternitatis amatores, diligentes invicem, in veritate sociati, mansuetudine domini alterutri praestolantes, nullum despicientes.

Stand fast, therefore, in these things and follow the example of the Lord, firm and immovable in faith, loving the brotherhood, cherishing one another, united in the truth, giving way to one another in the gentleness of the Lord, despising no one.

Pol. *Phil.* chs. 10-12 are only preserved in Latin. Since judgments about literary dependence often depend upon verbal similarities it will be evident how much more tentative we must be in this section than in the sections preserved in Greek. Where necessary, either the back-translation into Greek of Lightfoot[226] or that of Zahn[227] will be employed.

After Polycarp implores the Philippians to stand firm in the things he has written and to follow the example of the Lord, he begins the first item in the virtue list which follows *firmi in fide et immutabiles* ("firm and immovable in faith"). The juxtaposition of the two adjectives *firmi* and *immutabiles* with *in fide* makes one think of Col 1:23. Col 1:23 reads εἴ γε ἐπιμένετε τῇ πίστει τεθεμελιωμένοι καὶ ἑδραῖοι ("if indeed you continue in the faith firmly established and steadfast"). A similar expression is found in 1 Cor 15:58 which reads Ὥστε, ἀδελφοί μου ἀγαπητοί, ἑδραῖοι γίνεσθε, ἀμετακίνητοι... ("So then, my beloved brothers, be steadfast, immovable..."). In favor of Col 1:23 is the presence of Polycarp's *in fide* which is lacking in 1 Cor 15:58. Against this suggestion is the absence of other clear allusions to Colossians in Pol. *Phil.* In favor of 1 Cor 15:58 is the suggestion that Polycarp originally wrote ἑδραῖοι τῇ πίστει καὶ ἀμετακίνητοι (both Lightfoot[228] and Zahn[229]) and the other supporting references to that letter in Polycarp's own, though it must be emphasized that their suggestions are conjectural and influenced by their preference for 1 Cor 15:58. Against 1 Cor 15:58 is the lack of τῇ πίστει there. It is very probable that Polycarp is influenced by Paul via one or the other (or possibly both) of these texts, though there is no certain way of determining which.[230]

---

[226] Lightfoot, *The Apostolic Fathers*, part 2, vol. 3, 338-347.

[227] Theodor Zahn, *Ignatii et Polycarpi*, Patrum Apostolicorum Opera II (Lipsiae: J.C. Hinrichs, 1876), 124-130.

[228] Lightfoot, *The Apostolic Fathers*, part 2, vol. 3, 338.

[229] Zahn, *Ignatii et Polycarpi*, 124.

[230] Lightfoot considers this to be a quotation of 1 Cor 15:58 and/or Col 1:23.

The next of Polycarp's encouragements is *fraternitatis amatores* ("loving the brotherhood"). This phrase may have come from 1 Pet 2:17 (τὴν ἀδελφότητα ἀγαπᾶτε "love the brotherhood")[231] or 1 Pet 3:8 Τὸ δὲ τέλος πάντες ὁμόφρονες, συμπαθεῖς, φιλάδελφοι... ("To sum up, let all be harmonious, sympathetic, brotherly...) where the Vulgate contains the exact phrase *fraternitatis amatores*.[232] But a decision between the two depends largely upon what Polycarp wrote originally which is anyway conjectural. And in light of Polycarp's apparent connection to Rom 12:10 immediately following, it may be that Polycarp is here merely giving a loose rendering of Rom 12:10 τῇ φιλαδελφίᾳ εἰς ἀλλήλους φιλόστοργοι, τῇ τιμῇ ἀλλήλους προηγούμενοι ("Be devoted to one another in brotherly love; give preference to one another in honor")[233] and that 1 Peter is not in his mind at all.

Even if the τῇ φιλαδελφίᾳ of Rom 12:10 is not the source of *fraternitatis amatores* (though it may be) it is probably the source of two other phrases in this list. The phrase *diligentes invicem* ("cherishing one another") very likely is dependent upon the ἀλλήλους φιλόστοργοι of Rom 12:10 and Polycarp may be employing that exact phrase.[234] This is strengthened by the fact that both Rom 12:10 and Pol. *Phil.* 10.1 are found in virtue lists and contain overlapping content and expressions.

The meaning of the phrase *alterutri praestolantes* is difficult because of

---

Lightfoot, *The Apostolic Fathers*, part 2, vol. 3, 338. These connections are also suggested by Massaux, *Influence*, 39-40; Kleist, *The Didache...*, 194 n. 71; Charles M. Nielsen, 'Polycarp, Paul and the Scriptures,' *ATR* 47 (1965): 215. Less convincing are parallels with Ign. *Eph.* 10.2 or Ign. *Smyrn.* 1.1, suggested alongside of Col 1:23 and 1 Cor 15:58 by W. Bauer, *Die apostolischen Väter II*, 293-294 and J. B. Bauer, *Die Polykarpbriefe*, 63. Oxford Society gives any connection to Col 1:23 the lowest possible rating (D, d). But this seems to be influenced by an unnecessary skepticism toward the possibility that Polycarp knows Colossians. Such skepticism is unwarranted. Is a piece of literature judged guilty (i.e. unknown) until proven innocent (i.e. known)? Or is it not just as likely that this particular letter is known to Polycarp (particularly in light of his knowledge of Ephesians) but just happens to not appear in such a short letter? What should strike us in Pol. *Phil.* is not how few sources Polycarp draws upon but how many he draws upon in such a short space. The Oxford Committee is saying in essence that Polycarp probably does *not* know Colossians. It is more accurate, in light of Polycarp's place in early church history and the evidence from his letter that he knows many writings, to say that he could have known Colossians but the evidence from his letter is inconclusive.

[231] Lightfoot, *The Apostolic Fathers*, part 2, vol. 3, 338.

[232] Massaux, *Influence*, 40; Schoedel, *Polycarp*, 30.

[233] "ein Rückgriff auf Paul. Rom. 12:10.." W. Bauer, *Die apostolischen Väter II*, 293-294.

[234] Lightfoot, *The Apostolic Fathers*, part 2, vol. 3, 338-339. Also, Barnett, *Paul*, 177; Schoedel, *Polycarp*, 30; Nielsen, 'Polycarp, Paul,' 215.

the semantic range of *praestolantes*. Does it mean 'giving way' [to one another], as an extension of its common meaning 'await'? Or does it mean 'serve' or 'wait on,' a meaning attested by Aelius Donatus in *Eunuchus* 5.5.5? If it means the second ('serve'), then the source of the phrase could be Gal 5:13 διὰ τῆς ἀγάπης δουλεύετε ἀλλήλοις ("through love serve one another").[235] If it means the first ('giving way'), then the source is probably Rom 12:10 τῇ τιμῇ ἀλλήλους προηγούμενοι ("giving way to one another in honor").[236] The various points of contact with Rom 12:10 here make it more likely that Rom 12:10 is the source of Polycarp's expression though again we do not know what Polycarp originally wrote.

The *mansuetudine domini* ("gentleness of the Lord") may be an allusion to 2 Cor 10:1 Αὐτὸς δὲ ἐγὼ Παῦλος παρακαλῶ ὑμᾶς διὰ τῆς πραΰτητος καὶ ἐπιεικείας τοῦ Χριστοῦ, ὃς κατὰ πρόσωπον μὲν ταπεινὸς ἐν ὑμῖν, ἀπὼν δὲ θαρρῶ εἰς ὑμᾶς ("Now I, Paul, myself urge you by the meekness and gentleness of Christ – I who am meek when face to face with you, but bold toward you when absent!"). This cannot be pressed, but the context also includes Paul himself in an attitude of 'giving way' to the Corinthians which fits well the context of Pol. *Phil.* 10.1.

The two phrases *in veritate sociati* ("united in truth")[237] and *nullum despicientes* ("despising no one")[238] are so general that no definite connection with an earlier text can be argued.

Summary of 10.1: A probable allusion to a Pauline phrase either from 1 Cor 15:58 or Col 1:23. A possible allusion to 1 Pet 2:17 or 3:8. Two probable allusions to Rom 12:10. A possible allusion to 2 Cor 10:1.

Pol. Phil. *10.2-3*

Cum potestis benefacere, nolite differre, quia eleemosyna de morte liberat. Omnes vobis invicem subiecti estote, conversationem vestram irreprehensibilem habentes in gentibus, ut ex bonis operibus vestris et vos laudem accipiatis et dominus in vobis non blasphemetur. Vae autem per quem nomen domini blasphematur. Sobrietatem ergo docete omnes in qua et vos conversamini.

"When you are able to do good, do not put it off, because almsgiving

[235] See discussion in Schoedel, *Polycarp*, 30.
[236] See discussion in Lightfoot, *The Apostolic Fathers*, part 2, vol. 3, 339.
[237] John 17:17, 19; 1 John 3:18; 2 John 1-4; 3 John 1-4 all connect unity with 'in truth.'
[238] 1 Cor 16:11; Gal 4:4; Matt 18:10 all contain similarities.

delivers from death. All of you be subject to one another, and maintain an irreproachable standard of conduct among the Gentiles, so that you may be praised for your good deeds and the Lord may not be blasphemed because of you. But woe to him through whom the name of the Lord is blasphemed. Therefore teach to all the self-control by which you yourselves live."

First we come to *Cum potestis benefacere, nolite differre* ("When you are able to do good, do not put it off"). The similarity in content to Prov 3:27 has been pointed out regularly ("Do not withhold good from those to whom it is due, when it is in your power to do it").[239] The only verbal connection is at the point of 'doing good.' Otherwise it would have to be considered a contextual reminiscence. Sir 29:8-9 may also be regarded as a possible source for this quotation (though Sir 29:8-9 itself may have been shaped by the teaching of Prov 3:27[240]). Sir 29:8-9 reads πλὴν ἐπὶ ταπεινῷ μακροθύμησον καὶ ἐπ᾽ ἐλεημοσύνῃ μὴ παρελκύσῃς αὐτόν. χάριν ἐντολῆς ἀντιλαβοῦ πένητος καὶ κατὰ τὴν ἔνδειαν αὐτοῦ μὴ ἀποστρέψῃς αὐτὸν κενόν ("However, be patient with a man of humble circumstances, and do not make him wait for your alms. Help a poor man for the commandment's sake, and because of his need do not send him away empty.") This lacks the verbal 'doing good' that Prov 3:27 has but has the advantage of containing the word ἐλεημοσύνη which could have been a verbal link in Pol. *Phil.* 10.2 to the following quotation from Tobit. However, such teaching exists elsewhere (note esp. Luke 11:5-13; James 2:15f) and makes reference to Prov 3:27 or Sir 29:8-9 no more than a possibility.[241]

This is followed by the explanation *quia eleemosyna de morte liberat* ("because almsgiving delivers from death"). That here we have a quotation of Tobit (4:10 and/or 12:9) is evident.[242] Tob 4:10 reads διότι ἐλεημοσύνη ἐκ θανάτου ῥύεται ("because almsgiving delivers from death"). Tob 12:9 reads ἐλεημοσύνη γὰρ ἐκ θανάτου ῥύεται ("for almsgiving delivers from death"). Assuming that the Latin translator of Pol. *Phil.* accurately reproduced the sentence from Polycarp and was

---

[239] W. Bauer, *Die apostolischen Väter II*, 294; Kleist, *The Didache...*, 194 n. 73; Garrison, *The Graeco-Roman Context*, 78. Schoedel, *Polycarp*, 30-31 considers it a probable quotation of Prov 3:28.

[240] Garrison, *The Graeco-Roman Context*, 78.

[241] See comments in J. B. Bauer, *Die Polykarpbriefe*, 64.

[242] Grant, *Introduction*, 65; Schoedel, *Polycarp*, 31; McNatt, 'Old Testament Usage,' 153-155; Sanday, *The Gospels*, 36; Oxford Society, 84; Swete, *Introduction*, 414; Lightfoot, *The Apostolic Fathers*, part 2, vol. 3, 339; J. B. Bauer, *Die Polykarpbriefe*, 64.

not himself influenced by the form found in Tob 4:10 or 12:9, Polycarp apparently cites Tobit exactly. The juxtaposition of almsgiving with deliverance from death is unusual enough to make influence from Tobit almost certain. Beckwith has suggested that the *quia* ('because') is an abbreviated form of "for it is written").[243] Polycarp then would be the first writer to use this short formula in reference to Tobit.[244] Assuming for the moment that Beckwith is correct, it still does not tell us how much authority Polycarp accords to this book. A better explanation for the presence of the *quia*, however, is that Polycarp is *exactly* reproducing the quotation from Tobit which includes either Tob 4:10's διότι or Tob 12:9's γάρ. If this is the case, here it is not a formula at all, but rather is part of the quotation.[245]

Polycarp's exhortation *Omnes vobis invicem subiecti estote* ("All of you be subject to one another") could perhaps reflect any of four sources. Eph 5:21 reads Ὑποτασσόμενοι ἀλλήλοις ἐν φόβῳ Χριστοῦ ("being subject to one another in the fear of Christ"). 1 Pet 5:15 reads Ὁμοίως, νεώτεροι, ὑποτάγητε πρεσβυτέροις· πάντες δὲ ἀλλήλοις τὴν ταπεινοφροσύνην ἐγκομβώσασθε ("Likewise, you younger men, be subject to the elders; and all of you, clothe yourselves with humility toward one another"). *1 Clem.* 38.1 reads καὶ ὑποτασσέσθω ἕκαστος τῷ πλησίον αὐτοῦ ("and let each one be subject to his neighbor"). Ign. *Magn.* 13.2 reads ὑποτάγητε τῷ ἐπισκόπῳ καὶ ἀλλήλοις ("be subject to the bishop and to one another"). Eph 5:21 has all the necessary correspondences, and though it lacks Polycarp's 'all of you' its context (5:21-6:9) implies it strongly. 1 Pet 5:5, though it has all the necessary elements does not link the subjection directly to one another, though Polycarp could still have derived it from that context. *1 Clem.* 38.1 contains the 'each of you' but lacks the expression 'to one another.' Ign. *Magn.* 13.2 contains all the elements but also adds 'to the bishop' – a somewhat foreign element in the context of Polycarp's exhortation. (In addition, literary correspondences to the letters of Ignatius exist in Pol. *Phil.* but are not very strong.) All things considered, any or none of these could be the primary source of the exhortation found here in Pol. *Phil.* It should be admitted that

---

[243] Roger Beckwith, *The Old Testament Canon of the New Testament Church and its Background in Early Judaism* (Grand Rapids: William B. Eerdmans Publishing Company, 1985), 336 n. 186; 388 compares it to Rom 10:13; 11:34f; 1 Cor 2:16; 10:26; 15:27; 1 Pet 1:24f; 3:10-12; 4:8 and 5:5.

[244] Ibid., 138.

[245] Note that Origen (*Orat.* 14) does not include Tobit in the writings for the Jews.

Polycarp may simply be reflecting the same general idea of mutual submission reflected in these other documents.[246]

Polycarp writes *conversationem vestram irreprehensibilem habentes in gentibus, ut ex bonis operibus vestris et vos laudem accipiatis* ("maintain an irreproachable standard of conduct among the Gentiles, so that you may be praised for your good deeds"). This is almost certainly a loose, compressed citation of 1 Pet 2:12 which reads τὴν ἀναστροφὴν ὑμῶν ἐν τοῖς ἔθνεσιν ἔχοντες καλήν, ἵνα ἐν ᾧ καταλαλοῦσιν ὑμῶν ὡς κακοποιῶν ἐκ τῶν καλῶν ἔργων ἐποπτεύοντες δοξάσωσιν τὸν θεὸν ἐν ἡμέρᾳ ἐπισκοπῆς ("Keep your behavior excellent among the Gentiles, so that in the thing in which they slander you as evildoers, they may on account of your good deeds, as they observe them, glorify God in the day of visitation.")[247] There are too many common elements to posit independence from one another in these two passages. The following items seal the link: 1) Conduct; 2) 'Among the Gentiles' (why would a Gentile like Polycarp use the term 'Gentiles' if it was not part of a quotation?); 3) Praise for good deeds; 4) Not being slandered/blasphemed[248] (which is picked up in the next phrase in Pol. *Phil.* 10.2 and into 10.3 as well and is present in 1 Pet 2:12 in ἐν ᾧ καταλαλοῦσιν ὑμῶν ὡς κακοποιῶν – "in that which they slander you as evildoers".)

At the end of 10.2 and in 10.3 are the following: *et dominus in vobis non blasphemetur. Vae autem per quem nomen domini blasphematur.* ("...and the Lord may not be blasphemed because of you. But woe to him through whom the name of the Lord is blasphemed.") There is little question that the original source of Polycarp's words is the clause in Isa 52:5. Note that Polycarp's usage arrives via the LXX δι᾽ ὑμᾶς διὰ παντὸς τὸ ὄνομά μου βλασφημεῖται ἐν τοῖς ἔθνεσιν ("Because of you my name is continually blasphemed among the Gentiles").[249] The main question is whether or

---

[246] Lightfoot, *The Apostolic Fathers*, part 2, vol. 3, 339 suggests perhaps influence form Eph 5:21, 1 Pet 5:5 or Ign. *Magn.* 13.2. Massaux, *Influence*, 44 think that the dependence is actually upon *1 Clem.* 38.1. Schoedel, *Polycarp*, 31 thinks it is a probable quotation of 1 Pet 5:5. J. B. Bauer, *Die Polykarpbriefe*, 64 and P. N. Harrison, *Two Epistles*, 293 think that the primary possibility is Eph 5:21 in the context in which it falls (though Harrison calls it a 'minor correspondence').
[247] Massaux, *Influence*, 44; Oxford Society, 87; Schoedel, *Polycarp*, 31; Lightfoot, *The Apostolic Fathers*, part 2, vol. 3, 339.
[248] J. B. Bauer, *Die Polykarpbriefe*, 64.
[249] Hernando, 'Irenaeus,' 193; Swete, *Introduction*, 414 link this text directly to Isa 52:5. Others see influence from Ign. *Trall.* 8.2, including Kleist, *The Didache...*, 194 n. 76; W. Bauer, *Die apostolischen Väter II*, 294; Schoedel, *Polycarp*, 31; McNatt, 'Old Testament Usage,' 155-156.

not it has been mediated through Rom 2:24 τὸ γὰρ ὄνομα τοῦ θεοῦ δι᾽ ὑμᾶς βλασφημεῖται ἐν τοῖς ἔθνεσιν, καθὼς γέγραπται ("For the name of God is blasphemed among the Gentiles because of you, just as it is written") or through Ign. *Trall.* 8.2 μὴ ἀφορμὰς δίδοτε τοῖς ἔθνεσιν, ἵνα μὴ δι᾽ ὀλίγους ἄφρονας τὸ ἔθεον πλῆθος βλασφημῆται. οὐαὶ γάρ, δι᾽ οὖ ἐπὶ ματαιότητι τὸ ὄνομά μου ἐπί τινων βλασφημεῖται ("Do not give any opportunity to the pagans, lest the godly majority be blasphemed on account of a few foolish people. For woe to him through whose folly my name is blasphemed among any.") Both Rom 2:24 and Ign. *Trall.* 8.2 are dependent upon Isa 52:5 and both are documents which Polycarp knows. In favor of Rom 2:24 is the brevity of Polycarp's use, including the absence of the 'continually' found in Isa 52:5. Against is the absence of the 'woe.' The 'woe' is found in Ign. *Trall.* 8.2 and is the most plausible source for the inclusion in Polycarp.[250] But the form of the quotation appears to be derived, not from the expanded form used by Ignatius, but either from Rom 2:24 or directly from Isa 52:5. Though Polycarp could have bypassed Rom 2:24 and used Isa 52:5 directly, in light of Polycarp's special attachment to Paul in this letter, it remains a distinct possibility that his quotation still is mediated through Rom 2:24. But the 'woe' is probably derived from Ign. *Trall.* 8.2, though even that is not certain.[251]

Summary of 10.2-3: A possible reminiscence of Prov 3:27 or Sir 29:8-9. An almost certain exact citation of Tob 4:10 and/or Tob 12:9. A possible loose citation of Eph 5:21, 1 Pet 5:5, *1 Clem 38.1*, or Ign. *Magn.* 13.2. An almost certain loose citation of 1 Pet 2:12. A probable loose citation of Isa 52:5 with possible influence from Ign. *Trall.* 8.2 and Rom 2:24.

Pol. Phil. *11.1*

Nimis contristatus sum pro Valente, qui presbyter factus est aliquando apud vos, quod sic ignoret is locum qui datus est ei. Moneo itaque, ut abstineatis vos ab avaritia et sitis casti veraces. Abstinete vos ab omni malo.

---

[250] See Eberhard Nestle, 'Two Interesting Biblical Quotations in the "Apostolic Constitutions,"' *ExpTim* 9 (1897-1898): 14-15 for a discussion of other Christian texts from the second century which in common include the 'woe' and such phrases as 'among the Gentiles' or 'among you' etc. He wonders where these additional phrases arose but does not have an answer.

[251] For example, Grant, *Introduction*, 65 suggests that Polycarp's dependence upon Isa 52:5 is mediated through *2 Clem.* 13.2. This is possible, but unlikely in the absence of other allusions to *2 Clement*, particularly if Pol. *Phil.* is to be dated earlier that *2 Clement*.

> I have been deeply grieved for Valens, who once was a presbyter among you, because he so fails to understand the office that was entrusted to him. I warn you, therefore: avoid love of money, and be pure and truthful. Avoid every kind of evil.

Polycarp expresses his grief at the falling of a former presbyter of the Philippian church named Valens along with his wife. Their sin was avarice of some sort, though the details of the sin are not evident from the letter. Polycarp's desire is for them to repent and to be restored to fellowship. The biblical allusions in ch. 11 center around this problem.

In 11.1 there is only one sentence which is of interest for our analysis of Polycarp's dependence upon earlier writings: *Abstinete vos ab omni malo* ("Avoid every kind of evil"). Similarities exist with 1 Thess 5:22 ἀπὸ παντὸς εἴδους πονηροῦ ἀπέχεσθε ("avoid every form of evil").[252] The brevity and suddenness of the sentence argues, if ever so slightly, that this is in fact a quotation of some sort. If, when Polycarp wrote this sentence in Greek, the forms of the sentence were identical or extremely verbally close (which is possible), dependence upon 1 Thess 5:22 would become probable. But in the absence of a Greek text, and in light of the brevity and conventional terms and ideas involved, dependence upon 1 Thess 5:22 can only be said to be possible. 1 Thessalonians, it should be remembered, is not clearly quoted elsewhere in the letter.

Summary of 11.1: A possible citation of 1 Thess 5:22.

Pol. Phil. *11.2*

> *Qui autem non potest se in his gubarnare, quomodo alii pronuntiat hoc? Si quis non se abstinuerit ab avaritia, ab idololatria coinquinabitur, et tanquam inter gentes iudicabitur, qui ignorant iudicium domini. Aut nescimus, quia sancti mundum iudicabunt, sicut Paulus docet?*

> But how can a man who is unable to control himself in these matters preach self-control to someone else? If a man does not avoid love of money, he will be polluted by idolatry, and will be judged as one of the Gentiles, who are ignorant of the Lord's judgment. Or do we not know that the saints will judge the world, as Paul teaches?

When Polycarp writes *Qui autem non potest se in his gubarnare, quomodo alii pronuntiat hoc?* ("But how can a man who is unable to control himself

---

[252] Kleist, *The Didache...*, 194 n. 79, Harnack, *Miscellen*, 87, and J. B. Bauer, *Die Polykarpbriefe*,, 65 all appear to think this is probably a quotation. Perhaps also Lightfoot, *The Apostolic Fathers*, part 2, vol. 3, 341.

in these matters preach self-control to someone else?") there may be a reminiscence of 1 Tim 3:5 εἰ δέ τις τοῦ ἰδίου οἴκου προστῆναι οὐκ οἶδεν, πῶς ἐκκλησίας θεοῦ ἐπιμελήσεται; ("but if a man does not know how to manage his own household, how will he take care of the church of God?").[253] The contexts are similar; both discuss the connection of public and private life in a presbyter. But the context of 1 Tim 3:5 is about disciplining one's children, whereas in Pol. *Phil.* 11.2 it is disciplining oneself. Still, there are enough similarities to consider a reminiscence a serious possibility.

The connection of avarice with idolatry may suggest influence from Eph 5:5 or Col 3:5.[254] In Pol. *Phil.* 11.2 is written, *Si quis non se abstinuerit ab avaritia, ab idololatria coinquinabitur* ("If a man does not avoid love of money, he will be polluted by idolatry"). In Eph 5:5, τοῦτο γὰρ ἴστε γινώσκοντες, ὅτι πᾶς πόρνος ἢ ἀκάθαρτος ἢ πλεονέκτης, ὅ ἐστιν εἰδωλολάτρης, οὐκ ἔχει κληρονομίαν ἐν τῇ βασιλείᾳ τοῦ Χριστοῦ καὶ θεοῦ ("For this you know with certainty, that no immoral or impure person or covetous man, who is an idolater, has an inheritance in the kingdom of Christ and God.") In Col 3:5, Νεκρώσατε οὖν τὰ μέλη τὰ ἐπὶ τῆς γῆς, πορνείαν ἀκαθαρσίαν πάθος ἐπιθυμίαν κακήν, καὶ τὴν πλεονεξίαν, ἥτις ἐστὶν εἰδωλολατρία ("Therefore consider the members of your earthly body as dead to immorality, impurity, passion, evil desire, and greed, which amounts to idolatry"). The connection of avarice and idolatry in all these texts is what makes a reminiscence of Paul by Polycarp a possibility. The context of Col 3:5 may be a little more compatible with Pol. *Phil.* 11.2 but Ephesians is better attested in general in Polycarp's letter. A decision between the two seems impossible. Certainty of literary dependence also is prohibited when we remember that Polycarp may simply have shared a common understanding with Paul concerning the connection of avarice and idolatry. This may be reinforced by the similar conceptual connection (though lacking the operative word 'idolatry' and cognates) in the teachings of Jesus (cf. Matt 6:24; Luke 16:13-14).

---

[253] Massaux, *Influence*, 40; Schoedel, *Polycarp*, 32. Oxford Society, 97, thinks it unlikely.

[254] Oxford Society, 93, 101 prefers dependence upon Eph 5:5 because of lack of other supporting references to Colossians in Pol. *Phil.* Harnack, *Miscellen*, 87 prefers dependence upon Col 3:5. For either as a possibility, see Lightfoot, *The Apostolic Fathers*, part 2, vol. 3, 341; Rensberger, 'As the Apostle Teaches,' 114; Giordani, *Social Message*, 260. Massaux, *Influence*, 42 rejects any influence of Eph 5:5 or Col 3:5 on Pol. *Phil.* 11.2.

When Polycarp speaks of the Gentiles *qui ignorant iudicium domini* ("who
are ignorant of the Lord's judgment") there is a probable allusion to
the LXX of Jer 5:4-5.[255] Jer 5:4 (LXX) reads ὅτι οὐκ ἔγνωσαν ὁδὸν
κυρίου καὶ κρίσιν θεοῦ ("because they do not know the way of the Lord
and the judgment of God"). In 5:5 this clause is repeated, though it is
positive – they do "know the way of the Lord and the judgment of
God." Polycarp seems perhaps to have condensed Jer 5:4, leaving out
the ὁδὸν and the θεοῦ found in both Jer 5:4-5 and bringing κρίσιν κυρίου
together. We have seen Polycarp compress citations elsewhere (5.3, 1
Cor 6:9; 7.1, 1 John 4:2-3; 10.2, 1 Pet 2:12) so it should not surprise us
in this instance. Notice the mention of the πτωχοί ('poor') in Jer 5:4,
providing another possible link from that passage to the discussion of
avarice in Pol. *Phil.* 11. The fact that the clause in Polycarp is a relative
clause may help support (if only slightly) its function as an allusion to
Jer 5:4-5.[256]

The final sentence in Pol. *Phil.* 11.2 is an almost certain, almost exact citation of 1 Cor 6:2.[257] It reads *Aut nescimus, quia sancti mundum
iudicabunt, sicut Paulus docet?* ("Or do we not know that the saints will
judge the world, as Paul teaches?"). 1 Cor 6:2 reads ἢ οὐκ οἴδατε ὅτι οἱ
ἅγιοι τὸν κόσμον κρινοῦσιν ("Or do you not know that the saints will
judge the world?"). The only difference is the change from the second
to the first person in Pol. *Phil.* 11.2. The formula 'as Paul teaches' would
make Polycarp's dependence upon 1 Cor 6:2 seem certain. There remains, however, the slight possibility that the Latin translator either
harmonized to a text of 1 Corinthians that he knew[258] or inserted the
sicut Paulus docet into the text.[259] Three considerations, however, militate
against the suggestion that the Latin translator inserted the *sicut Paulus
docet*. The high regard given elsewhere to Paul in Pol. *Phil.* would make
an additional mention of Paul normal (see my arguments in ch. 3). The

---

[255] Oxford Society, 84; Harnack, *Miscellen*, 87; Hernando, 'Irenaeus,' 193; Lightfoot,
The Apostolic Fathers, part 2, vol. 3, 342; Schoedel, *Polycarp*, 32-33; J. B. Bauer, *Die
Polykarpbriefe*, 65.

[256] It is not necessary to look outside of Jer 5:4-5 to connect judgment with Gen-
tiles in the previous clause (Lightfoot, *The Apostolic Fathers*, part 2, vol. 3, 342 compares
Isa 42:1; Dan 7:22; Wis 3:8; Matt 18:17 – also Harnack, *Miscellen*, 87 for Matt 18:17).
But the idea of judgment of the Gentiles is implicit in the context of Jer 5.

[257] Oxford Society, 85; Rensberger, 'As the Apostle Teaches,' 119; Grant, 'Polycarp
of Smyrna,' 143; Harnack, *Miscellen*, 87; Lightfoot, *The Apostolic Fathers*, part 2, vol. 3,
342; J. B. Bauer, *Die Polykarpbriefe*, 66; Barnett, *Paul*, 177-178.

[258] Hagner, *Use*, 284 n. 2.

[259] Massaux, *Influence*, 37; Lindemann, *Paulus im ältesten Christentum*, 90 n. 113; 228.

clustering of allusions to Paul's writings around this naming of Paul both here in 11.2-12.1 and elsewhere (3.2-4.1; 9.1-10.1) also argues for the original presence of Paul's name in this case (see my argument in ch. 4). The mention of *beatus Paulus* which immediately follows is best explained as that which gives rise to the content of 11.3 where Polycarp's paraenesis is based upon Paul's historical connection to the Philippian church. If one takes away the *sicut Paulus docet* in 11.2, the appearance of Paul's name in the following verse is not as contextually smooth (though it cannot be said to be impossible). In light of these considerations, the *sicut Paulus docet* should be considered original and the quotation which precedes it an almost certain citation of 1 Cor 6:2.

Summary of 11.2: A possible reminiscence of 1 Tim 3:5. A possible reminiscence of Eph 5:5 or Col 3:5. A probable allusion to Jer 5:4-5. An almost certain, almost exact citation of 1 Cor 6:2.

Pol. Phil. *11.3*

Ego autem nihil tale sensi in vobis vel audivi, in quibus laboravit beatus Paulus, qui estis in principio epistulae eius: de vobis etenim gloriatur in omnibus ecclesiis, quae solae tunc dominum cognoverant; nos autem nondum cognoveramus.

But I have not observed or heard of any such thing among you, in whose midst the blessed Paul labored, and who were his letters of recommendation in the beginning. For he boasts of you in all the churches – those alone, that is, which at that time had come to know the Lord, for we had not yet come to know him.

The clause in 11.3 *qui estis in principio epistulae eius*, is difficult because it appears something was lost or altered either in translating from Greek to Latin or in the Greek or Latin process of transmission. The most widely adopted solution is that attributed to Thomas Smith and supported by Michael W. Holmes. Polycarp, it is suggested, originally wrote τοῖς ἐπαινουμένοις ἐν ἀρχῇ τῆς ἐπιστολῆς αὐτοῦ. A copyist of the Greek text skipped the participle via homoeoteleuton, his sight being drawn to the dative plural ending of the participle instead of returning to the dative, plural article.[260] As to whether or not there is dependence upon an earlier text, the ἐν ἀρχῇ may suggest a reminiscence of Phil 4:15 where Paul praises the Philippians for their sharing with him from the

---

[260] Michael W. Holmes, 'A Note on the Text of Polycarp *Philippians* 11.3,' *VC* 51 (1997): 207-210.

beginning of preaching the gospel in that region.[261] If the above mentioned emendation is not accepted, an allusion to 2 Cor 3:2 where Paul
refers to the Corinthians as his letter may provide parallels to Polycarp
reference to the Philippians as Paul's letter of recommendations.[262]

When in Pol. *Phil.* 11.3 we read *de vobis etenim gloriatur in omnibus ecclesiis*
("for he boasts about you in all the churches"), the parallels to 2 Thess
1:4 ὥστε αὐτοὺς ἡμᾶς ἐν ὑμῖν ἐγκαυχᾶσθαι ἐν ταῖς ἐκκλησίαις τοῦ θεοῦ
("so then, we ourselves boast of you among the churches of God") are
obvious. There would be little question that Polycarp is alluding to 2
Thess 1:4 and the praise contained therein (1:3-4) if it were not for the
obvious fact that Polycarp is addressing the Philippians rather than the
Thessalonians. Most who have looked at the question think that an
allusion to 2 Thess 1:4 is still likely.[263] So why does Polycarp apply that
praise to the Philippians?

The two most common explanations are the following:

1) Polycarp is quoting from 2 Thess 1:4 but has a memory lapse,
thinking that the sentence in question is actually addressed to the
Philippians.[264] This is possible, though one wonders if the extensive
knowledge of Christian literature demonstrated by Polycarp would suggest such a lapse of memory.

2) Harnack suggests that Polycarp considers the Thessalonian letters
among those directed toward the Philippian church by Paul, perhaps
even knowing a collection which includes them together.[265] In other
words, all letters to the Macedonians (whether to the Thessalonians or
to the Philippians) are shared by both congregations. This is supported
by the quotation from 2 Thess 3:15 in the next verse (Pol. *Phil.* 11.4),
especially when one considers Polycarp's clustering tendencies. It would
also solve the problem of Polycarp's plural ἐπιστολάς in 3.2. If the letters to the Thessalonians could also be regarded as belonging to the
Philippians, the difficulty of the plural in 3.2 is alleviated. An additional argument in favor of Harnack's view is that 1 Thess 2:2 contains
the only mention of Philippi in Paul's letters outside the canonical

---

[261] Grant, *Formation*, 103.
[262] See notes by Oxford Society, 91.
[263] Harnack, *Miscellen*, 88-89; Lucetta Mowry, 'The Early Circulation of Paul's
Letters,' *JBL* 63 (1944): 84; P. N. Harrison, *Two Epistles*, 293; Massaux, *Influence*, 40;
Oxford Society, 95: Barnett, *Paul*, 178-179.
[264] Oxford Society, 95; Massaux, *Influence*, 40.
[265] See entire discussion in Harnack, *Miscellen*, 86-93. Barnett, *Paul*, 178-179 also
adopts Harnack's position. J. B. Bauer, *Die Polykarpbriefe*, 67 is much more cautious
about Harnack's position.

Philippians. In 1 Thess 2:2 Paul says to the Thessalonians, "but after we had already suffered and been mistreated in Philippi, as you know, we..." This little phrase 'as you know' plus the mention of Philippi could have helped Polycarp *link* the two communities together as two parts of one community. Though not conclusive, Harnack's view seems to account for the most data and explains why Polycarp would apply Paul's boasting in 2 Thess 1:4 to the Philippians.

Summary of 11.3: A possible reminiscence of Phil 4:15 or 2 Cor 3:2. A probable allusion to 2 Thess 1:4.

Pol. Phil. *11.4*

> *Valde ergo, fratres, contristor pro illo et pro coniuge eius, quibus det dominus poenitentiam veram. Sobrii ergo estote et vos in hoc, et non sicut inimicos tales existimetis, sed sicut passibilia membra et errantia eos revocate, ut omnium vestrum corpus salvetis. Hoc enim agentes, vos ipsos aedificatis.*

> Therefore, brothers, I am deeply grieved for him and for his wife; may the Lord grant them true repentance. You, therefore, for your part must be reasonable in this matter, and do not regard such people as enemies, but, as sick and straying members, restore them, in order that you may save your body in its entirety. For by doing this you build up one another.

In Polycarp's comment *quibus det dominus poenitentiam veram* ("may the Lord give true repentance") we encounter a possible literary connection with 2 Tim 2:25.[266] 2 Tim 2:25 contains instruction on how to deal with antagonists: ἐν πραΰτητι παιδεύοντα τοὺς ἀντιδιατιθεμένους, μήποτε δώῃ αὐτοῖς ὁ θεὸς μετάνοιαν εἰς ἐπίγνωσιν ἀληθείας ("with gentleness correcting those who are in opposition, if perhaps God may grant them repentance leading to knowledge of truth"). The literary connections are in 'may the Lord give,' the word 'repentance' and in 'true/truth.' Still, all these are fairly conventional. Depending upon the exact wording of the Greek, verbal similarities could be either more exact or more distant. Beyond that we can only say that literary dependence on 2 Tim 2:25 is a possibility.

When Polycarp says *et non sicut inimicos tales existimetis* ("and do not

---

[266] Harnack, *Miscellen*, 89 uses the sign =, which means he thinks dependence is probable. Apart from him (and Oxford Society, 97-98, which contradictorily gives the uncertain B, c rating but adds, "The words of Polycarp certainly recall 2 Timothy..."), others are unsure. See Lightfoot, *The Apostolic Fathers*, part 2, vol. 3, 343; Kleist, *The Didache...*, 195 n. 85.

regard such people as enemies") it appears that he is purposely adapting 2 Thess 3:15.[267] 2 Thess 3:15 reads καὶ μὴ ὡς ἐχθρὸν ἡγεῖσθε, ἀλλὰ νουθετεῖτε ὡς ἀδελφόν ("and do not regard him as an enemy, but admonish him as a brother"). Though the expression common to both texts is short and Pol. *Phil.* 11 is only preserved in Latin, the expression is distinctive enough to make conscious literary dependence upon 2 Thess 3:15 probable.

After Polycarp recommends that the Philippians deal with people like Valens not as enemies but as sick and straying members, he counsels the church to restore them so as to "save your entire body as well." Then he adds, "For by doing this you build up one another." A number of scholars think a reminiscence of Paul's body metaphor is possible here (cf. esp. 1 Cor 12:12-27; Rom 4:4-8; Eph 1:23; 4:4-16; 5:23-32; Col 1:18-24; 3:15).[268] The following ideas make the connection probable: 1) The mention of members/parts (cf. 1 Cor 12:12, 27; Rom 12:4-5); 2) The idea of a unified body in its entirety (1 Cor 12:19, 25; Rom 12:5; Eph 4:4); 3) The idea of building up one another (1 Cor 12:7; 14:12, 26; Rom 14:19; 15:2; Eph 4:12, 16, 29; 1 Thess 5:11); and 4) Shared suffering ('sick and straying members' in Pol. *Phil.*) (1 Cor 12:26). It can also be noted that the body metaphor is also present in *1 Clem.* 37.5, the final phrase being εἰς τὸ σῴζεσθαι ὅλον τὸ σῶμα ("that the whole body may be saved"). This is similar to Polycarp's *ut omnium vestrum corpus salvetis* ("in order that you may save your body in its entirety").[269] But without the original Greek it is impossible to know how exact the verbal parallels are and, anyway, the idea is easily derived from Paul. It seems unlikely that either 'Clement' or Polycarp, both of whom were well-acquainted with 1 Corinthians and Romans, would have used the body metaphor without conscious awareness that Paul

---

[267] Oxford Society, 95; Rensberger, 'As the Apostle Teaches,' 114; Barnett, *Paul*, 180; P. N. Harrison, *Two Epistles*, 293; Harnack, *Miscellen*, 89; Lightfoot, *The Apostolic Fathers*, part 2, vol. 3, 343; Schoedel, *Polycarp*, 34; Grant, *Introduction*, 139-140 (but note that in an earlier work, 'Polycarp of Smyrna,' 143-144, Grant states that Polycarp's knowledge of the Thessalonian epistles "is more doubtful," though in that work he does not even address the probable dependence of 11.4 upon 2 Thess 3:15).

[268] Barnett, *Paul*, 180; Lightfoot, *The Apostolic Fathers*, part 2, vol. 3, 344; Harnack, *Miscellen*, 90; Grant, *Introduction*, 139-140; J. B. Bauer, *Die Polykarpbriefe*, 67; Massaux, *Influence*, 37-38.

[269] Schoedel, *Polycarp*, 34 considers this a probable quotation of *1 Clem.* 37.5 (Schoedel seems to have a decided tendency toward optimistic decisions when faced with possible literary dependence on *1 Clement* throughout Pol. *Phil*). Harnack, *Miscellen*, 90 may also suggest influence from *1 Clem.* 37.5 (though Harnack also sees influence from Paul's metaphor of the body).

had used it as well. I conclude that a reminiscence of Paul's use of the body metaphor is probable and influence from *1 Clem.* 37.5 is still a possibility.

Summary of 11.4: A possible allusion to 2 Tim 2:25. A probable loose citation of 2 Thess 3:15. A probable reminiscence of Paul's body metaphor (cf. esp. 1 Cor 12:12-27; Rom 4:4-8; Eph 4:4-13) with possible influence from *1 Clem.* 37.5.

Pol. Phil. *12.1*

Confido enim vos bene exercitatos esse in sacris literis et nihil vos latet; mihi autem non est concessum. Modo, ut his scripturis dictum est, irascimini et nolite peccare, et sol non occidat super iracundiam vestram. Beatus, qui meminerit; quod ego credo esse in vobis.

For I am convinced that you are well trained in the sacred Scriptures and that nothing is hidden from you (something not granted to me). Only, as it is said in these Scriptures, be angry but do not sin, and do not let the sun set on your anger. Blessed is the one who remembers this, which I believe to be the case with you.

The first issue to be addressed in this passage is the problem of why Polycarp says that the Philippians are well versed in the sacred Scriptures whereas he says that such knowledge has not been granted to him. Is Polycarp depreciating his knowledge of the OT?

Some scholars take Polycarp's statement at face value. He really does not know the OT well, and that is why he does not often quote it.[270] Against this is the simple observation that Polycarp is the *teacher*, whereas the Philippians are the recipients of his teaching. They had *requested* Polycarp to write this letter. If he were truly not versed in the OT, their request is difficult to understand.[271]

Another approach is that Polycarp is simply displaying his humility

---

[270] Carrington, *The Early Christian Church*, vol. 1, 460; Rensberger, 'As the Apostle Teaches,' 346; Shepherd, 'The Letter of Polycarp,' 123; Nielsen, 'Polycarp, Paul,' 201. Also, Schoedel, 'Polycarp, Epistle of,' 392, but in so saying has contradicted earlier statements. Refer to the discussion in the main text. In the introduction (ch. 1) I showed evidence that Polycarp has been regarded by many as a simpleton. Taking the statement found here at face value appears to have been one of the reasons that some who have looked at Polycarp's letter have drawn this conclusion.

[271] One suggestion that has not been followed by many scholars (or by Fischer himself who suggests it) is that the phrase has been mistranslated. According to Fischer, an alternate translation could be "mir aber steht es nicht zu." Joseph A. Fischer, *Die Apostolischen Väter* (Darmstadt: Wissenschaftliche Buchgesellschaft, 1976), 263 n. 141.

because he is in fact humble.[272] It can hardly be doubted that Polycarp displays humility in this letter (his modesty in relationship to Paul in 3.2 is evidence enough[273]). This solution is acceptable as far as it goes. It, however, does not say enough.

Schoedel in his commentary (not in his later article in *ABD*[274]) takes pains to argue that Polycarp is *not* depreciating his knowledge of the OT. Schoedel says it "seems out of place here" particularly when we consider Polycarp's role as a church leader and the fact that he had been a Christian from his youth (*Mart. Pol.* 9.3). Schoedel suggests that Polycarp is saying merely that his point is not to teach them about the OT. Thus Schoedel punctuates the sentence so that it is set off from the previous phrase and translates it, "But that has not been left for me..." (i.e. to do).[275] Though Schoedel's grammatical interpretation seems strained, he has accurately recognized how unlikely it is that Polycarp would actually *not* know the OT.

In my opinion, the most plausible solution is that Polycarp is employing a 'humility statement' (here I am using J. B. Bauer's designation 'eine Demutsformel'[276]) as a rhetorical device. He does not simply make a statement of humility because he is humble (though that may in fact be the case). I think that Polycarp's statement also carries with it paraenetic intent. Though his knowledge of the 'Scriptures' is actually superior to that of the Philippians, he depreciates his knowledge in order to spur them to more learning and obedience to the Scriptures. Thus, he begins by commenting that they are well trained in the Scriptures, a statement which itself would have spurred the Philippians to learn the Scriptures better (since they know that Polycarp actually exceeds them in this area). Polycarp's praise (also with paraenetic intent) can be compared with Acts 26:2-3 where Paul praises Agrippa's knowledge of the customs of the Jews to win a hearing for the other things he wishes to say. Note that Polycarp has already praised the Philippians in 10.3 "by which you yourselves live" and in 11.3 "but I have not observed or heard of any such thing among you." Polycarp's 'humility' is

---

[272] Nielsen, 'Polycarp, Paul,' 204.
[273] See comments in Rensberger, 'As the Apostle Teaches,' 116.
[274] In his later article in *ABD*, Schoedel says without qualification, "Yet Polycarp makes relatively little use of the OT and professes inferiority to the Philippians in the knowledge of Scripture (*Phil.* 12.1)." Schoedel, 'Polycarp, Epistle of,' 392. This contradicts his more extensive discussion in Schoedel, *Polycarp*, 34-35 which are represented in my discussion.
[275] Schoedel, *Polycarp*, 34-35.
[276] J. B. Bauer, *Die Polykarpbriefe*, 69.

comparable to Ign. *Eph.* 3.1 where Ignatius says that he will not command them as though he were important ('a humility statement') though he is in fact giving commands throughout.

In summary, Polycarp first praises the Philippians' knowledge of the Scriptures with paraenetic intent and then makes a statement of humility also with paraenetic intent. Polycarp probably knew the Scriptures well. The reason he does not draw heavily upon the OT writings in his letter is because connecting his readers to Christian writings, and Paul in particular, *better fits his purpose*, which is to give instruct about 'righteousness' *like Paul.*[277]

The second major issue in Pol. *Phil. 12.1* is the employment of two more quotations. Probably the most discussed quotations in the entire letter are the quotations found here in Pol. *Phil.* 12.1: *Modo, ut his scripturis dictum est, irascimini et nolite peccare, et sol non occidat super iracundiam vestram* ("Only, as it is said in these Scriptures, be angry but do not sin, and do not let the sun set on your anger"). These two exhortations are introduced by the formula *ut his scripturis dictum est* ("as it is said in these Scriptures") – the clearest example of a citation formula in all of Polycarp's letter. It is followed by the first exhortation: *irascimini et nolite peccare* ("be angry and do not sin"). It can hardly be doubted that this was derived originally from the LXX rendering of Ps 4:5a (English, 4:4a) – ὀργίζεσθε καὶ μὴ ἁμαρτάνετε (cf. רגזו ואל־תחטאו). Whether Polycarp cites it directly is another issue.

Polycarp's second exhortation is linked to the first with an *et* and reads: *sol non occidat super iracundiam vestram* ("do not let the sun set on your anger"). The majority of those who have looked at this issue consider it clear that Polycarp is in this instance citing Eph 4:26 since Eph 4:26 contains both the citation from Ps 4:5 found in Pol. *Phil.* 12.1 *along with* this second exhortation. Eph 4:26 reads ὀργίζεσθε καὶ μὴ ἁμαρτάνετε· ὁ ἥλιος μὴ ἐπιδυέτω ἐπὶ [τῷ] παροργισμῷ ὑμῶν ("be angry and do not sin; do not let the sun set on your anger"). Unless the Latin translator harmonized this text when he translated it or it was otherwise harmonized to a known form by a copyist somewhere during its transmission,[278] it appears that Polycarp in both exhortations is quot-

---

[277] Note other possible parallels for praise and humility statements with Ign. *Eph.* 14.1; Ign. *Trall.* 3.2; *1 Clem.* 53.1; 2 Tim 1:5; 3:15 and 1 John 2:20-21. Dehandschutter, 'Polycarp's Epistle,' 285 thinks that the lack of specific OT quotations is not because Polycarp did not know the OT, but because he wants his paraenesis to be specifically Christian rather than Jewish or Hellenistic.

[278] Hagner, *Use*, 284 suggests this (of course possible) situation.

ing almost word for word from Eph 4:26. The juxtaposition of the two
commands is reason enough for most who have looked at this issue to
convince them that Polycarp has Eph 4:26 in mind in some way here.[279]

The obvious problem with a literary connection with Eph 4:26 is
that at face value it appears that Polycarp has linked under his introductory formula a quotation from Ps 4:5a (also found in Eph 4:26a)
with a quotation only found in this form in Eph 4:26b *and called them
both Scripture*. The fact that in Pol. *Phil.* 12.1 appears an *et* between the
two exhortations (which are juxtaposed without a coordinating conjunction in Eph 4:26) combined with Polycarp's plural *scripturis* makes
it appear on the surface that Polycarp is including the quotation of Eph
4:26b as Scripture. Some of the various solutions to this difficulty are
given here:

1. Polycarp knowingly quotes Ps 4:5a and intentionally follows it
with a quotation from Eph 4:26b. Since he considers Ephesians also to
be Scripture, he labels both the quotation from Ps 4:5a and Eph 4:26b
as such.[280]

2. Polycarp thinks he is quoting Ps 4:5 but does not realize that the
second exhortation is only found in Eph 4:26b, not in Ps 4:5. In other
words, he knows Eph 4:26 and in fact that passage controls his use of
Ps 4:5, but he is thinking of Ps 4:5 when he uses the term Scripture.[281]

3. Polycarp quotes Eph 4:26 directly and does not even realize that
part of it is found in Ps 4:5a. Thus, he only has Eph 4:26 in mind for
both exhortations and intends to call both exhortations Scripture.[282]

4. Polycarp quotes Ps 4:5a knowing that it is also in Eph 4:26a and
follows it with the second exhortation which he knows is found in Eph
4:26b. But Polycarp is also aware that the exhortation to not let the sun
go down on one's anger in Eph 4:26b could itself be alluding to similar
OT exhortations (such as Jer 15:9 or Deut 24:13). Since Polycarp is
aware that these other OT allusions are present in Eph 4:26b, he refers
to both clauses as Scripture – not because he thinks Ephesians is Scrip-

---

[279] Oxford Society, 93; Lightfoot, *The Apostolic Fathers*, part 2, vol. 3, 345; P. N.
Harrison, *Two Epistles*, 293; Massaux, *Influence*, 38.

[280] Maurice F. Wiles, *The Divine Apostle: The Interpretation of St. Paul's Epistles in the
Early Church* (Cambridge: Cambridge University Press, 1967), 4; Metzger, *Canon*, 62.

[281] Koester, *Synoptische Überlieferung*, 113; Schoedel, *Polycarp*, 35; Knox, *Marcion*, 30
n. 15. Anyone arguing this position has to reckon with a substantial weight of evidence
in Pol. *Phil.* that Polycarp has a very good memory and appears repeatedly to be able to
connect Pauline quotations and allusions with the name of Paul (see argument of ch.
4).

[282] Nielsen, 'Polycarp, Paul,' 201.

ture, but because of the OT allusions contained therein.[283]

5. Polycarp quotes Ps 4:5a in the first exhortation and, though he knows both are in Eph 4:26, considers the second exhortation found there also to be anchored in Ps 4:5b. J. B. Bauer suggests that the second clause "do not let the sun set on your anger" is an analogous paraphrase of the second half of Ps 4:5 (λέγετε ἐν ταῖς καρδίαις ὑμῶν καὶ ἐπὶ ταῖς κοίταις ὑμῶν κατανύγητε, "speak in your hearts and upon your bed feel remorse"). J. B. Bauer shows evidence of the possibility of the pain of remorse of κατανύγητε in Ps 4:5 being instead read as κατανύετε ('bring to an end') by some Hellenistic readers. As a result, a Hellenistic reader could have understood the second part of Psalm 4:5 to have read, "And upon your beds bring to an end (i.e. your anger)." This would have paved the way for the loose paraphrase in Eph 4:26 and Polycarp's awareness and appropriation thereof.[284]

With some uncertainty, J. B. Bauer's solution is the one adopted here. The plural of *his scripturis* may argue against locating both phrases in Ps 4:5, but, as Hagner notes, this cannot be pressed.[285] The location of Polycarp's second exhortation along with the first in Ps 4:5 (though not denying knowledge of Eph 4:26) would then mitigate against Polycarp identifying Eph 4:26 as Scripture. I am not arguing that Polycarp *cannot* refer to Paul's writings as Scripture in the early parts of the second century, only that the evidence here is not a clear argument that he does.[286] Awareness of both passages (Ps 4:5 and Eph 4:26) by Polycarp, then, is being argued though it appears that the primary dependence in the first exhortation is upon Ps 4:5a whereas the second exhortation is primarily dependent upon Eph 4:26b.

Summary of 12.1: A probable true citation of Ps 4:5a (with awareness of Eph 4:26a) followed by a probable true citation of Eph 4:26b (with awareness of Ps 4:5b).

---

[283] Barnett, *Paul*, 180-181. Bernard Weiss, *A Manual of Introduction to the New Testament*, vol. 1, trans A. J. K. Davidson (New York: Funk & Wagnalls, n.d.), 44 takes a more extreme variation of this view. He thinks that there is no reference at all to Eph 4:26 in this passage, but thinks that Polycarp refers to Ps 4:5 in the first quotation and to Deut 24:15 in the second.

[284] See discussion in J. B. Bauer, *Die Polykarpbriefe*, 69-71.

[285] Hagner, *Use*, 274 n. 1.

[286] It cannot be maintained that in the first half of the second century there were never equivalencies drawn between the OT and the NT, though it is rare. Hanson lists examples before the middle of the second century where γραφή or ὡς γέγραπται was used. He includes 2 Pet 3:16 citing Paul, Basilides citing 1 Cor 2:13 (in Hippolytus, *Elenchos* 7.26.3 – also see 7.25.2 and 7.27.8), the Epistle of Barnabas citing 'many are called but few chosen,' and *2 Clem* 2.4 'another Scripture'). Hanson, *Tradition*, 206-207.

Pol. Phil. *12.2*

Deus autem et pater domini nostri Iesu Christi et ipse sempiternus pontifex, dei filius Iesus Christus, aedificet vos in fide et veritate et in omni mansuetudine et sine iracundia et in patientia et in longanimitate et tolerantia et castitate; et det vobis sortem et partem inter sanctos suos, et nobis vobiscum, et omnibus qui sunt sub caelo, qui credituri sunt in dominum nostrum et deum Iesum Christum et in ipsius patrem qui resuscitavit eum a mortuis.

Now may the God and Father of our Lord Jesus Christ, and the eternal High Priest himself, the Son of God Jesus Christ, build you up in faith and truth and in all gentleness and in all freedom from anger and forbearance and steadfastness and patient endurance and purity, and may he give to you a share and a place among his saints, and to us with you, and to all those under heaven who will yet believe in our Lord and God Jesus Christ and in his Father who raised him from the dead.

The prayer of 12.2 is a pastiche of early Christian expressions, *all* of which are found in similar form somewhere in the NT,[287] but *none* of which can be definitively connected with any particular text. Because of the conventionality of these expressions, only a couple of the more likely literary connections will be mentioned.

The placement of the expression *sempiternus pontifex* ('eternal high priest) next to *dei filius* ('son of God') looks as if some influence from Hebrews may be present. Jesus is called both ἀρχιερεύς ('high priest') and υἱὸς τοῦ θεοῦ ('son of God') in Heb. 4:14. In Heb 6:20 it is said about Jesus ἀρχιερεὺς γενόμενος εἰς τὸν αἰῶνα ("having become a high priest forever"). Three verses later (7:3) we find the statement ἀφωμοιωμένος δὲ τῷ υἱῷ τοῦ θεοῦ, μένει ἱερεὺς εἰς τὸ διηνεκές ("but made like the Son of God, he abides a priest perpetually"). Both the designation as priest (not high priest) and the continuity of his priesthood are present in 7:3. The combination of these ideas make literary influence from Hebrews a real possibility.[288] *Mart. Pol.* 14.3 contains a very similar expression in the mouth of Polycarp and may give evidence that this is a meaningful idea for Polycarp. Still, it should be admitted that the idea of Christ as high priest is also found various places in *1 Clement* (cf. also Ign. *Phil.* 9.1) though the specific idea that Christ is eternal and

---

[287] See, for example, the list in Schoedel, *Polycarp*, 35-36.

[288] Metzger, *Canon*, 61; J. B. Bauer, *Die Polykarpbriefe*, 71; Clayton N. Jefford, *Reading the Apostolic Fathers: An Introduction* (Peabody, Mass.: Hendrickson Publishers, 1996), 81 all seem fairly confident of literary dependence on Hebrews. Massaux, *Influence*, 40 and Oxford Society, 99-100 admit the possibility but are tentative.

the identification as son of God is not present there.[289]

Some have found in Polycarp's expression *et det vobis sortem et partem inter sanctos suos* ("and may he give to you a share and a place among his saints") a possible literary connection to Acts 26:18 or 8:21 or perhaps even to Deut 12:12 or 14:26-28 because of 'share' and 'inheritance' language there.[290] The brevity of these, however, makes any literary connection inconclusive.

The final part of 12.2 contains the expression ...*Iesum Christum et in ipsius patrem qui resuscitavit eum a mortuis* ("...Jesus Christ and in his Father who raised him from the dead"). It seems that Polycarp shares an expression that had very early become stereotyped.[291] The parallel to Gal 1:1 is the closest; Paul says that he had been sent διὰ Ἰησοῦ Χριστοῦ καὶ θεοῦ πατρὸς τοῦ ἐγείραντος αὐτὸν ἐκ νεκρῶν ("through Jesus Christ, and God the Father, who raised Him from the dead"). However, parallels also exist with Col 2:12 and 1 Pet 1:21 and similar language is used elsewhere. Literary influence may be limited to Polycarp being influenced by an expression which is already commonplace by his time. The possibility, however, of a more direct influence by the closest parallel passage, Gal 1:1, cannot be ruled out.

Summary of 12.2: A possible allusion to the conception of Christ as 'eternal high priest' and 'son of God' by the author of Hebrews (cf. Heb 4:14, 6:20, 7:3). A possible loose citation of Gal 1:1.

Pol. Phil. *12.3*

> *Pro omnibus sanctis orate. Orate etiam pro regibus et potestatibus et principibus atque pro persequentibus et odientibus vos et pro inimicis crucis, ut fructus vester manifestus sit in omnibus, ut sitis in illo perfecti.*

Pray for all the saints. Pray also for kings and powers and rulers, and for those who persecute and hate you, and for the enemies of the cross, in order that your fruit may be evident among all people, that you may be perfect in him.

The first call to prayer is *Pro omnibus sanctis orate* ("Pray for all the saints"). This could be an abbreviated form of Eph 6:18 Διὰ πάσης

---

[289] Could there be here an allusion to the tradition that Jesus said that he was the Son of God as he stood before the high priest, as in Matt 26:23?

[290] Oxford Society, 99; Lightfoot, *The Apostolic Fathers*, part 2, vol. 3, 345; Hagner, 'The Sayings of Jesus,' 240, 263 n. 38 all suggest it but consider it inconclusive.

[291] Barnett, *Paul*, 182.

προσευχῆς καὶ δεήσεως προσευχόμενοι ἐν παντὶ καιρῷ ἐν πνεύματι, καὶ εἰς αὐτὸ ἀγρυπνοῦντες ἐν πάσῃ προσκαρτερήσει καὶ δεήσει περὶ πάντων τῶν ἁγίων ("With all prayer and petition pray at all times in the Spirit, and with this in view, be on the alert with all perseverance and petition for all the saints").[292] Its brevity, lack of exactness, and commonplace idea[293] prohibits any more than it being judged possibly dependent.

From a syntactical standpoint, the first phrase "pray for all the saints" is separate from the prayers for: 1) Kings, powers, rulers; 2) Those who persecute and hate you; and for 3) The enemies of the cross. The ease with which Polycarp links these three may give a hint as to some of the pressures placed upon Christians by the local government.

Polycarp says *Orate etiam pro regibus et potestatibus et principibus* ("Pray also for kings and powers and rulers"). This may be a loose citation of 1 Tim 2:2 where prayers are encouraged ὑπὲρ βασιλέων καὶ πάντων τῶν ἐν ὑπεροχῇ ὄντων ("for kings and all who are in authority")[294] and where the background in both cases seems to be some hostility from those rulers.[295] Still, the idea is general and literary dependence is only possible.

After Polycarp enjoins prayer for governmental rulers, he continues *atque pro persequentibus et odientibus vos* ("and for those who persecute and hate you"). This is possibly another allusion to the teaching of Jesus,

---

[292] J. B. Bauer, *Die Polykarpbriefe*, 72; Schoedel, *Polycarp*, 36; Kleist, *The Didache...*, 196 n. 94; P. N. Harrison, *Two Epistles*, 293; Massaux, *Influence*, 40.

[293] Oxford Society, 94.

[294] Sanday, *The Gospels*, 83-84; Rensberger, 'As the Apostle Teaches,' 114, see also 125; N. White, *Timothy and Titus*, 79; W. Bauer, *Die apostolischen Väter II*, 297; Lightfoot, *The Apostolic Fathers*, part 2, vol. 3, 346 all think a literary connection is possible. Also Helmut Koester, *History and Literature of Early Christianity, vol. 2: Introduction to the New Testament* (Philadelphia: Fortress Press and Berlin: Walter de Gruyter, 1982), 307, but note that he's reticent to allow much possibility for the *quoting* of the Pastorals even though he does recognize that Pol. *Phil.* 4.1 is from 1 Tim 6:10. He comments on p. 307, "However, passages that look like quotations from the Pastoral Epistles are rare in Polycarp's writing." Rare indeed! Polycarp's letter is so short that the number that do exist are really quite significant, especially when frequency of quotation is compared with general frequency of quotation in the writings of the other of the Apostolic Fathers.

[295] Dennis Ronald MacDonald suggests that the prayer for kings, powers and rulers is not just a private matter but is "a demonstration of goodwill toward the empire." Dennis Ronald MacDonald, *The Legend and the Apostle: The Battle for Paul in Story and Canon* (Philadelphia: The Westminster Press, 1983), 67. But this is unlikely in light of the fact that it is linked with prayers 'for those who persecute and hate you, and for the enemies of the cross.' Are the prayers for the 'enemies of the cross' (i.e. the docetists) also prayers to show goodwill?

and appears to be a conflation of Matt 5:44 and Luke 6:27.[296] Matt
5:44 reads ἀγαπᾶτε τοὺς ἐχθροὺς ὑμῶν καὶ προσεύχεσθε ὑπὲρ τῶν
διωκόντων ὑμᾶς ("love your enemies and pray for those who persecute
you"). Luke 6:27 reads ἀγαπᾶτε τοὺς ἐχθροὺς ὑμῶν, καλῶς ποιεῖτε τοῖς
μισοῦσιν ὑμᾶς ("love your enemies, do good to those who hate you").
Dependence upon Matt 5:44 is more strongly suggested by the contextual presence in both Pol. *Phil.* 12.3 and in Matt 5:48 of the exhortation
to be perfect. But as has been observed elsewhere, Polycarp does not
slavishly follow the text of Matthew, and sometimes prefers a reading
found in Luke. Dependence upon an oral source or early catechetical
source is of course possible, but the solution adopted here is the simplest. Still, literary dependence upon Matt 5:44 and Luke 6:27 cannot
be judged to be any more than a possibility.

The phrase *et pro inimicis crucis* ("and for the enemies of the cross") is
so striking that it is probably dependent upon Phil 3:18 where Paul
calls his opponents τοὺς ἐχθροὺς τοῦ σταυροῦ τοῦ Χριστοῦ ("the enemies
of the cross of Christ").[297] There is no other NT parallel and similar
expressions appear nowhere in the writings of the Apostolic Fathers.
The many allusions to Paul's Philippians in Pol. *Phil.* support the contention of probable dependence here.

Polycarp's expression *ut fructus vester manifestus sit in omnibus* ("in order
that your fruit may be evident among all") appears at first glance to be
a citation of 1 Tim 4:15 ἵνα σου ἡ προκοπὴ φανερὰ ᾖ πᾶσιν ("in order
that your progress may be evident to all"). It is possible that the Latin
translator of Pol. *Phil.* rendered ἡ προκοπή as *fructus*, in which case this
citation might have originally been an almost exact quotation of 1 Tim
4:15 (except for the plural). But if Polycarp originally wrote ὁ καρπός,
1 Tim 4:15 may not have been in his mind at all – he could have been
evincing a reminiscence of John 15:16. The *only* literary parallel with
John 15:16, however, is in 'fruit'. Since we do not have access to

---

[296] Koester, *Synoptische Überlieferung*, 119-120 suggests possible influence by Luke 6:27
but thinks Matt 5:44 is primary; also J. B. Bauer, *Die Polykarpbriefe*, 73; Schoedel, *Polycarp*,
37. Dehandschutter, 'Polycarp's Epistle,' 289 and Hernando, 'Irenaeus,' 193 limit literary dependence to Matthew. Sanday, *The Gospels*, 86-87 is unsure whether dependence
is upon one of our synoptic gospels or from a written document similar to our triple
tradition.

[297] Barnett, *Paul*, 181; Grant, *Formation*, 103. Oxford Society, 94 says it is 'probable'
but then for some reason gives it a B, c rating. A little less certain are Lightfoot, *The
Apostolic Fathers*, part 2, vol. 3, 346; J. B. Bauer, *Die Polykarpbriefe*, 73; and Schoedel,
Polycarp, 37.

Polycarp's Greek, literary dependence in this instance must be judged inconclusive.[298]

The final phrase *ut sitis in illo perfecti* ("that you may be perfect in him") is, in light of the allusion to the Sermon on the Mount a few lines earlier, more likely an allusion to Matt 5:48. James 1:4 and Colossians 2:10 also contain similar clauses[299] but are a less likely influence than is the Sermon on the Mount. Neither James nor Colossians are clearly attested in Pol. *Phil.*, whereas the Sermon on the Mount is (cf. 2.2-3; 6.2; 7.2).

Summary of 12.3: A possible abbreviated citation of Eph 6:18. A possible loose citation of 1 Tim 2:2. A possible conflated citation of Matt 5:44 and Luke 6:27. A probable allusion to Phil 3:18. A possible allusion to Matt 5:48.

Pol. Phil. *13-14*

No apparent literary connections exist in chs. 13-14.

Tendencies

1. For the most part, when Polycarp quotes from an earlier writer, he tends to use the quotation in a contextually similar way. An exception is his probable allusion to Gal 4:26 in Pol. *Phil.* 3.3 where the contexts are quite distinct.

2. Polycarp often summarizes the teaching of a particular passage into an abbreviated form while still drawing upon the terminology of that passage. Some clear examples include: the citation of Eph 2:5, 8-9 in Pol. *Phil.* 1.3; the citation of 1 Cor 6:9-10 in Pol. *Phil.* 5.3; the citation of 1 John 4:2-3 in Pol. *Phil.* 7.1; the citation of 1 Pet 2:12 in Pol. *Phil.* 10.2; the probable allusion to Jer 5:4-5 in Pol. *Phil.* 11.2.

3. Polycarp also has a tendency to add additional comments to texts he quotes. Some clear examples include the following: in Pol. *Phil.* 1.3

---

[298] J. B. Bauer, *Die Polykarpbriefe*, 73 considers this expression to be a *combination* of John 15:16 and 1 Tim 4:15. So also J. Duncan M. Derrett, 'Scripture and Norms in the Apostolic Fathers,' in *Principat 27,1: Religion*, ed. Wolfgang Haase (Berlin and New York: Walter de Gruyter, 1993), 676.

[299] Barnett, *Paul*, 182; Lightfoot, *The Apostolic Fathers*, part 2, vol. 3, 346; P. N. Harrison, *Two Epistles*, 301, 294 all tentatively suggest possible dependence upon James 1:4 or Col 2:10.

he adds "but by the will of God through Jesus Christ" to the citation of Eph 2:5, 8-9; in Pol. *Phil.* 2.1 he adds "and a throne at his right hand" to the probable citation of 1 Pet 1:21; in Pol. *Phil.* 2.2 he adds "or blow for blow or curse for curse" to the citation from 1 Pet 3:9; in Pol. *Phil.* 5.3 he adds "nor those who do perverse things" to the citation of 1 Cor 6:9-10.

4. For text critics, the only passages bearing any weight are the quotations of Acts 2:24 in Pol. *Phil.* 1.3 and the quotation of Gal 4:26 in Pol. *Phil.* 3.3 (see relevant discussions earlier in this chapter).

CHAPTER THREE

POLYCARP, AN IMITATOR OF PAUL?

There can be little doubt that in Pol. *Phil.*, Polycarp holds Paul in high esteem. This esteem has been observed by many.[1] But is esteem all that we encounter in the letter? Does Polycarp, perhaps, make intentional connections to Paul in order to support his goal of encouraging righteous living among the Philippians?

In this chapter, I will argue that in Pol. *Phil.*, Polycarp is linked to Paul through imitation (Greek: μίμησις; Latin: *imitatio*). Because Polycarp is 1) writing to a Pauline congregation, 2) responding to a request to write about 'righteousness', and 3) may have been requested (as I have previously suggested) to write them a letter *as Paul did*, Polycarp purposely seeks to imitate both the literary style and the ethical example of Paul as he writes to the Philippians. In so doing, he is influenced by a general and widespread value accorded imitation in the Graeco-Roman world of the second century.

---

[1] D. Richard Stuckwish, 'Saint Polycarp of Smyrna: Johannine or Pauline Figure?' *CTQ* 61 (1997): 121 comments, "In addition to the proliferation of quotations and allusions from the Pauline Epistles, the person of Saint Paul is also highly regarded in the epistle of Polycarp..." Dennis Ronald MacDonald, *The Legend and the Apostle: The Battle for Paul in Story and Canon* (Philadelphia: The Westminster Press, 1983), 114 n. 4 writes, "His letter to the Philippians resonates with the authority of a Pauline letter." Albert E. Barnett, *Paul Becomes a Literary Influence* (Chicago: The University of Chicago Press, 1941), 171 notes, "In several passages Polycarp shows that he writes under the conscious influence of Paul and his letters." Andreas Lindemann, *Paulus im ältesten Christentum: Das Bild des Apostels und die Rezeption der paulinischen Theologie in der frühchristlichen Literatur bis Marcion*, BHT 58 (Tübingen: J.C.B. Mohr [Paul Siebeck], 1979), 89 comments on how unusual such regard is, "Die hier sichtbar werdende Hochschätzung des Paulus ist außerordentlich." Helmut Koester, *History and Literature of Early Christianity, vol. 2: Introduction to the New Testament* (Philadelphia: Fortress Press and Berlin: Walter de Gruyter, 1982), 307 opines, "For Polycarp there is no apostolic authority other than Paul..." Charles M. Nielsen, 'Polycarp and Marcion: A Note,' *TS* 47 (1986): 299 agrees, "While Polycarp does not regard Paul as the only apostle, Paul is clearly the only *important* apostle." See also comments in David K. Rensberger, 'As the Apostle Teaches: The Development of the Use of Paul's Letters in Second-Century Christianity,' (Ph.D. diss., Yale University, 1981), 117.

Graeco-Roman Imitation[2]

Polycarp lived in a time when imitation of earlier masters, both in speech and literature, was highly valued. Innovation was not esteemed in the way it is today.[3] Quintilian (*Institutio Oratoria* 10.2.1) comments that "it is expedient to imitate whatever has been invented with success."[4] There are regular discussions of the concept of imitation among rhetorical theorists from the time of the writing of *On Imitation* by Dionysius of Halicanassus (written a few years before the birth of Christ) onward. Imitation, as a concept, is foundational to all of Dionysius' writings on rhetoric and is a central concern of many ancient rhetoricians.[5]

---

[2] This section will argue that Polycarp reflects the Graeco-Roman value placed upon imitation. But note that imitation was not only a value for the Greeks and Romans. The retelling of Israel's history and the recreating of a 'biblical atmosphere' was common in the Jewish literature of the Second Temple period. See Devorah Dimant, 'Use and Interpretation of Mikra in the Apocrypha and Pseudepigrapha,' in *Mikra: Text, Translation, Reading and Interpretation of the Hebrew Bible in Ancient Judaism and Early Christianity*, ed. Martin Jan Mulder (Assen/Maastricht: Van Gorcum and Minneapolis: Fortress Press, 1990): 379-419 and James L. Kugel, 'Early Interpretation: The Common Background of Later Forms of Biblical Exegesis,' in *Early Biblical Interpretation*, by James L. Kugel and Rowan A. Greer (Philadelphia: The Westminster Press, 1986). Such characteristics are sometimes also seen in Josephus. See Louis H. Feldman, 'Use, Authority and Exegesis of Mikra in the Writings of Josephus,' in *Mikra: Text, Translation, Reading and Interpretation of the Hebrew Bible in Ancient Judaism and Early Christianity*, ed. Martin Jan Mulder (Assen/Maastricht: Van Gorcum and Minneapolis: Fortress Press, 1990): 470-518. There is strong evidence that the Rabbis were conscious that not only their teaching, but also their conduct would and should be imitated by their pupils. See discussion in Birger Gerhardsson, *Memory and Manuscript: Oral and Written Transmission in Rabbinic Judaism and Early Christianity*, trans. Eric J. Sharpe (Uppsala: Almqvist & Wiksells, 1961), 181-189. As a non-Jewish speaker of Greek, it is much more likely that Polycarp would have been influenced by the value accorded imitation in the Hellenistic world than by any of these other models.

[3] Donald Lemen Clark, 'Imitation: Theory and Practice in Roman Rhetoric,' *QJS* 37 (1951): 11. Elaine Fantham, 'Imitation and Decline: Rhetorical Theory and Practice in the First Century after Christ,' *CP* 73 (1978): 115 comments, "Mistrust of *imitatio* is natural to modern critics in the light of the Romantic antithesis between imitation and originality, but they do little justice to the insight, subtlety, and flexibility with which imitation was encouraged by the best ancient teachers."

[4] Cited by Thomas Louis Brodie, 'Greco-Roman Imitation of Texts as a Partial Guide to Luke's Use of Sources,' in *Luke-Acts: New Perspectives from the Society of Biblical Literature Seminar*, ed. Charles H. Talbert (New York: Crossroad, 1984), 18.

[5] See the discussion of Dionysius of Halicarnassus in George Kennedy, *The Art of Rhetoric in the Roman World 300 B.C.- A.D. 300* (Princeton: Princeton University Press, 1972), 342-363. Dionysius describes the extent of his work: "The first of these contains an abstract inquiry into the nature of imitation. The second asks what

George Kennedy summarizes the regard and practice of imitation:

> More common, however, in late Hellenistic and imperial times is the
> concept of imitation as a technique of literary creativity by which a
> writer or student deliberately imitates the form or thought or especially
> the style of a great literary model who thus becomes a touchstone of
> taste. Imitation in this sense is a feature of the classroom and often
> reflects a pedagogic point of view: the teacher has presented a student
> with a classical model to imitate, copy, or emulate.[6]

Imitation is a common feature in paraenetic discourse. Malherbe
calls the invitation to imitate found in Pseudo-Isocrates, *To Demonicus*
9-15 the 'classic example of paraenesis.'[7] Not surprisingly, the passage Malherbe quotes from Pseudo-Isocrates is no less than the author trying to exhort Demonicus to various honorable duties by list-
ing all the honorable principles and activities represented by
Demonicus's own father. In paragraph after paragraph, including
many lists of duties, Demonicus is called upon to 'imitate and emulate' his father. Polycarp, it will be shown later, calls upon the
Philippians to imitate their spiritual father, Paul.

Because of the dependence upon earlier writers in a classical edu-
cation, it is more assumed by rhetoricians than directly discussed that
quotations and allusions can bolster one's arguments.[8] Occasionally,
however, we find explicit comments in this regard. Quintilian (*Institutio
Oratoria* 1.8.12) encourages the reader that such quotations of earlier writers "have the additional advantage of helping the speaker's
case..."[9] Lying behind such exhortations, of course, is the concept
of *assimilation*, in which the students are influenced because they know
the earlier writings so well, and indeed have memorized their expressions and absorbed their style.[10] Those practicing imitation do not,
however, (at least in most cases) slavishly reproduce the model's words.

---

particular poets and philosophers, historians and orators, should be imitated. The
third, which treats of proper manner of imitation, remains unfinished." Cited in
Elizabeth A. Castelli, *Imitating Paul: A Discourse of Power* (Louisville, Ky.: Westminster/
John Knox Press, 1991), 148 n. 34.

[6] Kennedy, *The Art of Rhetoric*, 347.

[7] Abraham J. Malherbe, *Moral Exhortation, A Greco-Roman Sourcebook* (Philadelphia:
The Westminster Press, 1986), 125. *To Demonicus* 9-15 is quoted in full by Malherbe
on pp. 125-126.

[8] Frances M. Young, *Biblical Exegesis and the Formation of the Christian Culture* (Cambridge: Cambridge University Press, 1997), 100.

[9] Quoted in Ibid., 101.

[10] Fantham, 'Imitation and Decline,' 110.

Rather, they often emulate his style while appropriating some of his expressions, and thereby actualize both the form and content of the model into their own writing.[11]

Some disagreement exists among Greek and Roman rhetorical theorists about whether one should imitate only one model or should use many models. Clark comments on this, "The consensus of antiquity was against the continued or slavish imitation of one model."[12]

Kennedy mentions four areas in which students would be exhorted to imitate the (in this case oral) example of their teachers: "This kind of imitation would involve subject, arrangement, style and delivery." Kennedy adds, "but it is likely that style was often the most conspicuous element."[13]

Polycarp lived at the peak of Atticism, which appears to have crested in the mid-second century.[14] Atticism varies in degree, but on the far extreme it is "the rule that the Attic orators and such other Attic writers as Thucydides and Plato are the only sound models for choice and use of words. This doctrine 'froze' literary Greek into a classical pattern..."[15] What is relevant for this study is that the only way such a 'freezing of style' could have developed was if the general concept of imitation of earlier writers was so well regarded as to allow for such a development.

But Polycarp is a Christian and his concerns are not primarily in imitating Hellenistic literature.[16] His authorities are the writings of the OT, the words of Jesus and the apostolic writings.[17] Still, there is considerable evidence from his letter that he is influenced by the literary conventions of the Hellenistic world concerning the value of

---

[11] F. M. Young, *Biblical Exegesis*, 101.

[12] Clark, 'Imitation,' 14.

[13] George A. Kennedy, *Classical Rhetoric and Its Christian and Secular Tradition from Ancient to Modern Times* (Chapel Hill: The University of North Carolina Press, 1980), 117.

[14] Ibid., 118-119.

[15] Ibid., 119.

[16] "We think, however, that Polycarp was primarily looking for a specifically *Christian* paraenetical tradition, capable also of being similarly identified by the Philippians." Boudewijn Dehandschutter, 'Polycarp's Epistle to the Philippians: An Early Example of "Reception"' in *The New Testament in Early Christianity: La réception des écrits néotestmentarios dans le christianisme primitif*, ed. Jean-Marie Sevrin (Leuven: Leuven University Press, 1989), 285.

[17] That Christian writers of the second century considered their authorities to be a new set of classics is supported by the way that Justin and Tatian had to argue against the charge that they were introducing something novel in place of the classics. See discussion in F. M. Young, *Biblical Exegesis*, 52-54.

imitation. F. M. Young comments that "...patristic exegesis took for granted principles of interpretation and composition drawn from classical rhetoric..."[18] Though most of Young's examples are from a later stage, and Polycarp appears to be representative of a transitional period in Christian literature, nevertheless the structure and method of Polycarp's letter is to some degree indebted to the rhetorical tradition.[19] Polycarp is an author who, without necessarily intending to use classical rhetorical conventions, is nonetheless influenced by the atmosphere of opinion on how an effective argument should be made. He does not necessarily *analyze* this process; nevertheless he is influenced by a common understanding in his culture and time that imitation is valuable.[20]

In the two sections which follow, I will highlight arguments from Pol. *Phil.* which support the contention that Polycarp is imitating Paul (they will be numbered for the sake of clarity). Since Graeco-Roman imitation often focuses both upon *literary imitation* (including style, structure and phraseology) and imitation of a model's *ethical example* (as in *Demonicus* 9-15, discussed above), the arguments will be divided into two categories representing these two emphases (though overlap exists in some cases). Evidence of literary imitation will first be detailed and will be followed by arguments for ethical imitation. No individual assertion in this section can prove that imitation is taking place, but the cumulative effect of these arguments point to a man (Polycarp) who knows the value of imitation and employs it to persuade his readers to pursue lives of practical righteousness.[21]

---

[18] Ibid., 47 (and the discussion of Part II as a whole).

[19] Polycarp's letter would be included under Aune's judgment that "...early Christian letters...owed far more to Hellenistic than to oriental epistolary conventions." David E. Aune, *The New Testament in Its Literary Environment* (Philadelphia: The Westminster Press, 1987), 180.

[20] His letter is too short and focused to determine whether Polycarp had any rhetorical training.

[21] There is, however, no attempt to write pseudepigraphically. Lindemann comments on all of the so-called Apostolic Fathers, "...the fathers appear openly in their writings; they do not hide their identities behind a famous pseudonym." Andreas Lindemann, 'Paul in the Writings of the Apostolic Fathers,' in *Paul and the Legacies of Paul*, ed. William S. Babcock (Dallas: Southern Methodist University Press, 1990), 26. This includes the *Epistle of Barnabas* (c. 130) in which the name 'Barnabas' never appears in the text. Polycarp writes in his own name and explicitly distinguishes between his own attempt at letter writing and that of the great founder of the Philippian church, the Apostle Paul (3.2).

Evidence of Literary Imitation of Paul by Polycarp

1. It is propitious to begin with the obvious. Polycarp is writing to the church of Philippi, a church founded by Paul.[22] The letter itself indicates that Polycarp thinks there is persuasive potential in making explicit connection with the founder of their church (cf. 3.2; 9.1-2; 11.2-3).[23]

2. The sheer number of citations, allusions and reminiscences from the Pauline epistles is considerably higher than from any other source (including the words of Jesus). Though, for various reasons, it is difficult to count, a reasonable tallying of the conclusions drawn in ch. 2 include the following results in their categories:

Almost Certain: 10 are from non-Pauline sources; 9 from Paul.[24]

Probable: 22 are from non-Pauline sources; 19 are from Paul.

Possible: 27 are from non-Pauline sources; 24 are from Paul.

It can be seen that a little less than half of all references to earlier literature in Pol. *Phil.* are from the letters of Paul. Among non-Pauline sources, 1 Peter is represented most (5 almost certain; 6 probable; 3 possible).[25] Thus it can be seen that in shear force of citations, allu-

---

[22] "Polycarp...regarded St. Paul's letter to the Philippians as the foundationstone of their faith." J. N. D. Kelly, *Early Christian Doctrines*, 5th rev. ed. (London: Adam & Charles Black, 1958; repr. 1980), 33. "As the Philippians had been instructed by St. Paul he would not have dared to teach them Christian doctrine had they not pressed this upon him. They had better study St. Paul's letters (2-3)." F. L. Cross, *The Early Christian Fathers* (London: Gerald Duckworth & Co. Ltd., 1960), 20.

[23] Compare this with the letters of Ignatius. Ignatius only mentions Paul in his letter to the Ephesians and in his letter to the Romans, the only two congregations which have a tradition of a Pauline presence. See Frederick W. Norris, 'Asia Minor before Ignatius: Walter Bauer Reconsidered,' in *Studia Evangelica*, vol. 7, papers presented to the Fifth International Congress on Biblical Studies (1973), ed. Elizabeth A. Livingstone, TU 126 (Berlin: Akademie-Verlag, 1982), 372. This shows a tendency by Ignatius to bring in Paul where relevant for his readers. This may be the same reason Paul is so emphasized in Pol. *Phil.*

[24] All the NT letters purported to be from Paul which are referred to in Pol. *Phil.* are listed since in *Polycarp's* view there were no deutero-Pauline letters.

[25] There are more citations and allusions from 1 Peter than from any other *single* source. But when put against the Pauline letters as a group 1 Peter pales in comparison (refer to numbers in the main text above). The simple fact that Eusebius (*H.E.* 4.14.9) notes the references to 1 Peter in Pol. *Phil.* has, I believe, been a reason that more scholars have not concentrated upon the relationship of Polycarp to Paul's writings, even though references from Paul's writings far surpass references to 1 Peter when taken as a whole. The reader should also remember that many scholars have compared the style of 1 Peter with the Pauline epistles; it is arguably the letter which is closest in style to Paul's letters. Brooke Foss Westcott, *A General*

sions and reminiscences to earlier writings, the Apostle Paul stands out clearly from the rest.

3. When we analyzed Polycarp's use of earlier writings, we observed repeatedly that when Polycarp uses a phrase which we suspect is dependent upon an earlier writing – but which lacks the distinctives necessary to be classified as 'almost certain' or 'probable' – that phrase most often parallels some Pauline expression. Again, this points to a deep dependence upon Paul in Pol. *Phil.* It is also the kind of evidence one expects to find when literary imitation is occurring.

Not only phrases, but individual words point toward profound dependence upon Paul. Westcott points out a number of words unique to 1) Polycarp, 2) Paul, and 3) 1 Peter (among the writings of the NT and the Apostolic Fathers). These include: ἀνακόπτεσθαι, ψευδάδελφος, ψευδοδιδασκαλία, μεθοδεύειν and μεθοδεία, ἀπότομος and ἀποτομία. He also lists words shared by Polycarp and Paul alone, including ἀποπλανᾶν, ἀρραβών, ἀφιλάργυρος, τὸ καλόν, ματαιολογία, προνοεῖν.[26] Moreover, Polycarp uses many other terms and expressions which are prominent in Paul, though not necessarily unique to him: καρποφορέω in 1.2 (Rom 7:4; Col 1:6, 10), οἰκοδομέω in 3.2 (Rom 15:20; 1 Cor 8:1, 10; 10:23; 14:4, 17; Gal 2:18; 1 Thess 5:11), κατὰ πρόσωπον in 3.2 (2 Cor 10:1, 7; Gal 2:11), τὰ κρύπτα τῆς καρδίας in 4.3 (1 Cor 14:25), δίλογοι with reference to deacons in 5.2 (1 Tim 3:8), ὁ νῦν αἰών in 9.2 (1 Tim 6:17; 2 Tim 4:10; Tit 2:12), *poenitentiam veram* in 11.4 (2 Tim 2:25).[27] Four times Polycarp uses the formula εἰδότες ὅτι which is a particularly Pauline expression (Rom 5:3; 6:9; 13:11; 1 Cor 15:58; 2 Cor 1:7; 5:14; 5:11; Gal 2:16; Eph 6:8; Phil 1:16; Col 3:24 – though it is also to be found in James 3:1 and 1

Survey of the History of the Canon of the New Testament (Cambridge and London: Macmillan and Co., 1881), 37-39 comments, "The style of St Peter, it is well known, is most akin to that of the later epistles of St Paul." This could have been a reason why Polycarp was comfortable sprinkling references from 1 Peter in his letter even though Paul is his central concentration. 1 Peter also has a large concentration of paraenetic material (1 Pet 1:13-4:11) which would be of use in Polycarp's argument.

[26] Westcott, *A General Survey*, 39. But note that ἀποπλανᾶν also appears in Mark 13:22.

[27] Édouard Massaux, *The Influence of the Gospel of Saint Matthew on Christian Literature before Irenaeus. Book 2: The Later Christian Writings*, trans. Norman J. Belval and Suzanne Hecht, ed. Arthur J. Bellinzoni (Macon, Ga.: Mercer University Press, 1990), 41.

Peter 1:18). Finally, κυρίῳ ἡμῶν Ἰησοῦ Χριστῷ in 1.1 is, as Harrison says, 'a Pauline combination.'[28]

4. Just as telling are the numerous subtle and underlying reminiscences of Paul's letter to the Philippians in particular.[29] Three probable allusions (cf. Phil 1:27 in 5.2; Phil 2:16 in 9.1; and Phil 3:18 in 12.3) and an explicit mention of Paul's letter writing activity to the Philippians (3.2) makes dependence upon that letter virtually certain. But Polycarp's letter abounds with what appear to be many subtle hints of that letter in his own. These are found in 1.1 (Phil 4:10 and 2:17); 1.2 (Paul's commendations of the Philippian church); 2.1 (Phil 3:21 and 2:10); 3.2 (Phil 1:27); 4.3 (Paul's idea in Philippians of a person's actions being a sacrifice to God, cf. Phil 2:17; 4:18); 9.1 (Phil 1:29-30); and 11.3 (Phil 4:15).[30] Though Pol. *Phil.* contains more numerous clear citations of other letters (such as 1 Corinthians and 1 Peter), there appear to be more subtle connections to the canonical Philippians than to any other source Polycarp uses. This should not be a surprise which we remember that Polycarp explicitly mentions Paul's letter writing activity to the Philippians (3.2). The numerous subtle connections to Paul's Philippians support the contention that imitation of Paul is occurring in Polycarp's letter to the Philippians.

5. I have already argued in ch. 2 that the *Haustafeln* which are concentrated in Pol. *Phil.* 4.2-6.2 provide many pieces of evidence that, when taken together, indicate the likelihood of a general reliance upon 1 Timothy's many similar instructions.[31] Campenhausen has overemphasized these similarities, arguing that Polycarp or someone near him authored the Pastoral Epistles.[32] But almost all of the similarities with 1 Timothy are concentrated in Pol. *Phil.* 4.2-6.2 and should only be considered one aspect of Polycarp's reliance upon Paul

---

[28] P. N. Harrison, *Polycarp's Two Epistles to the Philippians* (Cambridge: Cambridge University Press, 1936), 301.

[29] "The reminiscences of S. Paul's Epistle are numerous, besides one direct reference to it." J. B. Lightfoot, *The Apostolic Fathers: Clement, Ignatius and Polycarp*, 2d ed., part 2, vol. 3 (London: Macmillan and Co., 1890; repr., Peabody, Mass.: Hendrickson Publishers, 1989), 322.

[30] See relevant discussions of each in ch. 2.

[31] Aune, *Literary Environment*, 196 comments on the close correspondence of these two passages.

[32] See Hans von Campenhausen, 'Polykarp von Smyrna und die Pastoralbriefe,' chap. in *Aus der Frühzeit des Christentums: Studien zur Kirchengeschichte des ersten und zweiten Jahrhunderts* (Tübingen: J.C.B. Mohr [Paul Siebeck], 1963.

(whom he considers the author of the Pastoral Epistles; see my argument, ch. 4).

6. The opening (and perhaps the closing) of Pol. *Phil.* gives an indication of Polycarp's use of Pauline style. R. Brown compares Pol. *Phil.* 1.1-2 with NT letters, "Perhaps one should speak of a step in Christian letter format wherein the blessed state of the addressees was acknowledged by using either *eucharistein*, 'to give thanks,' or *chairein*, 'to rejoice.'"[33] Many of Paul's letters contain a prayer of thanksgiving beginning with the verb εὐχαριστεῖν after the salutation (such as Rom 1:8-17; 1 Cor 1:4-9; Phil 1:3-11).[34] Paul Schubert points out that such 'thanksgivings' are sometimes found in Hellenistic letters but usually center on thanksgiving for rescue from danger.[35] In Pol. *Phil.* 1.1-2 the terminology is Συνεχάρην ὑμῖν μεγάλως... but the idea is the same as in Paul, namely, thanking God for the recipients of the letter. Thus, Polycarp is well within the Pauline letter tradition in the way that he begins his letter.[36]

It is more difficult to evaluate the relationship of the closing of Pol. *Phil.* with Paul's closings because of uncertainty about whether Pol. *Phil.* is one or two letters. If two, as I think, the 'second' (chs. 1-12) either contained an ending which was not preserved when the letters were fused or else ended with ch. 14. As it stands, Pol. *Phil.* 14 does end with a χάρις benediction like Paul's (1 Cor 16:23; 2 Cor 13:14; Gal 6:18; Eph 6:24; Phil 4:23; Col 4:18; 1 Thess 5:28; 2 Thess 3:18; 1 Tim 6:21; 2 Tim 4:22; Tit 3:15; Phil 25), though the wording belongs to Polycarp.

---

[33] Raymond E. Brown, *An Introduction to the New Testament* (New York: Doubleday, 1997), 416 n. 17. Paul often replaces the simple Greek greeting (χαίρειν) with an expanded phrase such as 'grace to you and peace'. These are, if you will, a spiritual health wish akin to the health wishes found at the beginning of many Greek letters. See John L. White, 'Saint Paul and the Apostolic Letter Tradition,' *The Catholic Biblical Quarterly* 45 (1983): 437.

[34] Aune, *Literary Environment*, 185.

[35] Paul Schubert, *Form and Function of the Pauline Thanksgivings* (Berlin: Töpelmann, 1939), 158-179.

[36] For further study on how Polycarp might intersect with Pauline and other Hellenistic letter forms refer to John L. White, 'New Testament Epistolary Literature in the Framework of Ancient Epistolography,' in *Aufstieg und Niedergang der Römischen Welt*, ed. H. Temporini and W. Haase, 1730-1756 (Berlin: Walter de Gruyter, 1984); Franz Schnider and Werner Stenger, *Studien zum neutestamentlichen Briefformular*. New Testament Tools and Studies, XI (Leiden: E. J. Brill, 1987); and especially Heikki Koskenniemi, *Studien zur Idee und Phraseologie des griechischen Briefes bis 400 n. Chr.* Soumalaisen Tiedekatemian Toimituksia; Annales Academiae Scientarium Fennicae 102.2 (Helsinki: Akateeminen Kirjakauppa, 1952).

7. The way Polycarp uses introductory formulae also argues for imitation of Paul, not as much in the *way* that Paul uses such formulae, but in the *fact* that Polycarp once again is flagging his intention to connect his letter to Paul and particular sayings of Paul. Polycarp surprisingly avoids formulae for his OT references (except in 12.1, though a connection to Paul exists there too). Of the eight passages containing formulae that are more or less clearly functioning as formulae[37] (1.3; 2.3; 4.1; 5.1; 6.1-2; 7.2; 11.2; 12.1) four are from Paul (1.3; 4.1; 5.1; 11.2), one is a Psalm quotation mediated through Paul (12.1), and three refer to the teaching of Jesus (2.3; 6:1-2; 7.2). Whereas clear references to 1 Peter exist in the letter, Polycarp never uses an introductory formula before a quotation from 1 Peter. These formulae and their primary use for sayings from Paul strongly indicates conscious connection to the teaching and letters of Paul. Though it does not in itself prove literary imitation, it does support the contention that imitation is occurring.

8. The argument which will be developed in the following chapter (ch. 4) that Polycarp clusters citations from Paul around the name of Paul may also support purposeful imitation of Paul. The clearest examples of clustering of references from a single writer by Polycarp are the three instances where Polycarp mentions the name of Paul (3.2-4.1; 9.1-10.1; 11.2-12.1). The apparent clustering of allusions to *1 Clement* in Pol. *Phil.* 4.2-3 or the even less clear possible cluster of references to 1 John in Pol. *Phil.* 7.1 or to the words of Peter in Pol. *Phil.* 1.2-3 are not nearly so obvious as the clustering of Pauline references around the name of Paul.

9. Even the length of Pol. *Phil.* is compatible with Paul's letters and contrasts with the lengths of most secular letters of the time (which, on average, are significantly shorter).[38] Paul's letters average 1,300 words in length. Polycarp's letter (chs. 1-14) has about 1,580 words on my count, and around 1,440 if we take away chs. 13-14. Philippians (by way of comparison) has 1,624 words.[39]

---

[37] Some less clear examples of formulae are the γάρ in 7.1 (before a quotation from 1 John 4:2-3 and 1 John 3:8), the γάρ in 9.2 (before a quotation from 2 Tim 4:10) and the *quia* in 10.2 (before a quotation from Tob 4:10 and/or Tob 12:9).

[38] D. A. Carson, Douglas J. Moo, and Leon Morris, *An Introduction to the New Testament* (Grand Rapids: Zondervan Publishing House, 1992), 232, comment that "...many of the New Testament letters stand out from their contemporary secular models in length. (Cicero wrote 776 letters, ranging in length from 22 to 2,530 words; Seneca 124 letters, from 149 to 4,134 words in length; Paul averages 1,300 words in length, and Romans has 7,114)."

[39] Aune, *Literary Environment*, 205.

Evidence of Ethical Imitation of Paul by Polycarp

Graeco-Roman imitation is not only limited to the modeling of style, structure and phraseology, it also is sometimes concerned with emulation of the model as a person (as we observed earlier in this discussion). These two aspects of imitation, of course, are not mutually exclusive. In the rhetorical tradition, one of the ways that an argument can be strengthened is via its foundation in the character of the person who speaks it. Indications are strong in Pol. *Phil.* that Polycarp intends to imitate Paul's moral example and to recommend such imitation to his readers.

1. Polycarp singles out Paul from among the other apostles. Paul is the only apostle mentioned by name, though the general terms 'the apostles' (6.3) and 'the rest of the apostles' (9.1) are present in the letter. Paul is called 'blessed and glorious' (3.2), 'Paul himself' (9.1), and 'the blessed Paul' (11.3).[40] Paul's wisdom and accurate teaching of the truth are lauded (3.2). His letter writing activity toward the Philippians is mentioned explicitly (3.2). Statements made by Polycarp about Paul transcend anything found in *1 Clement* or the letters of Ignatius.[41]

2. Polycarp's humility statements in relation to Paul in 3.2 are an indication that Polycarp is consciously imitating Paul, both in terms of his moral/spiritual example, and in terms of his letter composition (which are related).[42] In 3.2 Polycarp says, "For neither I nor anyone like me can keep pace with the wisdom of the blessed and glorious Paul, who, when he was among you in the presence of the men of that time, accurately and reliably taught the word concerning the truth." The formulation of this sentence by Polycarp is best explained by the notion that Polycarp was *requested* to write a letter *like Paul's* to the Philippians. This is supported by the previous sentence where Polycarp says he is not writing by his own direction but

---

[40] Ferdinand Christian Baur, *The Church History of the First Three Centuries*, trans. Allan Menzies, vol. 1 (London: Williams and Norgate, 1878), 140 mentions what are to him clear indications of Paulinism in Pol. *Phil.* He is especially impressed by the number of glowing statements about Paul found in the letter.

[41] Lindemann, *Paulus im ältesten Christentum*, 87.

[42] Lightfoot, while not raising the question of imitation, comments, "Was it not natural that, finding himself thus engaged in writing to the Philippian Church, he should remember that he was doing what a far greater man had done before, and should institute a comparison humiliating to himself?" Lightfoot, *The Apostolic Fathers*, part 2, vol. 1, 584.

because they asked him to write. Thus, Polycarp's response in 3.2 shows that his letter is an attempt to respond to their request but that he feels less than adequate to do so. Though his assessment of his ability in comparison to Paul is negative, he nevertheless *compares* himself to Paul. Such a comparison (even if stated emphatically), of course, does not itself prove imitation. But the presence of such a comparison is what one might expect in a letter where imitation is occurring.

His comparison indicates that he knows that he is (inadequately in his own mind) emulating the person of Paul, a person of 'wisdom' who was 'glorious' and who taught 'accurately and reliably'. Polycarp upholds Paul as a model for himself and for the Philippians throughout the letter.

3. One of Polycarp's subthemes in his letter is (relevantly) the theme of imitation. This is relevant because of the possible window into Polycarp's thought processes it might provide. The fact that Paul himself develops a subtheme of imitation may itself be telling, particularly if Polycarp is working to any degree within this stream.

Polycarp specifically develops a theme of imitation in chs. 8-10 where he uses the terminology of imitation. Polycarp talks about becoming 'imitators' (μιμηταί) of the endurance of Christ when faced with suffering (8.2) for the sake of his name. In doing this Christ has become an 'example' or 'pattern' (ὑπογραμμός) to be followed. Moreover, in 10.1 Polycarp exhorts the Philippians to 'follow the example of the Lord' (*domini exemplar sequimini*) and adds a list of Christian virtues. In other words, though imitation of endurance in suffering is pronounced in the previous context, a life of righteousness is also something to be imitated.

Examples of endurance in suffering are also seen in Ignatius, Zosimus and Rufus, and in 'Paul himself' and the other apostles (9.1). These examples are bracketed by the charges we just looked at in the previous paragraph to be imitators of Christ in enduring suffering (8.2) and to follow the example of the Lord (10.1). By extension, then, these other martyrs are being held forth by Polycarp as examples who, like the Lord, need to be imitated. Since 'Paul himself' is singled out in the list of these to be imitated, we are again given a clue that, in this letter, imitation of Paul is an issue.

The theme of imitation is not only limited to Pol. *Phil.* 8-10, though it is there that it is dealt with explicitly. The thanksgiving section at the beginning of the letter (1.1) refers to the μιμήματα of the true love.[43] Hort evidently preferred the translation 'copies'.[44] But a sub-theme of imitation also may be undergirding such phrases as "to follow the wisdom of the blessed and glorious Paul" (3.2), "if anyone is occupied with these" (3.3), "follow the commandment of the Lord" (4.1), "to live in a manner that is worthy" (5.1), "if we ask the Lord to forgive us, then we ourselves ought to forgive" (6.2), "let us return to the word delivered to us from the beginning" (7.2), "hold steadfastly...to our hope and...guarantee..." (8.1), as well as in the commendations of the letters of Ignatius in ch. 13 and the persons of Crescens and his sister in ch. 14. The theme of imitation appears to play an active role in the thought of Polycarp. This, then, makes the suggestion that he is consciously connecting to Paul through imitation more plausible.

The concept of imitation is already strong in Paul himself who has encouraged the readers of his letters to become imitators (μιμηταί) of him in all things, as he is of Christ (1 Cor 4:14f; 2 Thess 3:7, 9; 1 Cor 11:1; 1 Thess 1:6; cf. 1 Thess 2:14; Eph 5:1f).[45] Polycarp has apparently taken these exhortations to heart. In Paul's letter to the Philippians (4:9), Paul exhorts the Philippians to follow his example: "The things you have learned and received and heard and seen in me, practice these things; and the God of peace shall be with you." Perhaps Polycarp is influenced by this theme from Paul when he writes his own letter to the Philippians.[46]

4. Subject matter also points toward imitation of Paul by Polycarp. The question of theological influence on Polycarp by Paul will be opened in ch. 5. What is relevant here is the observation that Polycarp has consciously connected with the Pauline theme of righteousness (esp. 3.1; 3.3). Though Polycarp's own theological system (to the degree it can be ascertained) does not appear to be limited to ethics (he also is a transitional figure regarding eschatology) his central concern in

---

[43] i.e. Ignatius and company on their way to execution in Rome.

[44] See comments in T. F. Glasson, 'Hort's Renderings of Passages from Ignatius and Polycarp,' *CQR* 167 (1966): 308.

[45] "Paul thus considers that he is transmitting, not only in words, but also in his actions: on [sic] other words, with his whole life." Gerhardsson, *Memory and Manuscript*, 293. The theme of imitation is also mentioned in 1 Pet 2:21, *1 Clem.* 16:17; 33:8 and Ign. *Rom.* 6.3; *Eph.* 10.3. See comments by Johannes Bapt. Bauer, *Die Polykarpbriefe* (Göttingen: Vandenhoeck & Ruprecht, 1995), 62-63.

[46] But as has been mentioned in previous pages, Polycarp does not invite the Philippians to imitate himself, rather to imitate Christ and others who have suffered for Christ.

this letter (which he may consider the same central concern of Paul) is ethical righteousness. In light of the importance of this theme in Pol. *Phil.*, it suggests that Polycarp wants to model after Paul's own example of righteousness. And though I am most concerned with ethical imitation at this point, it should be observed that Polycarp's literary connections with Paul's letters are most often with Paul's paraenetic sections.[47]

Unlike most of Paul's letters, Pol. *Phil.* has no developed theological sections. Polycarp does, however, make the move in 1.3-2.1 from the (very brief) indicative to the imperative, a move that is so familiar to readers of Paul.[48] After Polycarp makes that move, the central focus of his letter is with living rightly (that is, 'righteousness'). Massaux comments,

> It is, therefore, a fact that Polycarp knows the Pauline literature: he uses it, he cites it in many passages and almost literally; he seems to have come under very strong influence from the writings of the apostle. But I wish to point out that all the Pauline passages on which he depends have a clearly marked moral character, or else they are introduced in moral contexts. Polycarp does not follow Paul on the path of high theological concepts.[49]

Depending upon how one defines 'ethical' and 'theological' and upon how one counts references to earlier writings, I estimate that between 60% and 80% of all of Polycarp's references to Paul's letters are from Pauline contexts which center upon ethical exhortation rather than foundational theology.

"In the whole section about Valens," observes Dehandschutter, "Polycarp's paraenesis is almost Pauline."[50] The same could have been said of much of Pol. *Phil.* The Paul after whom Polycarp seeks to model his own letter is (at least in this case) the Paul who teaches how to live righteously.

---

[47] Aune draws the useful distinction between *epistolary* paraenesis which are particularly paraenetic sections found at the end of Paul's letters such as in Rom 12:1-15:13; Gal 5:1-6:10; 1 Thess 4:1-5:22; Col 3:1-4:6 and *paraenetic styles* which 'permeate' letters such as 1 Thessalonians, Galatians or Colossians. Other letters, such as 1-2 Corinthians, Philippians, James and Hebrews have paraenetic teaching intermixed with non-paraenetic teaching. See Aune, *Literary Environment*, 191.

[48] Lindemann, 'Paul in...Apostolic Fathers,' 43.

[49] Massaux, *Influence*, 42.

[50] Dehandschutter, 'Polycarp's Epistle,' 283. In the section about Valens, it appears that Polycarp argues that the community has not lapsed into more serious sin largely because Paul ('the blessed Paul') himself was the one who labored among them (11.3).

Conclusion

The cumulative effect of these arguments supports the contention that Polycarp desires to imitate Paul, both literarily and ethically. Polycarp writes a letter which is *like* Paul's and brings to mind Paul's letter writing activity to the Philippian church. Thus, Polycarp makes conscious connections to Paul throughout his letter in many different ways. His purpose is to work within a narrow generic convention – not simply within a Hellenistic letter genre, nor even merely within a Christian letter genre, but within a Pauline letter genre. Polycarp's letter is evidence that he is somewhat *more* aware than other contemporary Christian authors of the generic conventions of Christian letters and wants to employ that knowledge in the way he composes his own letter.[51]

This special relationship to Paul does not necessarily prove something general about Polycarp, i.e. that he is in general Pauline (rather than, say, Johannine). "Unlike Marcion, Polycarp did not choose one apostle over all the others, even if he did prefer Saint Paul."[52] In light of the fact that Pol. *Phil.* is Polycarp's only extant writing, we do not even know if Polycarp would have shown the same regard for Paul if he had been writing to a church founded by another apostle. But at least for Pol. *Phil.*, the evidence indicates more than simply high regard for Paul; it suggests conscious imitation of Paul.

It may be noticed that purposeful imitation of Paul is perhaps less likely if the letter is a unity and more likely if P. N. Harrison's two-letter thesis is correct. For if it is a unity, then its immediate function is that of a cover letter for the letters of Ignatius. In that role, the effectiveness of imitating Paul for the Philippian readers could be diminished (since Ignatius would be at the forefront). Conscious imitation also implies a certain (though not excessive) amount of care in writing the letter; the letter presumably would have been a more hasty composition if its central function was that of a cover letter. But the evidence of the letter itself points toward care in its composition. Pol. *Phil.* does not seem to have been hastily composed (even if it is not the paragon of style). The arguments put forward for

---

[51] If this is the case, the commonly voiced opinion that "the only literary interest of Polycarp's epistle is to be found in its quotations" (Robert M. Grant, 'Polycarp of Smyrna,' *ATR* 28 (1948): 138) would be simplistic.

[52] Stuckwisch, 'Saint Polycarp,' 125.

purposeful imitation of Paul by Polycarp, then, appear to stand in a mutually supportive relationship with Harrison's two-letter thesis.

An implication of the argument made in this chapter is that Polycarp demonstrates that he is not the simpleton he has been made out to be by so many scholars (see discussion pp. 3-8). Though no one will argue brilliance for Polycarp, Polycarp evinces familiarity with the Christian epistolary genre and with the Graeco-Roman value placed upon imitation. He effectively employs this knowledge in his letter to the Philippians. Thus, when judged by the standards of *his* day, Polycarp succeeds in writing an effective, persuasive letter. As mentioned in the introduction, we should not be surprised by the value which was placed upon Pol. *Phil.* among Christians up until the time of Jerome.

CHAPTER FOUR

PAULINE CLUSTERS IN POL. *PHIL.*
AND THEIR IMPLICATION FOR
POLYCARP'S VIEW OF THE AUTHORSHIP OF
THE PASTORAL EPISTLES[1]

The authorship and dating of the so-called Pastoral Epistles is pe-rennially discussed in NT studies. In this chapter I will not try to resolve this discussion. I hope, however, to contribute to the schol-arly discussion of Polycarp and the Pastoral Epistles in two ways.

1. The first contribution will be to our understanding of Pol. *Phil.* in its own right. This chapter will document an unmistakable ten-dency in the letter of Polycarp to cluster Pauline citations, allusions and reminiscences after each of the three instances that Polycarp mentions the name of the Apostle Paul.

2. The second contribution flows from the first. Within the first two of these three clusters are citations almost certainly dependent upon 1 or 2 Timothy. If, as will be demonstrated in this chapter, Polycarp tends to group references from the Pauline Epistles around explicit namings of Paul, and if there is a quotation from 1 or 2 Timothy in two of these clusters, it can be plausibly argued that Polycarp (rightly or wrongly) understands Paul to be the author of these two epistles. The relevance of this observation is plain. Even if the late dating of the main body of Polycarp's letter, chs. 1-12 (P. N. Harrison's 'crisis letter'), is accepted, i.e. 135 C.E. (I prefer 120 C.E.), Polycarp becomes the earliest witness to the Pauline author-ship of two of the three 'Pastoral Epistles' by about 50 years.[2]

---

[1] An earlier version of this chapter appeared as Kenneth Berding, 'Polycarp of Smyrna's View of the Authorship of 1 and 2 Timothy,' *VC* 53 (1999): 349-360. The main difference between that article and the present chapter is this: in that article I attempted a *consensus* view of the Polycarp's use of earlier material; in this chapter I will base my decisions *on my own conclusions* reached in ch. 2. In both the article and in this chapter, the major conclusions are the same.

[2] In ch. 1, I argued for Harrison's suggestion that Polycarp's letter is actually two letters but against his date of c. 135 C.E. and in favor of a date around 120 C.E. See P. N. Harrison, *Polycarp's Two Epistles to the Philippians* (Cambridge: Cambridge University Press, 1936).

Thus, this chapter does not try to settle the question of Pauline authorship of the Pastoral Epistles, but does argue that Polycarp of Smyrna, writing in the early parts of the second century, considers at least 1 and 2 Timothy to be written by Paul.

References to the Pastoral Epistles in the Early Church and their Connections to Paul[3]

Two questions will be briefly revisited here to set the study in its proper context. First, when do traces of the Pastoral Epistles appear in the literature of the developing church? Second, when do writings begin explicitly calling them Pauline?[4]

The answer to the first question is somewhat disputed. There are some verbal similarities between the Pastoral Epistles and the so-called letter of Clement of Rome (c. 96 C.E.). Streeter reverses the dependence, however, and claims that the Pastorals quote 'Clement'.[5] The letters of Ignatius of Antioch (c. 110-117) may also show some dependence on the Pastorals, but it is not at all certain.[6] Polycarp is the first writer who almost certainly quotes from 1 and 2 Timothy (though not necessarily Titus). Curiously, von Campenhausen considers Polycarp himself (or a representative of Polycarp) to be the likely

---

[3] See J. H. Bernard, *The Pastoral Epistles* (Cambridge: Cambridge University Press, 1899; repr., Grand Rapids: Baker Book House, 1980) and Newport J. D. White, *The First and Second Epistles to Timothy and to Titus*, The Expositor's Greek New Testament IV (New York: George H. Doran Company, 1897; repr., Grand Rapids: Wm. B. Eerdmans Publishing Company, 1974) for citations of early church fathers who may be quoting or alluding to the Pastoral Epistles.

[4] We are not interested here primarily in the question of canonicity but in early church attestation of these letters and the degree to which they were considered Pauline.

[5] Burnett Hillman Streeter, *The Primitive Church* (New York: The Macmillan Company, 1929), 159.

[6] Oxford Society of Historical Theology, *The New Testament in the Apostolic Fathers* (Oxford: The Clarendon Press, 1905), 71-73. Separately, it is interesting, though disputed, that the majority (eight out of eleven) of possible 'echoes' (N. White, *Timothy and Titus*, 78) to the Pastoral Epistles found in Ignatius are in the letter he wrote to Polycarp. The four N. White lists as most likely are found in Ign. *Pol.* 2.3 (2 Tim 4:5; 2:5; 1:10), 3.1 (2 Tim 2:12); 4.3 (1 Tim 6:1, 2); 6.2 (2 Tim 2:4). Nevertheless, none of these 'echoes' are fully convincing. If they were, they would constitute an additional argument that Polycarp knew and in fact used the Pastoral Epistles in his own letter, for Ignatius hardly could have used so many unspecified reminiscences without the supposition that Polycarp would have known and been familiar with these letters.

author of the Pastorals,[7] and Walter Bauer considers the Pastorals to have derived their similarities to Polycarp through dependence upon Polycarp.[8] Scholarly opinion is now against them.[9] That Polycarp is literarily dependent upon 1 and 2 Timothy is generally accepted.[10] Soon after Polycarp, Justin Martyr (c. 140) probably evinces familiarity with the Pastorals.[11]

Thus, by the third decade of the second century (at the latest), the Pastoral Epistles were in general circulation. In light of the allusions in Clement and Ignatius, that date could be moved closer to the turn of the century.[12]

---

[7] Hans von Campenhausen, 'Polycarp von Smyrna und die Pastoralbriefe,' chap. in *Aus der Frühzeit des Christentums: Studien zur Kirchengeschichte des ersten und zweiten Jahrhunderts* (Tübingen: J.C.B. Mohr [Paul Siebeck], 1963. Campenhausen's alleged similarities between the Pastorals and Pol. *Phil.*, both in terms of historical correspondences and in terms of terminology, are too general to be valuable. They are off-set by a significant difference in literary style between the two sets of writings, including the density of Polycarp's allusions to apostolic writings, something not found in the Pastorals. Pol. *Phil.* is entirely lacking the formula πιστὸς ὁ λόγος which is so characteristic of the Pastorals (1 Tim 1:15; 3:1; 4:9; 2 Tim 2:11; Tit 3:8). Conversely, Polycarp repeats the formula εἰδότες ὅτι four times (in 1.3; 4.1; 5.1; 6.1) which is lacking in the Pastorals. Campenhausen's general similarities are not nearly as important as such differences. He himself has noted that there are some stylistic differences between the Pastorals and Pol. *Phil.* (for example, the language of the Pastorals being somewhat richer in comparison to the common language of Pol. *Phil.* – see p. 221). It should also be noted that the Polycarp who was so reticent to compare himself to Paul (Pol. *Phil.* 3.2) was not likely to write letters in the name of Paul.

[8] Walter Bauer, *Orthodoxy and Heresy in Earliest Christianity*, 2d German ed., with added appendices, by Georg Strecker, trans. by a team from the Philadelphia Seminar on Christian Origins, ed. Robert A. Kraft and Gerhard Krodel (Philadelphia: Fortress Press, 1971; repr., Mifflintown, Pa.: Sigler Press, 1996), 224.

[9] "In fact those who reject the authenticity of the letters have generally abandoned dates very far into the second century for their composition; most locate them at about the turn of the century." Philip H. Towner, *The Goal of our Instruction: The Structure of Theology and Ethics in the Pastoral Epistles*, JSNTsup 34 (Sheffield: Sheffield Academic Press, 1989), 22-23.

[10] "...most judge that Polycarp's letter (AD 120-130) has been influenced by the Pastorals and not vice versa." R. Brown, *Introduction*, 665. Edgar J. Goodspeed, *New Solutions of New Testament Problems* (Chicago: The University of Chicago Press, 1927), 50-51 and John Knox, *Marcion and the New Testament: An Essay in the Early History of the Canon* (Chicago: The University of Chicago Press, 1942), 58 (to mention only two) simply ignore the rather clear evidence of dependence upon 1 and 2 Timothy in Polycarp.

[11] See lists of possible connections between Polycarp and Justin in N. White, *Timothy and Titus*, 5; Bernard, *The Pastoral Epistles*, xiv. For a contrary view, see C. K. Barrett, *The Pastoral Epistles* (Oxford: Clarendon Press, 1963), 1.

[12] Frederick W. Norris, 'Asia Minor before Ignatius: Walter Bauer Reconsid-

When we inquire about the earliest evidence for a connection between the Pastoral Epistles and the church's understanding of Paul as its author a different picture emerges.[13] None of the above authors explicitly states that Paul is the author of the Pastorals, nor do they quote him by name. Marcion does not include the Pastorals in his collection of Pauline letters[14] (which, as many scholars have pointed out, does not mean he does not know them). Irenaeus (c. 188) is the first clear testimony to Pauline authorship, for he quotes phrases from the Pastorals as coming from Paul.[15] Theophilus of Antioch (c. 180) suggests the divine inspiration of these letters, which is unlikely, in view of the self-ascription of the letters, if he had not considered them to be Pauline.[16]

Thus, apart from the evidence of Polycarp presented in this chapter, there is considerable time (at least 50 years) between clear evidence of literary dependence on the Pastoral Epistles and the connection of that dependence with Paul as their author.

Polycarp and Paul

In the previous chapter, the close affinities between Pol. *Phil.* and the letters and person of Paul were detailed. It was there argued that Polycarp purposely imitates Paul in the composition of his letter and seeks to use Paul as both a literary and an ethical model. This close relationship to Paul is particularly noteworthy in light of the tradition that Polycarp at one time had a relationship with the Apostle John.[17] The pattern of clustering which emerges from a close study of Pol. *Phil.* solidifies this intimate connection between Paul and Polycarp in the letter he writes to the Philippians.

Polycarp in his letter seems to demonstrate very probable knowl-

---

ered,' in *Studia Evangelica*, vol. 7, papers presented to the Fifth International Congress on Biblical Studies (1973), ed. Elizabeth A. Livingstone, TU 126 (Berlin: Akadamie-Verlag, 1982), 370.

[13] Note that those who consider Paul to be the author of the Pastorals would claim that the church always knew they were Pauline, since Paul's name is written in each. The question which faces us, though, is the question of external attestation.

[14] Tertullian, *Adv. Marc.* 5.21. Tertullian's explanation for the absence of the Pastoral Epistles from Marcion's collection was that Marcion purposely deleted them.

[15] *Haer* 1.16.3; 2.14.7; 3.3.3; 4.16.3.

[16] Theophilus, *Ad Autolycum*, 3.14.

[17] Irenaeus in Eusebius, *H.E.* 5.20.6; Tertullian, *De Praescriptione* 32.

edge of many letters in our present Pauline corpus, including Romans, 1 and 2 Corinthians, Galatians, Ephesians, Philippians, 2 Thessalonians, and 1 and 2 Timothy. He also demonstrates knowledge of Tobit, 1 Peter, 1 John, *1 Clement*, the letters of Ignatius and probably also demonstrates knowledge of the Psalms, Proverbs, Isaiah, Jeremiah, Matthew, Luke, and Acts.[18] In addition, other possible affinities exist, as has been discussed in ch. 2 and can be observed on the list which follows below.

As we examine that list, the pattern of clustering references from Paul after the explicit mention of Paul's name readily emerges. It should come as no surprise that such clustering occurs.[19] In order to draw out the pattern of clustering especially around the name of Paul, a concise summary of the conclusions from ch. 2 will be included here. The 'almost certain' and 'probable' lists have here been joined together. Separately, a list of those deemed 'possible' are also included. In such a list we can only include dependencies upon *specific* texts (e.g. the use of Eph 2:5, 8, 9 in Pol. *Phil.* 1.3). Sometimes, however, there are instances where Polycarp may be dependent upon an earlier writer when no specific text can be demonstrated (e.g. an allusion to Paul's common expression 'the word of truth' or a contention of dependence upon 'Johannine language'). These instances are not included in the list which follows. But where they become relevant to the discussion, they will be included in the written text. Detailed discussion of the nature of literary dependencies is not included here. Explanations are available in ch. 2. Parentheses are used where there is possible influence from another source upon the same saying listed on the same line. Where Paul's name occurs in a passage it is marked by '**PAUL**'.

Pol. *Phil.*	'Almost Certain' / 'Probable'	'Possible'
1.1		Phil 4:10; 2:17
		Ign. *Smyrn.* 11.1 and
		Ign. *Eph.* 11.2
1.2	Acts 2:24	
1.3	1 Pet 1:8	

---

[18] My judgments are in general more optimistic than those of the Oxford Society, on the one hand, but are much more conservative than the conclusions of P. N. Harrison, *Two Epistles*, on the other.

[19] Eugene Harrison Lovering, 'The Collection, redaction, and early circulation of the corpus Paulinum,' (Ph.D. diss., Southern Methodist University, 1988), 229.

Pol. *Phil.*	'Almost Certain' / 'Probable'	'Possible'
	1 Pet 1:12	
	Eph 2:5, 8, 9	
2.1	1 Pet 1:13	
		Eph 6:14
	Ps 2:11	
	1 Pet 1:21	
		Phil 3:21; 2:10
		Acts 10:42
2.2		2 Cor 4:14
	1 Pet 3:9	
	Luke 6:28-29; Matt 5:39[20]	
2.3	*1 Clem.* 13.1-2	
		Matt 7:1
		Luke 6:38
	Luke 6:20; Matt 5:10	
3.1		
3.2	**'PAUL'**	*1 Clem.* 47.1
		Phil 1:27
3.3	Gal 4:26	(Rom 4:16)
	1 Cor 13:13	
	Rom 13:8-10/Gal 5:14 (cf. 6:2)	
4.1	1 Tim 6:10	
	1 Tim 6:7	
	2 Cor 6:7	
4.2	(General influence from	
	1 Timothy in 4.2-6.2)	
	1 Clem. 1.3	
	1 Clem. 21.6	
		1 Clem. 41.2
	1 Clem. 21.3	
	1 Cor 14:25	
5.1	Gal 6:7	
5.2		Mark 9:35
	Phil 1:27	(*1 Clem.* 21.1)
	2 Tim 2:12	
5.3	1 Pet 2:11	(Gal 5:17)

---

[20] Unclear whether it is through an oral or a written medium.

Pol. *Phil.*	'Almost Certain' / 'Probable'	'Possible'
	1 Cor 6:9-10	
		1 Clem. 1.3
6.1		Ezek 34:4
	Prov 3:4	(2 Cor 8:21)
		1 Tim 5:19
6.2	Matt 6:12, 14-15	
	Rom 14:10, 12 (2 Cor 5:10)	
6.3	Ps 2:11	
7.1	1 John 4:2-3	
		1 John 5:6-9
	1 John 3:8	
		1 John 3:12
7.2	1 Pet 4:7	
		1 Clem. 55.6; 64.1
	Matt 6:13	
	Matt 26:41	
8.1	1 Pet 2:22 (Isa 53:9b)	
	1 Pet 2:21	
		1 Pet 4:16
9.1		Heb 5:13
		Phil 1:29-30
	'PAUL'	
9.2	Phil 2:16	
		Rom 8:17
	2 Tim 4:10	
		2 Cor 5:15
10.1	1 Cor 15:58 or Col 1:23	
		1 Pet 2:17 or 3:8
	Rom 12:10	
	Rom 12:10 (again)	
10.2-3[21]		Prov 3:27 or
		Sir 29:8-9

---

[21] I have left out the possible loose citation of Eph 5:21, 1 Pet 5:5, *1 Clem.* 38.1, or Ign. *Magn.* 13.2 because of the difficulty in choosing between these four possible sources and the fact that it still ends up in the 'possible' category.

Pol. *Phil.*	'Almost Certain' / 'Probable'	'Possible'
	Tob 4:10 and/or 12:9	
	1 Pet 2:12	
	Isa 52:5	(Ign. *Trall.* 8.2 and Rom 2:24)
11.1		1 Thess 5:22
11.2		1 Tim 3:5
		Eph 5:5 or Col 3:5
	Jer 5:4-5	
	1 Cor 6:2 '**PAUL**'	
11.3	'**PAUL**'	
		Phil 4:15 or 2 Cor 3:2
	2 Thess 1:4	
11.4		2 Tim 2:25
	2 Thess 3:15	
12.1	Ps 4:5a (Eph 4:26a)	
	Eph 4:26b (Ps 4:5b)	
12.2		Gal 1:1
12.3		Eph 6:18
		1 Tim 2:2
		Matt 5:44/Luke 6:27
	Phil 3:18	
		Matt 5:48

Paul Referred to by Name

The first argument of this chapter is that Polycarp clusters Pauline citations and allusions around the mention of Paul's name. Polycarp mentions Paul in three contexts in this letter, which is itself striking.[22]

1. In 3.2 we read about 'the blessed and glorious Paul' (μακαρίου καὶ ἐνδόξου Παύλου).[23]

---

[22] Campenhausen, 'Polykarp von Smyrna,' 241.

[23] J. B. Bauer comments that μακάριος is a common term in the Greek church fathers for OT prophets like Job, Abraham or Joseph and also for significant NT

2. In 9.1 we find the phrase 'and in Paul himself' (καὶ ἐν αὐτῷ Παύλῳ) where Paul is listed as one of those who endured along with Ignatius, Zosimus, Rufus, 'others from your congregation' and 'the rest of the apostles'.[24]

3. The phrase, 'as Paul teaches' (*sicut Paulus docet*[25]) in 11.2 follows a clear citation of 1 Cor 6:2. In 11.3, Paul's name is mentioned again – 'the blessed Paul' (*beatus Paulus*). Each mention of Paul's name comes at the beginning of a cluster of Pauline citations, allusions and reminiscences.

Clusters in Polycarp

Pauline Cluster #1 (3.2-4.1) contains five phrases which are probably or almost certainly drawn from Gal 4:26 (with possible influence from Rom 4:16), 1 Cor 13:13, 1 Tim 6:10, 1 Tim 6:7, and 2 Cor 6:7. In 3.3 is also a probable reminiscence of Paul's use of the Jesus tradition in Rom 13:8-10 and/or Gal 5:14 (cf. 6:2). In addition to these is a probable allusion to the Pauline expression 'the word concerning the truth' (τὸν περὶ ἀληθείας λόγον) in 3.2 though no specific text is identifiable. Note also that 4.2 begins a section (4.2-6.2) which I have argued is probably generally dependent upon the *Haustafeln* of 1 Timothy. Thus, the first Pauline cluster contains seven probable or almost certain allusions to Pauline expressions though one of them cannot be linked with a particular text.

Pauline Cluster #2 (9.1-10.1) contains five probable or almost certain phrases from Paul: Phil 2:16, 2 Tim 4:10, 1 Cor 15:58 or Col 1:23, and Rom 12:10 (two times). The list which begins in 10.1 reminds us in a general sense of similar lists Paul made.[26] In fact, there are three fairly certain Pauline phrases in the first four phrases in this list, the first from 1 Cor 15:58 or Col 1:23, and the next two from Rom 12:10.[27] In addition, this Pauline cluster contains a pos-

---

characters such as the apostles, Mary, Elizabeth, Stephen and others. Johannes Bapt. Bauer, *Die Polykarpbriefe* (Göttingen: Vandenhoeck & Ruprecht, 1995), 46.

[24] Lindemann points out how striking it is that Paul is the only apostle named in this list. Even Peter is not mentioned. Lindemann, *Paulus im ältesten Christentum: Das Bild des Apostels und die Rezeption der paulinischen Theologie in der frühchristlichen Literatur bis Marcion*, BHT 58 (Tübingen: J.C.B. Mohr [Paul Siebeck], 1979), 89.

[25] 10:1-12:3 is only preserved in Latin.

[26] E.g. Rom 12:9-21.

[27] The phrase 'loving the brotherhood' (*fraternitatis amatores*) is possibly from 1 Pet 2:17.

sible reminiscence of Rom 8:17 in 9.2, a possible loose citation of 2 Cor 5:15 in 9.2 and a possible allusion to 2 Cor 10:1 in 10.1. Thus, there are five probable Pauline references in cluster #2 along with three that are less certain.

Pauline Cluster #3 (11.2-12.1) begins with a clear citation of 1 Cor 6:2 and the mention of Paul's name, 'as Paul teaches' (*sicut Paulus docet*). It is followed by probable phrases from 2 Thess 1:4, 2 Thess 3:15,[28] and two parts of one citation which show awareness both of Eph 4:26 and Ps 4:5 (see discussion in ch. 2). There is also a probable reminiscence of Paul's body metaphor (cf. 1 Cor 12:12-27; Rom 14:4-8; Eph 4:4-13). In addition, this cluster contains a possible reminiscence of Phil 4:15 or 2 Cor 3:2 in 11.3 and a possible allusion to 2 Tim 2:25 in 11.4. Thus there are five probable points of dependence upon Paul along with two that are less certain.

Not only has Polycarp clustered Pauline citations and allusions in this way, there appear to be smaller clusters, though none so dramatic as the three which are clustered around the name of Paul. There may be a short cluster of 'Petrine' references in Pol. *Phil.* 1.2-3 (Acts 2:24; 1 Pet 1:8; 1 Pet 1:12) though it is debatable whether the linking of Peter's speech in Acts 2 with the references from 1 Peter is any more than a simple coincidence. A stronger possibility exists in Pol. *Phil.* 4.2-3 where influence from *1 Clement* seems probable at three points and possible at one in a small cluster (*1 Clem.* 1.3; 21.6-8; 41.2; 21.3). There is also possibly a small cluster of phrases from 1 John in Pol. *Phil.* 7.1. That cluster would include an almost certain compressed citation of 1 John 4:2-3, a probable allusion to 1 John 3:8 and two possible reminiscences of 1 John 5:6-9 and 1 John 3:12 respectively. The presence of these (albeit) small clusters serves to reinforce the general observation of Polycarp's tendency to cluster writings from the same author together. At the same time, it should be observed that though Polycarp quotes 1 Peter with some frequency, apart from the one questionable cluster in Pol. *Phil.* 1.2-3, references from 1 Peter are scattered fairly randomly throughout the letter.

A synthesis of these findings yields the following results. Polycarp clusters references from the same author together at three major points. Each of these is around the name of Paul. Elsewhere Polycarp appears to briefly cluster references from a given author (as the case of

---

[28] "For 2 Thessalonians again the evidence, though small in bulk, is surely decisive." P. N. Harrison, *Two Epistles*, 293.

1 Clement illustrates) but does not always cluster them together (as the case of 1 Peter in general illustrates). Thus, when Polycarp does consistently cluster references from Paul around the name of Paul, it is worth noticing.

The clustering patterns around the name of Paul are illustrated in the graph on p. 153. The first graph only includes those references which are either 'probable' or 'almost certain'. The second includes the 'possible' references along with the 'probable' and the 'almost certain'. The numbers on the left of the graph indicate how many separate citations are included in a cluster. The numbers along the bottom of the graph follow the sequence of Polycarp's letter according to chapter. The point of the graph is to give a general visual illustration of what is discussed in the text. For details concerning those items listed as 'non-Pauline' or 'Pauline' on the chart, refer to the more complete discussion in chapter 2 of this monograph.

It can be seen from these diagrams that whether we limit ourselves to phrases which are almost certainly dependent, or whether we include all those which are plausibly drawn from an earlier source, they both support the contention of this chapter that Polycarp clusters references to Paul's writings around the mention of Paul's name.

Polycarp, Paul and the Pastoral Epistles

The recognition of the position of 1 Tim 6:10 and 6:7 in the first Pauline cluster and the position of 2 Tim 4:10 in the second Pauline cluster is the second main observation of this chapter.[29] That Polycarp has a tendency to cluster phrases from Paul around the mention of his name has already been supported. The implication is that Polycarp considers the phrases in each cluster to be Pauline. If this conclusion is accepted, then its most important implication is that Polycarp considers the phrases which he quotes from 1 and 2 Timothy also to be Pauline.

The Oxford Society of Historical Theology comments concerning 4.1 and its relationship to 1 Tim 6:10 and 6:7, "It is almost impos-

---

[29]   It is possible that 2 Tim 2:25 is alluded to in the third Pauline cluster in the phrase 'may the Lord grant them true repentance' (*quibus det dominus poenitentiam veram*, 11.4), but because it is less probable than the references from 1 and 2 Timothy in the first two clusters, it will not be argued here.

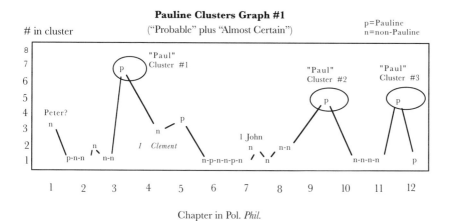

Pauline Clusters Graph #1
("Probable" plus "Almost Certain")

Chapter in Pol. *Phil.*

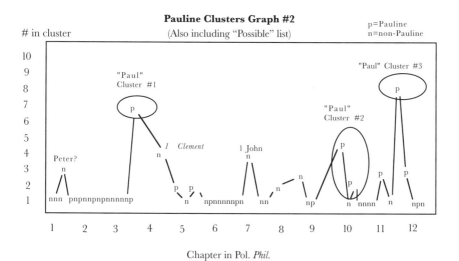

Pauline Clusters Graph #2
(Also including "Possible" list)

Chapter in Pol. *Phil.*

sible to believe that these passsages are independent."[30] Concerning
9.2 and its relationship to 2 Tim 4:10, "The dependence on 2 Timothy
seems almost certain, especially as ὁ νῦν αἰών occurs only in the
Pastoral Epistles among the books of the N.T. (cf. I Tim. 6[17]; Titus
2[12])."[31]

I do not think Polycarp deliberately created this clustering pattern, but there is no way to decide. Whether it occurred consciously
or unconsciously does not affect the thesis of this chapter. The fact
that such a clustering occurs three times in this short letter illustrates
Polycarp's assumption that the phrases surrounding Paul's name are
indeed Pauline.[32]

It will not be argued in this chapter, but it should be noted that
Harrison (following Benecke) is of the opinion that "if Polycarp knew
I and 2 Timothy, it becomes *a priori* more than likely that he knew
the Epistle to Titus also."[33] Harrison then attempts to show that there
are some points of contact between Polycarp's letter and Titus, but
they are inconclusive. It seems that his opinion is based (perhaps rightly
so) upon the weight of evidence that the three letters known as the
Pastoral Epistles (1 Timothy, 2 Timothy, and Titus) have historically
and generally in modern scholarship been viewed together.[34]

This, of course, does not prove that Polycarp is correct in his
assessment. But, as Koester says, Polycarp was "doubtlessly the most
significant ecclesiastical leader of the first half of II C.E."[35] Polycarp,
as Harrison comments, was in a position to answer "a group of problems, each in its own way fundamental, to which Polycarp was probably better qualified than any other man that ever lived to give
authoritative solutions."[36] If, as I have argued, Polycarp has given

---

[30] Oxford Society, 95.
[31] Ibid., 97.
[32] Harrison makes substantially the same point in regard to Polycarp's alter-
ation of the form of some of the quotations which he shares with Clement from the
Synoptic tradition. Harrison says, "Whether he made these corrections consciously
or unconsciously, the significant fact remains that he did make them." P. N. Harrison,
Two Epistles, 286-287.
[33] Ibid., 295.
[34] Though it is commonplace to view the three Pastoral Epistles as one homo-
geneous block of literature some have noted differences, particularly of 2 Timothy
over and against 1 Timothy and Titus. See Michael Prior, *Paul the Letter-Writer and
the Second Letter to Timothy*, JSNTSup 23 (Sheffield: Sheffield Academic Press, 1989),
61-67.
[35] Koester, *History and Literature*, 308.
[36] P. N. Harrison, *Two Epistles*, 3. Of course, Harrison himself argued vehe-

his opinion on the issue of the authorship of the Pastoral Epistles, it has come from the pen of an important early witness.

Conclusion

In this chapter I have sought to demonstrate a marked tendency in Polycarp's letter to the Philippians to cluster Pauline citations and allusions around Paul's name each of three times he mentions Paul's name. Included in the first two clusters are citations from 1 Timothy 6:10, 7 and 2 Tim 4:10 respectively. The most plausible conclusion which can be drawn is that Polycarp considers *these also* to be Pauline. If Harrison (and much of modern scholarship) is correct in linking Titus to 1 and 2 Timothy, Polycarp becomes the earliest external witness to the belief in the early church that Paul was the author of the Pastoral Epistles.

---

mently that the Pastorals were *not* written by Paul. See P. N. Harrison, *The Problem of the Pastoral Epistles* (London: Oxford University Press, 1921). See also P. N. Harrison, *Paulines and Pastorals* (London: Villiers Publications, 1964).

CHAPTER FIVE

PAUL'S INFLUENCE ON THE THEOLOGY
OF POLYCARP

How much is Polycarp influenced by Paul, not simply in terms of style, form or frequency of quotations, nor in terms of ethical example, but in terms of belief? To what degree and in what manner does Polycarp's theology bear the influence of Paul?

To even ask such a question is to invite misunderstanding. Do we know, for example, enough about the thought structures of Polycarp to say anything on this subject? The answer in one sense is no. All we possess are one or two short letters written to the Philippians to encourage them to live righteous lives.[1] Only hints exist about Polycarp's broader theological frame of reference.[2] But, as such hints do exist, it may prove to be fruitful to explore what might lie behind them, even if our conclusions remain tentative.

Nor is Polycarp's letter necessarily representative of Polycarp's views in general. Michael Prior comments about Pol. *Phil.*, "It should not be judged as a theological statement worked out in the calm atmosphere of study. There is no reason to imagine that it contains a rounded picture of Polycarp's view on the Christian life."[3] Still, in this chapter, our concern is to judge the theological influence of Paul rather than simply to try to uncover all of Polycarp's theological positions. Since it has been argued that Polycarp has purposely connected to the letters and person of Paul, and indeed has modeled his own letter after Paul, our concern will be to analyze the junctures at which the affirmations of Polycarp (to the degree they can be ascertained) intersect and, even more, depend upon Paul's thought.

---

[1] "*Philippians* first of all sets out a profile of righteousness. Polycarp mostly provides exterior specifics rather than theological or psychological ramifications, in contrast with Paul's theological reflection upon God, the cross and the parousia." Thomas H. Olbricht, 'Exegesis in the Second Century,' in *Handbook to Exegesis of the New Testament*, ed. Stanley E. Porter (Leiden: Brill, 1997), 412.

[2] "Zwar wird rasch deutlich, daß der Zweck des Briefes ethische Ermahnung ist; theologische Begründungen – meistens in Form von traditionellem Formelgut oder Zitaten – fehlen jedoch nicht gänzlich." Annegreth Bovon-Thurneysen, 'Ethik und Eschatologie im Philipperbrief des Polykarp von Smyrna,' *TZ* 29 (1973): 231.

[3] Michael Prior, *Paul the Letter-Writer and the Second Letter to Timothy*, JSNTSup 23 (Sheffield: Sheffield Academic Press, 1989), 188 n. 69.

An additional problem has to do with the question: which Paul? Since for Polycarp, there appear to be no deutero-Pauline texts (per the conclusion of ch. 4), in this chapter I will make no attempt to differentiate those letters widely accepted as Pauline in modern scholarship from those less commonly accepted as Pauline. Our point of departure is Polycarp's own appropriation of Paul and the way *he* has been influenced by Paul.[4]

There is also the constant danger of assuming that our understanding of Paul is adequate to such a task. The warning of Wiles is apropos. Wiles asks the question of (mostly later) patristic writers: how well did they understand Paul? Then he comments,

> Yet the very form in which the question arises is not without danger. It implies the assumption that we have a true interpretation of Paul's meaning – or at least a truer one than that of those whom we have studied – in the light of which theirs may be tested and judged.[5]

Nevertheless, since saying nothing is the only other option, with caution and with awareness of our own biases we move forward.

Nor will we attempt the impossible task of summarizing Paul's thought. We are more interested in the question of how Polycarp appropriates Paul than in simply comparing the thought of these two Christian leaders though such a task requires a certain amount of comparison.

Grant (correctly) comments, "Polycarp's ideas are largely Pauline."[6] This does not, however, mean that Polycarp is solely a 'Paulinist' (like Marcion), only that he depends upon Paul more than do any of the other Apostolic Fathers[7]: quoting him more often, naming him more often, and (as I have argued in ch. 3) even imitating him. Polycarp uses Paul to support his arguments throughout his letter. Lindemann

---

[4] See similar comments in Andreas Lindemann, 'Paul in the Writings of the Apostolic Fathers,' in *Paul and the Legacies of Paul*, ed. William S. Babcock (Dallas: Southern Methodist University Press, 1990), 25 and David K. Rensberger, 'As the Apostle Teaches: The Development of the Use of Paul's Letters in Second-Century Christianity,' (Ph.D. diss., Yale University, 1981), 58.

[5] Maurice F. Wiles, *The Divine Apostle: The Interpretation of St. Paul's Epistles in the Early Church* (Cambridge: Cambridge University Press, 1967), 132.

[6] Robert Grant, *An Introduction*, vol. 1, The Apostolic Fathers: A New Translation and Commentary, ed. Robert M. Grant (New York: Thomas Nelson & Sons, 1964), 140.

[7] Andreas Lindemann, *Paulus im ältesten Christentum: Das Bild des Apostels und die Rezeption der paulinischen Theologie in der frühchristlichen Literatur bis Marcion*, BHT 58 (Tübingen: J.C.B. Mohr [Paul Siebeck], 1979), 91.

argues that Polycarp, like 'Clement' and Ignatius before him, hides behind the image of Paul and his authority so as to attain the desired response. Polycarp's goal is not to understand Paul on his own terms. He actualizes the teachings and the portrait of the person of Paul for his setting and needs.[8]

The organization of a chapter such as this is also not without its problems. Since our point of departure is Polycarp rather than modern theological categories foreign to his letter, the categories themselves are represented by descriptions which Polycarp would have recognized. Thus, we employ the categories *Resurrection and Judgment*; *Christ*; *Righteousness, Grace, and Faith*; *The Church*; *Fulfillment of Law through Love*; *Money*; *Suffering and Martyrdom*; *The World*.

Excursus: Three Streams of Authority for Polycarp

Since our concern in this chapter is to judge the influence of Paul's theology on Polycarp, we need to know the extent of Paul's authority for Polycarp. How much is Paul an authority for Polycarp (if at all)? What are Polycarp's sources of authority in general? Does Polycarp work under the assumption of a single (canonical) authority?

Such questions are not simple when applied to an early second century author like Polycarp. But Pol. *Phil.* provides some helpful clues. Polycarp considers his authority to be something which he received ('the word delivered to us from the beginning', 7.2; the 'faith that has been given to you',[9] 3.2). Most notable among Polycarp's statements is his explicit mention of three streams of authority in Pol. *Phil.* 6.3:

---

[8] Ibid. It may be correct in one way (and not in another way) to suppose that Ignatius was more 'Pauline' than Polycarp. Lindemann, 'Paul in...Apostolic Fathers,' 40 comments, "Ignatius, we might say, was making an entirely unforced use of Paul, implicit rather than explicit, without rather than with any special thought or attention" which "demonstrate(s) just how far-reaching the Pauline influence on Ignatius apparently was." But Lindemann seems to suggest on p. 44 that though the deeper Pauline influences might not be as strong on Polycarp as on Ignatius, Polycarp was more intentional in employing those influences which he was aware of when he wrote Pol. *Phil.* So in this second sense he was more closely connected with Paul than was Ignatius.

[9] The 'faith' here seems to be the completed belief of the church. Johannes Bapt. Bauer, *Die Polykarpbriefe* (Göttingen: Vandenhoeck & Ruprecht, 1995), 47.

So, then, let us serve him [i.e. Christ] with fear and all reverence, just as he himself has commanded, as did the apostles, who preached the gospel to us, and the prophets, who announced in advance the coming of our Lord.

Three streams of authority are represented in this single sentence:

1. The first stream of authority (temporally but not in ranking) contain the OT prophets[10] who, in 6.3 'announced in advance the coming of our Lord'. The OT writings as a whole are for Polycarp the 'sacred Scriptures' (12.1).[11]

2. The words and example of the Lord are the second stream of authority. Obedience is required because 'he himself has commanded'. (Similar statements concerning the Lord's command are found in 2.2; 4.1; 5.1; 5.2; 6.3a; the Lord's example is discussed in 8.2 and 10.1).

3. The third stream of authority in 6.3 consists of the apostolic writings. As Christ 'commanded' so also have the apostles commanded. In Pol. *Phil.*, Paul is the one upon whom Polycarp most depends ('as Paul teaches', 11.2; 'accurate and reliable', 3.2), though references to 1 Peter and 1 John are very probable and other apostolic writings are possible.

The rub is that Polycarp never tries to equate these three streams or subsume them under a single 'canonical' rubric. He never asks whether the writings of the apostles are on the same level as the OT or the teaching of the Lord.[12] He simply understands them to be authoritative and binding upon one's actions.

---

[10] These prophets are pre-Christian prophets, unlike those in 1 Cor 12:28-29; Eph 2:20 and *Did.* 11.2-5.

[11] I have argued in ch. 2 that consciousness of Ps 4:5 stands behind the expression 'sacred Scriptures', though others (for example D. Richard Stuckwisch, 'Saint Polycarp of Smyrna: Johannine or Pauline Figure?' *CTQ* 61 [1997]: 122; Charles M. Nielsen, 'Polycarp, Paul and the Scriptures,' *ATR* 47 [1965]: 210; Lee M. McDonald, *The Formation of the Christian Biblical Canon* [Peabody, Mass.: Hendrickson Publishers, 1995], 148) have argued that Paul's writings are also included because of the connection with Eph 4:26. See discussion under 12.1 in ch. 2. The extent of these 'Scriptures' for Polycarp cannot be demonstrated. Following Roger Beckwith, *The Old Testament Canon of the New Testament Church and its Background in Early Judaism* (Grand Rapids: William B. Eerdmans Publishing Company, 1985), I am convinced that the canon of the Hebrew Scriptures was already in place by the time of Polycarp. Polycarp is probably dependent upon that. Polycarp may also have accepted Tobit (cf. 10.2) though the bare quotation of Tob 4:10 and/or 12:9 (without other supporting quotations from Tobit) makes it uncertain.

[12] According to Birger Gerhardsson, *Memory and Manuscript: Oral Tradition and Written Transmission in Rabbinic Judaism and Early Christianity*, trans. Eric J. Sharpe (Uppsala: Almqvist & Wiksells, 1961), 199 there is no question in the Apostolic Fathers that the words of Christ were considered absolute and on the same level as the OT writings.

Lindemann, in his comments about *1 Clement*, Ignatius and Polycarp seems to disagree with the notion that Polycarp cites Paul as an authority. He says that they

> ...were not citing Paul to prove or to secure their 'orthodoxy' but rather were quoting Paul's letters 'voluntarily.' By quoting Paul, they apparently hoped to 'impress' their addressees; and they seem to have believed that they could achieve their theological purposes more effectively with such quotations than without them.[13]

It is true that Pol. *Phil.* gives no indication that formal canonization of Paul's letters has yet taken place. But, at least in Polycarp's case, Lindemann (and others like him) have understated the case. Polycarp clearly is modeling and citing Paul as an *authority* to whom his readers should listen and whom they should obey.[14] If one had asked Polycarp, "Is this authority on the same level as the OT Scriptures and/or the words of the Lord?" he probably would have answered that it was different – but still authoritative and still to be obeyed. If asked whether Paul's writings were inspired like the writings of the Prophets, he may have answered that he had never asked the question in quite that way. In other words, it appears that Polycarp recognizes different categories of authority but is not yet at the point of trying to correlate them. Polycarp's understanding of authority for the apostolic writings, then, appears to be 'functional' rather than 'formal' or 'official' (as in Irenaeus).[15]

Polycarp, I am arguing, depends upon three streams of authority without answering (our) question of whether they are all Scripture.[16]

---

[13] Lindemann, 'Paul in...Apostolic Fathers,' 29.

[14] "The way he uses these documents is noteworthy: (1) while apparently none of the NT books are cited as 'Scripture' (the reference to Ephesians in Pol. *Phil.* 12.1 is a possible exception), (2) the manner in which he refers to them clearly shows that he considered them to be authoritative." Michael W. Holmes, 'Polycarp of Smyrna,' in *Dictionary of the Later New Testament & Its Developments*, ed. Ralph P. Martin and Peter H. Davids (Downers Grove and Leicester: InterVarsity Press, 1997), 936.

[15] James Daniel Hernando, 'Irenaeus and the Apostolic Fathers: An Inquiry into the development of the New Testament Canon,' (Ph.D. diss., Drew University, 1990), 35-37 (and throughout). Note that Hernando's well-executed study argues throughout for continuity between the Apostolic Father's understanding of authority and that of Irenaeus, only that by the time of Irenaeus, the authority has become official. He argues against the notion that Irenaeus has made a radical break with earlier conceptions of the authority of early Christian writings.

[16] "The question of 'scripture' was not as important as the question of 'the word of truth' set forth either orally or in writing." Robert M. Grant, *The Formation of the New Testament* (New York: Harper & Row, 1965), 106.

This actually explains *why* Polycarp does not feel compelled to use the OT writings or the teaching of the Lord *more* (though he does employ them both). He does not need to. The apostolic teaching (Paul, Peter, John) is authoritative and more suited to his compositional purpose (particularly those writings of Paul). If the apostolic teaching were somehow an inadequate authority, it is a reasonable inference that Polycarp would draw upon one of the other streams of authority more often. The fact that he does not shows that he invests a lot of authority in the teaching of Paul. It needs to be obeyed, if one wants to be obedient to the Lord.

These three streams of authority (the OT prophets, the teaching of the Lord and the apostolic writings) are only related by Polycarp insofar as the Lord himself is the fulcrum of the three. Pol. *Phil.* 6.2 (quoted above) makes this clear. The prophets 'announced in advance the coming of our Lord' while the apostles like the Lord commanded their audience to serve Christ with fear and reverence. Thus, the closest that Polycarp comes to relating these three streams of authority is to put Christ at the center.[17]

The same threesome is suggested in Rom 1:1-2, 2 Pet 3:2, and in Ign. *Phld.* 5.2, though in those passages it is implied rather than discussed. But Polycarp (6.2) explicitly mentions the three together as the foundational authorities for his exhortations. Polycarp, then, takes the 'first steps' (in Kümmel's words) toward a formal canonization of a new collection of Scriptures.[18]

In contrast to the authority accorded to these three streams,

---

[17] "The formula of Polycarp appears as the practical application of a principle: 'prophets and apostles' arranged in dependence on Christ and his commandments serve as norm of teaching in the church." Denis M. Farkasfalvy, "'Prophets and Apostles': The Conjunction of the Two Terms before Irenaeus,' in *Texts and Testaments: Critical Essays on the Bible and Early Church Fathers*, ed. W. Eugene March (San Antonio: Trinity University Press, 1980), 122-123; see also Bruce M. Metzger, *The Canon of the New Testament: Its Origin, Development, and Significance* (Oxford: Clarendon Press, 1987), 60.

[18] Werner Georg Kümmel, *Introduction to the New Testament*, rev. ed., trans. Howard Clark Kee (Nashville: Abington, 1975), 483-484; also Rensberger, 'As the Apostle Teaches,' 118. Farkasfalvy, 'Prophets and Apostles,' 127, calls it a 'proto-Canon'. Adolf von Harnack, *The Origin of the New Testament and the Most Important Consequences of the New Creation*, trans. J. R. Wilkinson (New York: The Macmillan Company, 1925), 26 comments, "Above all, it was because Christian writings were in public worship actually treated like the Old Testament, without being simply included in the body of the old Canon, that the idea of a second sacred collection could be realized."

Polycarp "...does not use the letters of Ignatius as authorities – even though they 'contain faith, endurance, and all the edification which pertains to our Lord' (13:2)."[19] Nor, arguably, does he use *1 Clement* as an authority, since it is unlikely that Polycarp would have *corrected* the form of an apostolic citation of the Lord, whereas that appears to be what Polycarp has done with *1 Clement* at a couple points in Pol. *Phil.* 2.3 (see discussion in ch. 2). Neither 'Clement' nor the letters of Ignatius are ever referred to with a citational formula in Pol. *Phil.* However, Polycarp in the eight clearest formulae which function as formulae in his letter (1.3; 2.3; 4.1; 5.1; 6.1-2; 7.2; 11.2; 12.1)[20] once refers to a Psalm quotation (mediated through Paul) (12.1); three times refers to the teaching of the Lord (2.3; 6.1-2; 7.2) and four times draws directly from Paul (1.3; 4.1; 5.1; 11.2). Polycarp's letter appears to contrast the period in which Polycarp lives with the apostolic period.[21]

In summary, Polycarp sees himself in continuity with earlier tradition, though for Polycarp that tradition is more developed than it was for the apostles (and, of course, less than for Irenaeus).[22] Polycarp depends upon three streams of authority: the writings of the OT, the words and example of Jesus, and the apostolic writings. He does not seem to be asking the question of whether the apostolic writings are on the same level as the OT. He (vigorously) uses the apostolic writings and assumes the authoritative and binding nature of their teaching. Thus, the theological influence of Paul upon Polycarp (to whatever extent it exists) is, in Polycarp's view, an influence by an authoritative teacher whose teaching Polycarp seeks to obey. We now turn to the question of the extent and nature of that influence.

Resurrection and Judgment

There are two aspects of resurrection for Polycarp: the past resurrection of Christ and the future resurrection of believers. Christ's resurrection is a central element of the gospel message which Polycarp

---

[19] Grant, *Formation*, 106.

[20] Less clear examples of formulae are the γάρ in 7.1 (before a quotations from 1 John 4:2-3 and 1 John 3:8), the γάρ in 9.2 (before a quotation from 2 Tim 4:10) and the *quia* in 10.2 (before a quotation from Tob 4:10 and/or Tob 12:9).

[21] Raymond F. Collins, *Introduction to the New Testament* (Garden City, N.Y.: Doubleday & Company, 1983), 19.

[22] Peter Steinmetz, 'Polykarp von Smyrna über die Gerechtigkeit,' *Hermes* 100 (1972): 73-74.

had been taught from childhood (see 1.2; 2.1; 9.2; 12.2b). That aspect will not need much discussion here since Polycarp's future concerns are never explicitly linked to Christ's resurrection.[23] Contrast this to Paul's discussion in 1 Corinthians 15 where the resurrection of Christ and the future resurrection of believers are two events in a single eschatological Event.[24]

The future resurrection of believers is of vital, practical, present concern for Polycarp (2.2; 5.2; 6.2; 7.1; 11.2; 12.2a). Still, his approach contrasts sharply to contemporary over-realized eschatologies, as F. F. Bruce notes in his comments about Pol. *Phil.* 7.1:

> He speaks out in forthright manner against anything that smacks of over-realized eschatology or of gnostic spiritualizing of the last things, putting it on a par with docetic misinterpretations of Christ's incarnation and passion...[25]

'Realized' elements of eschatology are mostly gone from Polycarp. For Polycarp, resurrection and judgment are part of a work that lies fundamentally in the future.[26] There may be a touch of realized eschatology in Polycarp's use of χάρα ('joy') in 1.2-3 – the church has a share of future joy when it presently experiences joy.[27] Moreover, the striking designation of Christ (not the Holy Spirit!) as 'our hope and the guarantee of our righteousness' (8.1) contains an eschatological impulse which is tied to our present relationship with Christ. But almost all other indications point to a primarily futuristic eschatology.

Paul, by way of comparison, while strongly affirming a future resurrection, not only affirms realized aspects of the resurrection but builds upon them. They function as one of the central structures for his theology of the Christian life (cf. Romans 6, Phil 3:7-16; Col 3:1-4). Christ's resurrection is the dynamic power of the Christian's present life through union with Christ. Polycarp's concern with such elements

---

[23] Only that in 2.2 the same God who raised Christ will raise us, too, cf. 2 Cor 4:14.

[24] Bovon-Thurneysen, 'Ethik,' 252.

[25] F. F. Bruce, 'Eschatology in the Apostolic Fathers,' in *The Heritage of the Early Church: Essays in Honor of Georges Vasilievich Florovsky*, ed. David Neiman and Margaret Schatkin (Rome: Pont. Institutum Studiorum Orientalium, 1973), 82.

[26] Bovon-Thurneysen, 'Ethik,' 251. In contrast, in Paul (and most of the NT): "And so what fills the forward view is not some ideal yet to be attained, but the Christian's position already attained in Christ and about to be revealed." Thomas F. Torrance, *The Doctrine of Grace in the Apostolic Fathers* (n.p.: Oliver and Boyd Ltd., 1948; repr. Pasadena: WIPF & Stock Publishers, 1996), 35.

[27] Bovon-Thurneysen, 'Ethik,' 254.

is minimal[28] and they do not seem to play the same central role in Polycarp's overarching theology as they do in Paul's.

Polycarp's eschatology is limited to three main ideas, none of which is fleshed out in Pol. *Phil.*[29] These are:

1. Resurrection of the dead (2.2; 5.2; 7.1).
2. The final judgment when Christ comes (2.1; cf. 6.2; 7.1; 11.2).
3. Future rewards (5.2; 9.2).[30]

Bovon-Thurneysen argues that Polycarp represents a transitional stage in the development of eschatological understanding.[31] For the most part, Paul and the other writings of the New Testament subsume ethics under eschatology. By the time of *2 Clement* in the middle of the second century, however, the situation (at least in the case of *2 Clement*) has changed. *2 Clem.* 12.1-6 makes the coming of the kingdom dependent upon sexual abstinence and thereby subsumes eschatology under ethics. Of course, writings from the first half of the second century are sparse. But even if we assume an uneven development of eschatological understanding, it may be significant that Polycarp's own position appears to straddle the two positions, as two passages in particular suggest. Pol. *Phil.* 2.2 and 5.2 suggest that Polycarp believes that the eschatological promises are conditionally activated.[32]

Pol. *Phil.* 2.2 reads, "But he who raised him from the dead will raise us also if we do his will and follow his commandments and love the things he loved..." Resurrection in this passage is conditionally linked with doing God's will and following his commandments, along with a long list of other actions.[33]

Pol. *Phil.* 5.2b reads "If we please him in this present world, we

---

[28] There may be a hint of Paul's idea of suffering with Christ (cf. Rom 8:17) in the expression ᾧ καὶ συνέπαθον ('with whom they also suffered') in Pol. *Phil.* 9.2.

[29] "The hope of Christians for the future, its images and its supposed conditions are not yet the object of reflection and explanation [in the Apostolic Fathers]; it is simply part of the Easter kerygma at the heart of the community's life and worship." Brian E. Daley, *The Hope of the Early Church: A Handbook of Patristic Eschatology* (Cambridge: Cambridge University Press, 1991), 14.

[30] Pierre Batiffol, 'Polycarp,' in *Dictionary of the Apostolic Church*, vol. 2, ed. James Hastings (Edinburgh: T.& T. Clark, 1918), 247.

[31] See Bovon-Thurneysen, 'Ethik,' 241-256.

[32] Ibid., 256.

[33] Schoedel considers contingency to be present here. William R. Schoedel, *Polycarp, Martyrdom of Polycarp, Fragments of Papias*, vol. 5 of *The Apostolic Fathers: A New Translation and Commentary*, ed. Robert M. Grant (Camden, N.J.: Thomas Nelson & Sons, 1967), 11.

will receive the world to come as well, inasmuch as he promised to raise us from the dead and that if we prove to be citizens worthy of him, we will also reign with him – if we are believing." Future resurrection is linked with three conditions here: 1) If we please him in this present world, 2) If we prove to be citizens worthy of him, and 3) If we are believing.[34] Note that these three conditional clauses show that Polycarp wants to emphasize the continuing working out of the faith of the Philippians.

Though God, through Christ, has activated grace apart from works (1.3), Polycarp appears to teach that future resurrection is contingent upon continuing to believe (note the summary position of εἴγε πιστεύομεν in 5.2) which works its way out in the believer's actions ('fruit' in 12.3 and 'bearing fruit' in 1.2).[35] Works, for Polycarp, are a demonstration of true faith. But, as in Paul, it is not always clear whether one may lose his/her standing if one fails to continue in faith, or whether such a falling demonstrates that they were not among the truly chosen (Pol. *Phil.* 1.1) in the first place.

Polycarp thus agrees with Paul about his understanding that true faith produces actions. Polycarp, however, more strongly emphasizes the human response over and against Paul who emphasizes the divine initiative. Nowhere does Paul explicitly link a conditional clause with a statement about future resurrection[36] (though a conditional clause is linked to salvation in 1 Cor 15:2; cf. Col 2:23; 2 Tim 2:12; and such passages as Gal 5:21, Phil 3:11, and Rom 11:22 seem to imply contingency). Still, Polycarp does not entirely misunderstand Paul, but evinces the beginning of a move toward greater human cooperation while at the same time not explicitly working out how that human interaction interfaces with God's grace.

How does Polycarp compare to Paul in terms of eschatological intensity? Both Schoedel and Jefford comment that expectation and eschatological intensity are less in Polycarp.[37] Such comments are accurate in one sense and misdirected in another. They are accu-

---

[34] All three conditional clauses are tied to future resurrection, as the repetition of such phrases as 'we will receive the world to come as well,' 'inasmuch as he promised to raise us from the dead,' and 'we will also reign with him' demonstrate. The three conditions, thus, can be considered parallel conditions.

[35] Refer also to the discussion below in the section entitled 'Righteousness, Grace, and Faith.'

[36] Bovon-Thurneysen, 'Ethik,' 248.

[37] Schoedel, *Polycarp*, 10; Clayton N. Jefford, *Reading the Apostolic Fathers: An Introduction* (Peabody, Mass.: Hendrickson Publishers, 1996), 79.

rate in the sense that Paul's expectation of an imminent parousia drove
and formed his life, both in terms of his mission and his theology.
Polycarp seems not as compelled in his expectation. But such comments are also misguided if they imply that Polycarp is a placid in-
structor of ethics. He is not. His ethics, as with Paul,[38] were formed
by his belief in a future resurrection, a theme he returns to repeatedly. The future is an issue of vital concern for Polycarp. But there
is still less of a sense with Polycarp that he expects Christ to return
any moment. For Polycarp, readiness has become less the expectation of the second coming as it is constant watchfulness in life.[39]
Moreover, some of Polycarp's insistence and repetition of the theme
of resurrection may simply be due to his antagonism toward docetists
who do not accept the idea of a bodily resurrection.[40]

Quasten opines that all the writings of the Apostolic Fathers have
a strong eschatological impulse. He says, "Typical of all these writings is their eschatological character. The second coming of Christ
is regarded as imminent."[41] Perhaps for a historian like Quasten who
spends most of his scholarly time working in later eras, the period
of the Apostolic Fathers could appear to speak in an eschatological
tone. But in comparison with NT writings, it can hardly be doubted
that the intensity of the expectation of the parousia is less. In terms
of eschatological expectation, Polycarp is a transitional figure.

In summary, though Polycarp evinces a common orthodox belief
in future resurrection, he depends upon Paul for many of his most
important statements. His uses of 2 Cor 4:14 (2.2), Rom 14:10, 12,
cf. 2 Cor 5:16 (6.2), and 1 Cor 6:2 (11.2)[42] in three of his statements
about resurrection, show the importance to Polycarp of standing in
continuity with Paul's belief in future resurrection. But, unlike Paul,
whose entire theological system is informed and driven by his escha-

---

[38] "Contrary to many popular assumptions about the detachment alleged to be
inherent within eschatological teaching, Paul's letters demonstrate a closes connection between eschatology and ethical exhortation." Larry J. Kreitzer, 'Eschatology,'
in *Dictionary of Paul and His Letters*, ed. Gerald F. Hawthorne, Ralph P. Martin and
Daniel E. Reid (Downers Grove, Ill. and Leicester, England: InterVarsity Press, 1993),
265.
[39] Bovon-Thurneysen, 'Ethik,' 256.
[40] J. N. D. Kelly, *Early Christian Doctrines*, 5th rev. ed. (London: Adam & Charles
Black, 1958; repr. 1980), 463.
[41] Johannes Quasten, *Patrology, vol. 1: The Beginnings of Patristic Literature* (Westminster, Md.: The Newman Press and Utrecht-Brussels: Spectrum Publishers, 1951),
40.
[42] Note also the way he uses Phil 1:27 in the discussion of Pol. *Phil.* 5.2.

tology, Polycarp's belief is more geared toward repeated affirmations of a future event. Polycarp also more closely links conditional statements concerning the human response with the prospect of attaining to the resurrection in a way not as common in Paul. Finally, though expectation of the end exists for Polycarp, its intensity is less than for Paul. The issue of resurrection, then, highlights both the nearness and the distance of Polycarp's thought to that of Paul.

Christ

Polycarp's Christology is high and his personal commitment to the exalted Christ appears on the pages of Pol. *Phil.* as a vibrant and compelling reality. His Christology, while not derived solely from Paul, for the most part shows continuity with Paul. There is no evidence in Pol. *Phil.* that Polycarp would have thought in terms of *differences* (even in emphasis) among the apostles on the question of Christology. His uses of various writings that touch upon the person of Christ are seamlessly woven together, usually without comment. Thus, the only way of approaching the question of Polycarp's relationship to Pauline Christology is to survey Polycarp's Christology and to highlight continuities, dependencies and divergences (the few that exist) between Paul and Polycarp as they arise.

Polycarp, as has just been stated, holds to a high Christology. Polycarp's most common term for Christ is 'the Lord' and 'our Lord'. This designation occurs especially in contexts where Christ's will is the authoritative standard for the Christian's conduct (2.2; 4.1; 5.3; 6.2-3).[43] Though he never expressly designates Christ as 'God' in the letter (except for the textually uncertain 12.2), Polycarp attributes to Christ the functions and perogatives of God. The subjection of everything to Christ is affirmed in 2.1, a teaching affirmed also by Paul in 1 Cor 15:26-28 and Phil 2:10; 3:21. Also in 2.1 it is Christ who is coming as "Judge of the living and the dead." Polycarp's salutation, "may mercy and peace from God Almighty and Jesus Christ our Savior be yours in abundance," conjoins 'Jesus Christ our Savior' with 'God Almighty'. The works of God are jointly exercised by Christ throughout the letter (1.2-3; 2.1-2; 9.2; 12.2). A striking feature of Polycarp's letter is the way he adds 'and Christ' or 'and our Lord'

---

[43] Stark, *Christology*, 35.

to 'God' where it seems (literarily) unneeded (1.1; 3.3; 5.2; 5.3). For Polycarp, it is evidence of the strong connection he makes in his mind between Christ and God.

A high view of Christ is also observable in Paul (Rom 9:5; Phil 2:6-7; Col 1:15-20), who, like Polycarp, usually speaks of functional rather than ontological relationships.

Polycarp's high view of Christ predominates throughout the letter. There may be hints of the subordination of Christ to God in 1.2-3; 2.1-2; 9.2; and especially 12.2 where Polycarp refers to God as the 'God and Father of our Lord Jesus Christ'.[44] But, as Stark comments,

> The thought of subordination, which occupies so large a place in Clement, has almost entirely disappeared in Polycarp...the dominant thought of his letter is that God and Christ are in a position of virtual equality in the work of salvation.[45]

Polycarp calls Christ the 'eternal high priest himself' and 'the son of God' in 12.2. Polycarp's concept of Christ as high priest is shared also with the writer of Hebrews (4:14-15; 6:20-7:3), with *1 Clement* (36.1; 61.3; ch. 64), and with Ignatius (Ign. *Phld.* 9.1). It is also reported to have been repeated by Polycarp in his doxology just before his death in a very similar form (*Mart. Pol.* 14.3).[46] The presence of priestly language in *Mart. Pol.* may indicate that Christ as high priest is more than a passing comment by Polycarp in his letter. The concept, of course, is not derived from Paul. As to the designation 'son of God', it does occur in Paul (cf. Rom 1:4; 2 Cor 1:19; Gal 2:20; Eph 4:13), though certainly Paul is not alone in this designation (which appears frequently in all four gospels, Hebrews and 1 John). There is, however, no way in Pol. *Phil.* 12.2 to tell what Polycarp might mean by such a designation and thus to locate conceptual dependence in any of these.

In 12.2, Christ is also the one who grants 'a share and a place among his saints'. In some manuscripts he is referred to both as 'our

---

[44] Kleist, *The Didache*..., 196 n. 91 calls this statement, "Polycarp's Christology in a nutshell."

[45] Alonzo Rosecrans Stark, *The Christology in the Apostolic Fathers* (Chicago: The University of Chicago Press, 1912), 36.

[46] "I glorify you, through the eternal and heavenly High Priest, Jesus Christ, your beloved child, through whom to you and with him and the Holy Spirit be glory both now and for the ages to come. Amen." The trinitarian formula points toward Christ being viewed as divine here. See comments in Grant, *Introduction*, 68-69.

Lord' and as 'God' though many do not contain 'and God'.[47]

Polycarp's understanding of the death of Christ is suggested primarily in three places: Pol. *Phil.* 2.1, 8.1 and 9.2. Christ bore our sins on the cross (8.1) which, in light of the connection of the quotation from 1 Pet 2:24, 22 with Isaiah 53 suggests that its meaning is that Christ bore the penalty of sins on behalf of others.[48] Thus, he died on our behalf (ὑπὲρ ἡμῶν) and was raised by God for our sakes (δι' ἡμᾶς)(9.2). Note the possible connection to Pauline phraseology in Polycarp's use of ὑπὲρ ἡμῶν in relation to the death of Christ in 9.2 (cf. Rom 5:8; 1 Thess 5:10; Eph 5:2; Tit 2:4). Christ, according to Polycarp, was able to die for us because he was sinless (8.1). God raised Jesus from the dead (2.1; 9.2) and gave him a throne at his right hand (2.1). Finally, Christ's death is a model for us when we endure suffering (8.2).

Polycarp's reference to Christ as the ἀρραβῶν ('pledge/down–payment') in 8.1, a term which can hardly have been used without a mental connection to Paul's use of the same term (Eph 1:14; 2 Cor 1:22; 5:5), is striking both in the fact that it is used at all and in light of Polycarp's differing use of the word. In Paul the ἀρραβῶν is the Holy Spirit who is the pledge of our inheritance. In Polycarp it is Christ himself who is the guarantee. But even in 8.1, Christ is the center of the life of the Christian who lives life ἐν αὐτῷ ('in order that we might live in him'). 'In Christ' terminology is no doubt derived from Paul, though once again there is no way to determine precisely what Polycarp may mean by its use.

In summary, Polycarp stands in continuity with Paul in the sense that his Christology is high (and like Paul's, primarily functional rather than ontological). He cannot be said to be solely dependent upon Paul for this high Christology since such a view is shared by many others besides Paul and Polycarp. Possible Pauline Christological influence may be detected in Polycarp's use of Paul's phrases ὑπὲρ ἡμῶν (9.2, cf. 8.1) in relation to the death of Christ and ἐν αὐτῷ (8.1) in relation to Christian living, though in the case of the second, it is uncertain what Polycarp may mean. Christ as the ἀρραβῶν in 8.1 is

---

[47] Grant, *Introduction*, 68 suggest that the Christology of Pol. *Phil.* 12 has been *lowered* in some of the Latin mss., just as the Latin Pseudo-Ignatian letters, to which Polycarp's letter is attached, has lowered the Christology of Ignatius. He thus thinks that 'God Jesus Christ' is original and that Polycarp is here referring to Jesus as God.

[48] Stark, *Christology*, 37.

both clearly dependent upon Paul and, at the same time, clearly different than Paul, who applies the word to the Holy Spirit. Finally, Polycarp, like Paul before him, demonstrates a living commitment to Christ, who is, for Polycarp, no less than 'the Lord' and 'our Lord'.

Righteousness, Grace, and Faith

Since Polycarp's stated purpose is to respond to the Philippians' request that he write to them about 'righteousness' (3.1), this is very evidently the item of most concern for Polycarp. It is also an item which will require concentration on our part. What do we learn by Polycarp's uses of the word 'righteousness', 'grace', and 'faith' in Pol. *Phil.*, and what theological commitments may lie behind them?

The term δικαιοσύνη ('righteousness') in Pol. *Phil.*, in five out of its seven appearances apparently means 'the practice of holy living'[49] with notable exceptions perhaps in 5.2 (i.e. God's righteous character) and 8.1 (i.e. Christ's righteous act on the cross[50]). Thus, at least in this letter, though the primary focus in Polycarp's thought is upon the way one should live rightly rather than on righteousness which has been given by God,[51] a relationship between right living and a righteous God and Christ (5.2; 8.1) may be (albeit subtly) suggested even in Polycarp's minority uses of δικαιοσύνη. The word χάρις ('grace') appears only once in the letter (1.3), though its location so early in the letter in a quotation from Eph 2:5, 8, 9 is probably significant. Polycarp's understanding of grace as a concept will be discussed below, but at this point it should be mentioned that Polycarp's

---

[49] "The word δικαιοσύνη (here rendered 'the practice of holy living'), which abounds in shades of meaning varying with the context, has unfortunately, through centuries of repetition, been forced into the straight jackets of 'justice' and 'righteousness'." James A. Kleist, *The Didache, the Epistle of Barnabas, the Epistles and the Martyrdom of St. Polycarp, the Fragments of Papias, the Epistle to Diognetus*, vol. 6, Ancient Christian Writers, ed. Johannes Quasten and Joseph C. Plumpe (Westminster, Md.: The Newman Press, 1948), 188 n. 25.

[50] It may be possible to read 'guarantee of our righteousness' ethically, i.e. someday we will *be righteous* but for now Jesus is the guarantee that it will happen. But the relative pronoun plus εἰμί when combined with the quotations and comments which follow in the rest of 8.1 point more toward a concept related to Christ's work on the cross.

[51] Lindemann, *Paulus im ältesten Christentum*, 88. Holmes, 'Polycarp of Smyrna,' 936, comments on the subject of Polycarp's view of 'righteousness' – "For him, orthopraxy is the other side of the coin of orthodoxy; if the community is behaving properly, it is also likely believing properly."

use of χάρις in a quotation from Eph 2:5, 8, 9 is strong evidence that
Polycarp sees himself in continuity with Paul on the teaching represented in the quotation. The word πίστις ('faith')[52] appears repeatedly in the letter (1.2; 3.2; 4.2; 9.2; 10.1; 12.2; 13.2). It sometimes
takes on more the nuance 'the faith' (i.e. the handed down system
of belief, as in 3.2; 4.2)[53] but elsewhere seems to be simply 'belief'
(i.e. the act of believing, as in 9.2; 12.2). The verbal form πιστεύω
also exists (5.2; 8.2).

A difficulty confronts any reader of Pol. *Phil.* who tries to determine Polycarp's view of how one stands rightly before God. Polycarp
affirms the active and necessary role of continuing in the faith throughout his letter (2.2-3; 3.3; 5.2-3; 6.2; 9.2; 11.2; 12.3). Meanwhile, in
a couple of key locations (1.2-3; 8.1; 12.2) he also emphasizes the
central role of Christ in the process. It is both necessary and useful
to interact with the well-known and influential thesis of Thomas F.
Torrance. In *The Doctrine of Grace in the Apostolic Fathers*,[54] Torrance
argues that there is a great gulf ('so great a divergence'[55]) between
the teaching of the NT concept of grace and that found in the Apostolic Fathers. He considers Polycarp to be one with the other
Apostolic Fathers "in a failure to apprehend the revolutionary and
distinctive character of the Gospel."[56] Concerning Polycarp, Torrance
writes,

> For Polycarp the death of Christ for our sins or on our account does
> not mean a forgiveness or a justification that cancels the power of sin.
> The Cross has not put men in the right with God but man is still re-
> garded as on the debit side of an account with God...Christ has set
> man on his feet again, and so put him in a position in which *he* can
> carry out the rest of his obligations towards God, namely, in fulfilling
> the command of righteousness.[57]

Torrance touches upon something important – the recognition of

---

[52] Or *in fide* in 10.1 and 12.2.

[53] J. B. Bauer, *Die Polykarpbriefe*, 47 in comments about 3.2.

[54] Torrance, *Doctrine of Grace*.

[55] Ibid., v.

[56] Ibid., 91. Adolf von Harnack, *History of Dogma*, vol. 1, trans. Neil Buchanan
(London: Williams & Norgate, 1905), 172-173 states his agreement with this general approach, "The moralistic view of sin, forgiveness of sin, and righteousness in
Clement, Barnabas, Polycarp and Ignatius, gives place to Pauline formulae; but the
uncertainty with which these are reproduced, shews that the Pauline idea has not
been clearly seen."

[57] Torrance, *Doctrine of Grace*, 94-95. He cites as evidence 1.1; 2.2f; 3.1f; 4.1f;
5.1f; 6.1; 9.2; 10.1f; 12.1f.

a historical move away from Paul's understanding of unmerited grace toward a theology where human action eventually takes a more central role. But, in the process, Torrance forces Polycarp into his general conclusions and thus seems to misrepresent Polycarp's individual position on the subject. F. C. Baur rightly comments that faith and works stand side by side in Pol. *Phil.* without any attempt by Polycarp to correlate them.[58] Polycarp's own questions are not the same as Torrance's who seems quite concerned about issues coming out of the Protestant Reformation. Torrance radicalizes his concerns by making Paul disinterested in ethics: "He is not really concerned to ask questions about ethical practice. He acts before questions can be asked."[59] He makes Polycarp, in contrast, almost wholly consumed with ethics under which faith is subsumed; Polycarp, says Torrance, "may be described as one unconsciously opposed to grace."[60] Moreover, "...trust comes also to be placed in human actions and in a life of love also."[61]

But Paul has thought deeply about ethics (consider only his discussions in 1 Cor 8, 10 and Rom 14) and Polycarp knows grace (Pol. *Phil.* 1.3, 12.2). It is not accurate to say that Polycarp does *not* understand forgiveness and release from the power of sin in Christ, as Torrance claims. The difference may lie more in emphasis than in fundamentals. This is not to say that Polycarp entirely apprehends Paul's concerns (he certainly does not emphasize them). But neither is his theology on this point markedly different from Paul.

Polycarp affirms God's grace *and* affirms a needed active human response. Polycarp does not anywhere clearly relate them. But what lies behind his concerns? 'Reciprocity' (to borrow a term from Danker) is a term which could be used to define Polycarp's theological position concerning grace.[62] Reciprocity may be defined as a responsive action taken by a beneficiary toward a benefactor. It is neither sim-

---

[58] Ferdinand Christian Baur, *The Church History of the First Three Centuries*, vol. 1, trans. Allan Menzies (London: Williams and Norgate, 1878), 140.

[59] Torrance, *Doctrine of Grace*, 34.

[60] Ibid., 97.

[61] Ibid., 34.

[62] See the discussion in Frederick W. Danker, 'Bridging St. Paul and the Apostolic Fathers: A Study in Reciprocity,' *CTM* 15 (1988): 84-94. Danker does not mention Polycarp at all. He is trying to present a model/matrix in which the differences between Paul and the Apostolic Fathers might be evaluated. Neither is he entirely clear about his meaning of the word 'reciprocity'. I am using a slightly narrower definition than he.

ple reception in gratefulness, on the one hand, nor meritoriously earning a gift through some deed, on the other. It is the culturally expected action taken by someone to *show* that they are grateful.[63] If Polycarp's thought is represented by this designation as I wish to argue, Torrance is wrong in concluding that humans still stand "on the debit side of an account with God."[64]

Torrance also concludes that the Apostolic Fathers, Polycarp included, wholly misunderstand the vital connection of God's grace to the concrete reality of Christ's work.[65] But, at least in the case of Polycarp, he overstates his case once again and almost admits it twice (but backs off both times). His admissions are included because they (paradoxically) illustrate the fact that a connection between God's grace and the work of Christ is present in Polycarp.

Torrance writes, "At other times Polycarp can speak of Christ as Savior, eternal High Priest, as having died on our behalf (ὑπὲρ ἡμῶν) and raised on our account (δι' ἡμᾶς); as having endured death for our sins (ὑπὲρ τῶν ἁμαρτιῶν ἡμῶν), an act regarded as the source of life to us..." Torrance however adds, "but there is nothing in all this to give us a different view of the relation of the death of Christ to the believer."[66] Once again Torrance argues against his own position: "As against this we must note that Polycarp does once allude to forgiveness, and to mercy and peace and election as coming from God and Christ; and throughout there is an emphasis on faith." But he adds, "Still, in spite of such Pauline language he makes salvation conditional."[67]

Torrance's comments do in fact argue against his position. Polycarp does speak of Christ as Savior (in the salutation), as eternal High Priest (12.2), as having died on our behalf (ὑπὲρ ἡμῶν, 9.2) and as having been raised on our account (δι' ἡμᾶς, 8.1). He speaks of him as having endured death for our sins (ὑπὲρ τῶν ἁμαρτιῶν ἡμῶν, 1.2). He does allude to forgiveness (6.2) and to God as the source of mercy and peace (salutation) and election (1.1) and to faith throughout. It seems

---

[63] See the Graeco-Roman examples in Danker, 'Bridging St. Paul and the Apostolic Fathers,' 84-94. Note that such cultural factors function in many parts of the Middle East today.

[64] Torrance, *Doctrine of Grace*, 94-95.

[65] "The great mistake has been to detach the thought of grace from the *person* of Jesus Christ." Ibid., v.

[66] Ibid., 93.

[67] Ibid., 93.

more consistent to interpret these allusions as evidence that Polycarp
does have at least some understanding of the connection between
God's grace and the reality of Christ's work than to argue, as Torrance
does, that he has *entirely missed* the connection. Moreover, conditionality
does not put Polycarp in a world entirely distinct from Paul, as
Torrance assumes (cf. 1 Cor 15:2). The question, as we discussed in
the section *Resurrection and Judgment* (pp. 162-167), is rather how
Polycarp understands his conditional statements. Though Polycarp
emphasizes more the human element in the process, we should understand it, as I have argued, under the framework of reciprocity,
which Polycarp would not have understood to be merit-oriented. The
fact that Polycarp repeatedly returns to the themes of the cross, the
resurrection and judgment give evidence that the totality of his thought
concerning righteousness is not merely ethical.[68]

Polycarp's understanding of faith also argues against it, as Lindemann comments:

> Pauline influence can also be discerned in Polycarp's understanding
> of faith: the content of the creed is Christological (2.1-2); Christian faith
> is a gift given (3.2[69]; 4.2); and faith is the condition of our eschatological
> salvation, the inheritance of the kingdom of God (5.2).[70]

It seems that one of the keys to understanding Polycarp is not that
he is driven simply by an ethical impulse, but that he wants to describe a *true* Christian. He wants to delineate the nature, in his own
words, of 'those who are truly chosen by God and our Lord' (1.1) or
those who have been granted 'true repentance' by the Lord (11.4).
He is concerned that many call themselves Christians who are not
(5.2-3; 6.3; 7.1-2).

The key location of Eph 2:5, 8, 9 in Pol. *Phil.* 1.3 may indicate
that grace is not just a passing issue for Polycarp, particularly when
one remembers that Paul's faith/works antithesis "is not characteristic of the Apostolic Fathers."[71] Goulder, however, goes too far when
he suggests that Polycarp's citation is "a continuation of Paul's fight

---

[68] Steinmetz, 'Polykarp von Smyrna,' 74.

[69] I disagree with one particular of this quotation from Lindemann. I understand
τὴν δοθεῖσαν ὑμῖν πίστιν in 3.2 to refer to the Christian faith that was passed on
rather than to a regenerating faith. This may also apply to 4.2.

[70] Lindemann, 'Paul in...Apostolic Fathers,' 44.

[71] "...and it is to be noted that the sharp Pauline antithesis of faith and works is
not characteristic of the Apostolic Fathers generally." Oxford Society of Historical
Theology, *The New Testament in the Apostolic Fathers* (Oxford: The Clarendon Press,
1905), 93.

against a Jewish Christian doctrine of salvation by works..."[72] There is nothing in the context to suggest such an interpretation. Polycarp brings ethics alongside of faith throughout his letter and, without explicating the relationship, affirms the importance of both.

In light of Polycarp's sustained warnings against avarice and greed in his letter, combined with some movement toward greater human participation, Garrison states his opinion that the allusion to Tob 4:10 'almsgiving delivers from death' (Pol. *Phil.* 10.2) is evidence that Polycarp believes in a doctrine of redemptive almsgiving. He says, "Presumably, Polycarp is anxious for the redemption of *post-baptismal* sin. Almsgiving is central to his remedy."[73] But this is reading more into the Polycarp's quotation than can be read out of it. Such statements need to be balanced by comparison with other quotations like the one from Eph 2:5, 8, 9 in 1.3 or the centrality of Christ's part in building up in the faith in the prayer of 12.2.

But is there not something substantial missing in Polycarp's discussion of righteousness, grace, and faith? Polycarp gladly uses Pauline terminology and raises a flag to indicate that he knows that these are important words for Paul (δικαιοσύνη, 3.1; χάρις, 1.3 in a Pauline quotation; and πίστις, 3.2 in a discussion of Paul's teaching ministry to the Philippians). But how can he knowingly use Pauline terminology if he does not employ Paul's meaning? This is particularly an issue for the term δικαιοσύνη ('righteousness') which Polycarp most often applies to ethical concerns.

The meaning(s) of δικαιοσύνη in Pauline thought has been, and continues to be hotly debated. But there is scholarly agreement that righteousness is one central element among the fundamental frameworks of Paul's thought (though many would argue about whether it is *the* center of his thought). What is significant for this discussion is that Polycarp's use of a word that he knows he has borrowed from Paul does not usually carry the Pauline associations (however they are to be understood). There is no attempt, for example, to connect to Paul's distinctive use of the expression δικαιοσύνη θεοῦ (Rom 1:17; 3:5, 21, 22; 10:3; 2 Cor 5:21, cf. Rom 3:25,26, Phil 3:9), particularly if we understand it to include an activity of God. If status is

---

[72] Michael D. Goulder, 'Ignatius' "Docetists",' *VC* 53 (1999): 19. According to Goulder, this is evidence of a struggle with Jewish Christianity that was taking place in Smyrna during the time of Polycarp.

[73] Roman Garrison, *The Graeco-Roman Context of Early Christian Literature,* JSNTSup 127 (Sheffield: Sheffield Academic Press, 1997), 79.

understood to be an element in this Pauline expression, it could be argued that it may be suggested in Polycarp's use of Eph 2:5, 8, 9 in 1.3, though δικαιοσύνη does not appear there. If understood as a quality of God, it could be argued that δικαιοσύνη θεοῦ may exercise some influence upon Polycarp's exhortation in Pol. *Phil.* 5.2 that deacons should be ἄμεμπτοι κατενώπιον αὐτοῦ τῆς δικαιοσύνης ('blameless in the presence of his righteousness'). But all these hints seem minor in comparison to Polycarp's general application of the term to righteous living. And despite the fact that Polycarp does imply some understanding of a connection between the death of Christ and the effect upon the believer (per discussion above), his letter never develops the doctrine of the imputation of righteousness to believers through faith in Christ – unless it is in the rather oblique clause, 'but by the will of God through Jesus Christ' after the quotation of Eph 2:5, 8, 9 in Pol. *Phil.* 1.3. If it were not for the fact that Polycarp seems to use Pauline terminology and signals that he knows it is from Paul, this would not be significant. As it stands, he apparently believes that he is in continuity with Paul's teaching on righteousness but still does not emphasize many elements that Paul emphasizes. Granted, he does derive many ethical elements from the Pauline letters. But he seems to ignore those elements of 'righteousness' that we usually associate as distinctively Pauline.

In summary, Polycarp's letter which he writes about 'righteousness' centers primarily upon Paul's teaching about ethical living and thus de-emphasizes Paul's distinctive teaching about how to be right with God. This does not mean that Polycarp entirely misunderstands all of Paul's concerns (e.g. he does affirm the centrality of God's grace apart from works). As discussed above, he may be functioning under a framework of 'reciprocity' (i.e. faith appropriates God's grace but also requires the believer to act). But whatever else may be said, it is clear that his priorities and emphases are different from Paul's, as least in this letter. His main concern is ethical righteousness where Paul's is the vindication of the righteous character of God through Christ. All the while, Polycarp apparently views his teaching about righteousness, grace, and faith as standing in continuity with Paul, a perspective which (from our vantage) seems to be only partially correct.

The Church

Paul's influence upon Polycarp is clearly seen in his teaching about relationships in the church, including his 'body' metaphor, the possibility of restoration of a sinner, leadership, and 1 Timothy's household codes.

Polycarp's general understanding of the function of the church is found in the final clauses of his instruction about how to handle the problem of Valens and his wife in ch. 11. He says, "...restore them, in order that you may save your body in its entirety. For by doing this you build up one another." In ch. 2 it was argued that there is probably conscious dependence here upon Paul's metaphor of the body (cf. esp. 1 Cor 12:12-27; Rom 14:4-8; Eph 4:4-13). The unity of the 'body' is very important to Polycarp.[74] Included in this 'body' are all 'those truly chosen by God' (1.1).[75] Outside this 'body' are the 'false brothers and those who bear the name of the Lord hypocritically' (6.3).

Valens and his wife appear to be on the fence. They have not experienced 'true repentance' (11.4) and are at risk of being 'judged as one of the Gentiles' (11.2) for their abuse of money (whatever it was), but they are also to be treated not 'as enemies, but as sick and straying members' (11.4). This statement implies the possibility of restoration.[76] Polycarp affirms the possibility of restoration and reception of Valens again into fellowship, even though some currents in the church of his time were beginning to question the possibility of restoration for members who fell into serious sin after their baptism.[77] Continuity with Paul on the restoration of a fallen member is evident (cf. Gal 6:1; 2 Cor 2:6-11; 2 Thess 3:15; though such teaching exists elsewhere, cf. Matt 18:15-20).

Concerning leadership, there is little of the authoritarianism of Ignatius in Polycarp's letter. The salutation begins, 'Polycarp and the presbyters with him...' Though Ignatius refers to Polycarp as *the* bishop

---

[74] Jefford, *Reading*, 79-80. Kleist, *The Didache...*, 188 n. 28 comments, "Since the purpose of the Church is to 'build up the body of Christ' (Eph. 4.12), a Christian's growth in virtue may be described as 'a building up.'" Cf. Pol. *Phil.* 3.2.

[75] "The early Christians had a very lively and practical conception of the doctrine of the Mystical Body." Kleist, *The Didache...*, 186 n. 4. Compare also with Ign. *Eph.* 8.2.

[76] Steinmetz, 'Polykarp von Smyrna,' 66.

[77] Kelly, *Early Christian Doctrines*, 198-199.

of Smyrna in his letter to Smyrna (Ign. *Smyrn.* 8-9), at least when Polycarp writes to the Philippians, he apparently does not view himself as a singular bishop. He is *one* of the presbyters at Smyrna. He also does not wield an authoritarian attitude, as the tone of his letter testifies. Campenhausen comments about this, "...the old Pauline idea of reciprocal subordination and mutual love of all the members is here still very much alive."[78] For Polycarp, says Campenhausen, "all Christians are still his brothers and sisters."[79] Polycarp says in 10.2, "All of you be subject to one another..." (cf. Eph 5:21).

Wives are instructed by Polycarp first to cherish their own husbands and then to love all others equally (4.1). The call to love all others equally is an (albeit unconscious) actualization of Paul's rejection of favoritism, as in Gal 3:28, "There is neither Jew nor Greek, there is neither slave nor free man, there is neither male nor female; for you are all one in Christ Jesus."

I have argued the probable influence of the *Haustafeln* of 1 Timothy upon the *Haustafeln* of Pol. *Phil.* 4.2-6.2 (see ch. 2). Since Polycarp understands 1 Timothy to be Pauline (see ch. 4), Paul's influence is readily seen throughout that entire section. J. B. Bauer compares the instructions about marriage in 4.2 with Paul's more detailed discussion in 1 Corinthians 7.[80]

Finally, Polycarp adopts Paul's expression of the Christian when he calls them 'saints' (12.2-3). The term 'saints' is a particularly Pauline expression (as in 1 Cor 6:1; 2 Cor 1:1; Eph 2:19; 3:8). In short, much of what Polycarp says about the church is in some way indebted to Paul.

Fulfilling the "Commandment of Righteousness" through Love

In Pol. *Phil.* 3.2-3 Polycarp writes,

> And when he [i.e. Paul] was absent he wrote you letters, if you study them carefully, you will be able to build yourselves up in the faith that has been given to you, which is the mother of us all, while hope follows and love for God and Christ and for our neighbor leads the way.

---

[78] Along with citations from Ignatius, Campenhausen cites the quotation in Pol. *Phil.* 10.2 (from Eph 5:21) as support. Hans von Campenhausen, *Ecclesiastical Authority and Spiritual Power in the Church of the First Three Centuries*, trans. J. A. Baker (Stanford: Stanford University Press, 1953), 102-103.

[79] Ibid., 103.

[80] J. B. Bauer, *Die Polykarpbriefe*, 51.

> For if anyone is occupied with these, he has fulfilled the commandment of righteousness, for one who has love is far from sin.

I have argued in ch. 2 that these sentences contain a probable allusion to Gal 4:26 (with possible influence from Rom 4:16); a probable allusion to 1 Cor 13:13 in the faith-hope-love triad and a probable reminiscence of Paul's use of the Jesus tradition in Rom 13:8-10 and/or Gal 5:14 (cf. 6:2). In ch. 4, I demonstrated that these allusions and reminiscences all fall within the first of three clusters of references from Paul that congregate around the name of Paul. Our concern for the moment is that we observe a substantial Pauline influence in this section.

But there are some differences between Polycarp's and Paul's respective applications of this shared tradition. What they share is the idea of love as a fulfillment. But that which is fulfilled for Paul is the Mosaic law (νόμος).[81] Polycarp never mentions νόμος in his letter. For Polycarp, that which is fulfilled is 'the commandment of righteousness' (ἐντολὴν δικαιοσύνης). What is 'the commandment of righteousness' for Polycarp? His use of 'commandment(s)' elsewhere in Pol. *Phil.* may help define it. In 2.2, 'his commandments' seem to be Christ's commands. Similarly, both 'the commandment of the Lord' in 4.1 and 'his commandment' in 5.1 are Christ's commands. In 6.3, we are to serve Christ with fear and all reverence 'just as he himself has commanded' along with the apostles and the prophets.[82] But in this passage (3.2-3) the commandment is 'of righteousness', and Polycarp employs the term (δικαιοσύνη) which he considers central to his compositional purpose (3.1) but which he usually defines ethically. In light of these, the 'commandment of righteousness' appears to be a collective singular (as in 5.1) and points primarily (though, not solely, as we shall see in a moment) to all the commands about right living which Christ issued.

But does this mean that Polycarp does not know that for Paul the Mosaic Law is what is fulfilled? In light of Polycarp's allusions to Gal 4:26 and perhaps to Rom 4:16 in the same sentence along with his fulfilling-the-commandment-of-righteousness phrase, it seems likely that Polycarp *does* know and includes the law of Moses (which he also

---

[81] Of course, Paul uses νόμος with different meanings, but in Rom 13:8-10 and Gal 5:14 he apparently intends the Mosaic Law.

[82] The 'teaching about righteousness' (λόγῳ τῆς δικαιοσύνης) may be a more general expression.

understands in terms of commands) among that which is fulfilled
through love. Love is (along with faith and hope), for Polycarp, at
the pinnacle of all that the Christian is supposed to do. The Christian still must serve God and do the commands which have been issued by Christ, the ancient prophets, and the apostles (6.3); but these
three – faith, hope, and particularly love – cover most of the bases
needed to live rightly ('for one who has love is far from all sin', 3.3).
Thus, even though the 'commandment of righteousness' centers upon
the commands of Christ, they also include any OT and apostolic commands. There is, anyway, for Polycarp no conflict between any of
these three streams of authority. Thus, in 3.3, the person who loves
fulfills them all.

But even this language of fulfillment highlights a conceptual difference between Paul and Polycarp. For Paul, fulfillment is the fo-
cusing and funneling of everything in history into the Christ event.
Yes, Paul would agree that love for God is a working out of that law
(just as Christ taught), but only because all the law has first been fulfilled
in the *person* and *work* of Christ. Thus, it is not surprising that the
passages where Paul teaches that love fulfills the law (Rom 13:8-10;
Gal 5:14) are found in the letters to the Romans and the Galatians
after Paul extensively develops the idea that *Christ* himself has fulfilled the law. Polycarp's teaching both here and throughout the letter
does not have the same organic relationship to the person and work
of Christ. For Polycarp, it seems to be limited to the idea that one
who loves is, of course, not committing sin and is obeying the Lord's
commands. Polycarp's center seems to be the action of love in relationship to obedience to commands, whereas Paul centers upon union
with Christ and the resultant life of love.

In summary, though Jesus is Paul's source for the idea that love
fulfills the law (cf. Matt 22:40), Polycarp is directly influenced by Paul's
teaching as found in Rom 13:8-10 and Gal 5:14/6:2 even though
he undoubtedly knows that Christ is the ultimate source of the teaching
(cf. Matt 22:40).[83] That Polycarp is influenced by Paul's teaching is
once again clear. But Polycarp's understanding of fulfillment seems
to focus more upon the action of love as a direct way to obey all the
commands which the Christian is supposed to do; whereas for Paul,

---

[83] J. B. Bauer, *Die Polykarpbriefe*, 47; Lindemann, 'Paul in...Apostolic Fathers,' 44;
Howard Carroll, 'Polycarp of Smyrna – With Special Reference to Early Christian
Martyrdom,' (Ph.D. diss., Duke University, 1946), 43.

fulfillment centers upon Christ himself, and love (and the fulfillment of the law through love) flows out of one's union with Christ.

Money

Polycarp evinces a strong Pauline influence in his understanding of the relationship of the believer to money. Polycarp vigorously denounces love of money throughout Pol. *Phil.* (2.2; 4.1-3; 6.1 and all of ch. 11).[84] Polycarp's use of 1 Tim 6:10 and 6:7 in Pol. *Phil.* 4.1 seems virtually certain. There Polycarp says, "But the love of money is the beginning of all troubles. Knowing therefore, that we brought nothing into the world, nor can we take anything out..." and begins various instructions. Thus his general antipathy toward avarice is, in his own mind, dependent upon Paul.

In Pol. *Phil.* 11, when Polycarp gives instructions about Valens who has fallen into some sort of sin related to abuse of money (we do not know exactly what), Polycarp repeatedly appeals to the teaching of Paul, almost to the exclusion of anyone else. There are three references which are probably or almost certainly from Paul and possibly as many as five others in Pol. *Phil.* 11. Only the probable allusion to Jer 5:4-5 is non-Pauline in this section. Notable among these is Polycarp's connection of love of money with idolatry (11.2), a connection also made by Paul in Eph 5:5 and Col 3:5.[85] Though dependence upon Paul on this point cannot be judged to be any more than a possibility, Polycarp here promotes a connection also promoted by Paul.

Paul's influence is felt throughout Polycarp's instructions about money and its abuse.

Suffering and Martyrdom

Polycarp repeatedly returns to exhortations about the need for endurance. Endurance is sometimes conceived as continuance in the faith (4.2; 5.2; 7.2; 10.1-2), but sometimes centers upon endurance

---

[84] See ch. 7 entitled 'The Love of Money in Polycarp's Letter to the Philippians,' in Garrison, *The Graeco-Roman Context*.

[85] The conceptual connection between money and idolatry is also found in the teaching of Jesus (cf. Matt 6:24; Luke 16:13-14).

under suffering even to the point of martyrdom (8.1-10.1). Additionally, these two ideas are not unconnected (cf. 1.2; 12.3; 13.2), for Polycarp appears to work under the assumption that Christians will (should?) suffer, an idea also promoted (not exclusively[86]) in Paul's writings (cf. Phil 1:29-30; 2 Tim 3:12). Polycarp, unlike Ignatius (cf. Ign. *Rom.* 5-6) does not have a fixation upon tortures and martyrdom. Rather, he says, "if we should suffer for the sake of his name, let us glorify him" (8.2).

Polycarp's teaching about suffering and martyrdom centers upon the imitation of Christ's sufferings (8.1-2; 10.1; cf. 1.2). Polycarp never discusses it directly, but a minor dependence upon Paul's idea of suffering with Christ may be present. Note the ᾧ καὶ συνέπαθον ('with whom they also suffered') in 9.2. Dying and rising with Christ is important in Paul's teaching (cf. Gal 2:20; Romans 6) as is the more general idea of suffering with him (Rom 8:17; Col 1:24). The verb συμπάσχω occurs only twice in the NT, both times in Paul (Rom 8:17 and 1 Cor 12:26). Massaux comments on the similarities between the uses of this verb here in 9.2 and in Rom 8:17.[87] But this is Polycarp's only possible connection with a concept that is extremely important for Paul.

The only important role that Paul plays in Polycarp's teaching about suffering is that (at least in this letter) 'Paul himself' stands as the epitome of those who have suffered as martyrs (9.1-2). Even though it is not explicitly stated, a sound inference from Pol. *Phil.* 8.1-10.1 is that these martyrs (especially Paul) should be imitated inasmuch as they have imitated Christ in their suffering. The strong theme of following Christ's example of suffering (8.2), combined with the call to follow the example of others who have suffered makes this a reasonable inference. In Polycarp's argument, it seems that these other examples, and Paul in particular, have done exactly what he enjoins the Philippians to do, that is, to follow Christ's example of suffering.

Thus, Paul's influence lies primarily in his own example of sharing in the sufferings of Christ, making him also worthy of imitation. There may be a whisper of Paul's teaching about suffering with Christ. It is, however, probably not an exaggeration to suggest that, whereas

---

[86] Cf. Matt 5:10-12; 1 Pet 1:6; 2:21.
[87] Édouard Massaux, *The Influence of the Gospel of Saint Matthew on Christian Literature before Saint Irenaeus, Book 2: The Later Christian Writings*, trans Norman J. Belval and Suzanne Hecht, ed. Arthur J. Bellinzoni (Macon, Ga.: Mercer University Press, 1990), 41.

for Paul the issue is suffering *with* Christ in union with his death and resurrection, the issue for Polycarp is suffering *like* Christ.

The World

'The world' is one of Polycarp's descriptions of the arena outside the community of faith (5.3; 7.2). What is Polycarp's understanding of how believers should relate to the world?

His concern with the world has five primary foci: 1) maintaining a good standard of conduct among unbelievers (10.2-3; 12.3 'fruit'); 2) avoiding their temptations (5.3; 6.3); 3) leading unbelievers to faith (12.2); 4) bearing up under persecution (8.2-9.2); and 5) praying for kings and powers (12.3). Docetists are a separate category of those outside the community of faith, who are false brothers to be avoided (6.3), though prayers for them are encouraged (12.3 'and for the enemies of the cross').

It is notable that Polycarp urges prayer for civil authorities (12.3).[88] 1 Tim 2:1-2 also solicits prayer for civil authorities, though influence from that passage upon Polycarp cannot be demonstrated. Polycarp may, however, be influenced by Paul's overall attitude of submission and honor toward the government (Rom 13:1-7; cf. Tit 3:1).

Jefford sees in the phrase ἐὰν πολιτευσώμεθα ἀξίως αὐτοῦ ('if we prove to be citizens worthy of him...') in 5.2 a situation in which "the church had gradually become an established segment of ancient culture and society." Thus, claims Jefford, Polycarp employs this imagery to show the responsibilities Christians were having in the increasingly institutionalized church.[89] This is doubtless reading a setting into this phrase which cannot be supported. The idea of counting oneself worthy is a Pauline concept (cf. Phil 1:27). Spiritualizing the imagery of citizenship is also found in Paul (Phil 3:20). Moreover, the ease with which Polycarp immediately moves from the phrase 'Pray also for kings and powers and rulers' in 12.3 into the phrase 'and for those who persecute and hate you' indicates that the church in Smyrna may have been living in a less-than-tranquil period in relation to the governing authorities. Thus, against Jefford, this phrase cannot tell us anything about the attitudes of Christians toward their society and, in particular, how they were viewed by their society.

---

[88] Quasten, *Patrology*, 81.
[89] Jefford, *Reading*, 80-81.

Most of Polycarp's teaching concerning the world is compatible with the teaching of Paul, though unique influence from Paul cannot be demonstrated except perhaps in Polycarp's supportive attitude toward the government.

What is Missing?

Polycarp clearly sees himself in continuity with the teaching of Paul, and in many cases we have seen that continuity indeed exists. But we have also observed numerous instances where Polycarp's ideas or underlying framework appears to be different from Paul's. In addition, there are issues which are important to Paul but which are absent in Polycarp. Each of these has already come out and been discussed to some extent in this chapter, but a highlighting of a few seems useful. There are five which seem more significant than others.

1. *History.* Polycarp's view of history and the history of redemption appears to be *flatter* than that of Paul. In other words, Pol. *Phil.* evinces less awareness of the aeon-changing dimensions of the death and resurrection of Christ than the letters of Paul. Admittedly, Polycarp does acknowledge that the prophets announced the coming of Christ (6.3) and that Christ in the future will judge the world (2.1; 6.2). He says that Christ died and was raised for us (2.1; 9.2) and was given a throne at God's right hand (2.1). The person of Christ is also given an exalted position in his letter. But Polycarp, unlike Paul, does not seem as much to espouse a dynamic view of redemptive history as a drama in which the entire history of Israel leads to Christ as the focal point, from whom also emerges the entire eschatological age.[90] Polycarp's view seems to be more concerned with promise and fulfillment and lacks the organic unity present in Paul's approach. Certainly it is true that Polycarp's compositional purpose and non-Jewish setting may be influencing him to draw less upon the writings of the OT than upon those written in the Christian era. Still, there are many points at which Polycarp's approach to history seems (for lack of a better word) *flatter.*

2. *The Holy Spirit.* In contrast to Paul's lively theology of the Holy

---

[90] Herman Ridderbos, *Paul: An Outline of His Theology*, trans. John Richard de Witt (Grand Rapids: William B. Eerdmans Publishing Company, 1975), 44-53.

Spirit (e.g. Rom 8; Gal 5; 1 Cor 12-14; 2 Cor 3), references to the Holy Spirit are absent from Polycarp's letter. Polycarp's one possible reference embedded in a loose citation of 1 Pet 2:11 (Pol. *Phil.* 5.3) is probably a reference to "the human spirit under the influence of the Divine"[91] rather than a reference to the Holy Spirit. In Polycarp's striking use of the Pauline term ἀρραβών ('pledge'/ 'downpayment'), the referent is not the Holy Spirit (as in Paul, cf. 1 Cor 1:22; 5:5; Eph 1:14) but is Christ himself. Once again, as we observed in our study of resurrection, a systemic difference between Paul and Polycarp may be observed. For Paul, the coming of the Spirit is an eschatological event. For Polycarp, eschatology lies primarily (though not solely) in the future.

3. *Sin*. Paul's idea of imputed sin (Rom 5:12-21) seems to have largely given way to the committing of sins in Polycarp (note the plural in 1.2 and 8.1; also in general 2.2-3; 3.3; 4.3; 5.2-3; 6.1; 6.3; 11.1; 12.1). This may be simply a function of Polycarp's compositional purpose – to write about practical righteousness (3.1) – but the difference in emphasis is noticeable. Moreover, Paul's understanding of sin as a cosmic entity of the old age plays no part in Polycarp's letter. Granted, Polycarp may once connect with a distinctive Pauline understanding of sin, as Lindemann comments:

> ...when, at the end of 6.1, Polycarp writes that 'we are all debtors of sin,' we should note that *hamartia* is in the singular. This linguistic usage, rarely found outside the Pauline literature, is the mark of a substantial Pauline theological influence.[92]

Still it is undeveloped and its lack of mention elsewhere is worth noticing.

4. *Union with Christ*. Polycarp nowhere develops the notion of the believer's union with Christ in his death and resurrection.[93] This has already been mentioned at various points in the discussion above. But it is an important dimension of Paul's theology (cf. Romans 6; Phil 3:7-16; Col 3:1-4) that is at best marginal in Pol. *Phil.*

5. *Deep Theological Reflection*. This is a general observation available to anyone who reads Pol. *Phil.* in even a cursory fashion. Polycarp

---

[91] Henry Barclay Swete, *The Holy Spirit in the Ancient Church: A Study of Christian Teaching in the Age of the Fathers* (London: Macmillan and Co., 1912), 17.

[92] Lindemann, 'Paul in...Apostolic Fathers,' 43.

[93] As has earlier been mentioned, there may be a hint of Paul's idea of suffering with Christ (cf. Rom 8:17) in the expression ᾧ καὶ συνέπαθον ('with whom they also suffered') in Pol. *Phil.* 9.2.

wants to encourage right living, not to search out the mysteries, say, of the righteous nature of God or how justice and mercy are resolved in Christ. Once again, it should be emphasized that this may simply be a function of Pol. *Phil.*; it should not be inferred that Polycarp *could not* have written deeply upon theological subjects.[94] Nevertheless, the letter he has written to the Philippians contains precious few theological expressions.

Conclusion

Even though Pol. *Phil.* is not lengthy, Polycarp evinces many points of dependence upon Paul theologically. Polycarp certainly considers himself to be in continuity with the teaching of the great apostle. In actual fact, his letter exhibits many points of contact and influence from the teaching of Paul, but lacks some of Paul's fundamental structures.

The significance of Polycarp theologically is partially due to the time in which he lived. Positively, his letter exhibits a certain amount of theological transition. In terms of eschatological expectation, Polycarp exhibits less intensity than Paul but more than many who come after him. He affirms God's grace apart from human works, while at the same time affirming faith and the outworking of that faith in righteous living without explicitly connecting them. He affirms three streams of authority (the OT writings, the words of Jesus, and the apostolic writings) without yet making the canonical connections found in Irenaeus. As such, Polycarp's letter deserves to be studied, not simply for his dependence upon earlier writings, but because his letter gives many tantalizing clues of continuities and discontinuities with earlier Christian authors, especially Paul. We can only wish he had written more.

---

[94] For example, Polycarp's application of the term ἀρραβῶν ('pledge'/ 'downpayment') to Christ, rather than to the Holy Spirit (8.1) could be a result of deeper thinking about the relationship of the work of Christ to the Holy Spirit, but there is no way to tell.

CHAPTER SIX

CONCLUSIONS

Following are summaries of the most important conclusions from this analysis of Polycarp's literary and theological relationship to Paul. Included also are other inferences which can be drawn from this study which are of value for biblical and patristic studies.

1. *Date.* P. N. Harrison's theory that Pol. *Phil.* is in fact two letters rather than a single letter has been adopted, but his dating of the second letter has not. The first (and shortest) letter was written as a cover letter for a collection of the letters of Ignatius; it consisted either of ch. 13 alone or of chs. 13-14 together. Chs. 1-12 were a separate letter written by Polycarp at a later time in response to a request from the Philippian church. However, P. N. Harrison's date of c. 135 C.E. has been abandoned as too late and as not fitting the evidence of the letter itself (the little evidence, that is, that exists). Instead, a date of c. 120 C.E. has been argued for the composition of chs. 1-12.

2. *Purpose.* The primary purpose of Pol. *Phil.* was to respond to the Philippians' request that Polycarp write to them about righteousness (Pol. *Phil.* 3.1). I have suggested that the request could have more narrowly been that Polycarp write to them 'as Paul did' in the past. Polycarp interpreted 'righteousness' throughout his letter primarily (but not solely) in terms of righteous living, that is, in terms of the ethical responsibilities of a follower of Christ.

3. *Literary Dependencies.* It is almost certain that Polycarp knew and drew upon the following sources: The Psalms, Matthew, Romans, 1 Corinthians, 2 Corinthians, Galatians, Ephesians, Philippians, 1 Timothy, 2 Timothy, 1 Peter, 1 John and *1 Clement.* Moreover, it is probable that he used the following: Proverbs, Isaiah, Jeremiah, Tobit, Luke, Acts, 2 Thessalonians, and the letters of Ignatius. Finally, influences from Ezekiel, Sirach, Mark, John, Colossians, 1 Thessalonians, and Hebrews are possible in individual instances. Among those sources deemed 'possible' certainly Hebrews deserves pride of place, but still cannot be judged probable.

Almost half of all Polycarp's citations, allusions and reminiscences in all three categories are from Paul.

4. *Pauline Letter Collection.* Despite the strong influence of the person

and writings of Paul throughout Pol. *Phil.* it cannot be stated with certainty that Polycarp possessed a collection consisting of an entire thirteen (or fourteen[1]) letter collection of the Pauline corpus. Nevertheless, we can be quite confident that he possessed most of these letters and assumed that the Philippians did as well. In ch. 2 it was argued that Polycarp very probably or almost certainly knew all the letters in the Pauline corpus except Colossians, 1 Thessalonians, Titus and Philemon. The extent to which Paul's letters were used in such a short letter is itself remarkable.[2] Polycarp quotes from Paul in a way that seems to assume that the Philippians had a collection of Paul's letters that was the same as his own.[3] Moreover, it is unlikely that Polycarp would have collected the letters of Ignatius together before a collection of Paul's letters existed,[4] particularly since his letter evinces far greater esteem for the letters of Paul than for the letters of Ignatius. The Philippians' request that they be included in Polycarp's distribution of the collected letters of Ignatius may itself suggest that such collections were common. Polycarp's use of the plural 'letters' in 3.2 may imply Polycarp's assumption that the Philippians possessed a collection of Paul's letters. Finally, the presence of 1 and 2 Timothy may suggest the inclusion also of Titus, and the presence of 2 Thessalonians may imply the inclusion also of 1 Thessalonians. Philemon is too short and particular in subject matter to have been quoted, leaving only Colossians. Thus, it would not be a surprise to learn that Polycarp had access to all of Paul's letters – since he certainly had most of them – but there is no way to prove it.[5]

5. *Neglect.* Polycarp's letter stands as one witness against the idea that

---

[1] I will not include Hebrews in this discussion even though it had a place in many of the earliest collections of Paul's letters. It is not included here because I have only judged dependence upon Hebrews to be a possibility whereas all the letters of Paul besides Colossians, 1 Thessalonians, Titus and Philemon are very probable or almost certain.

[2] "...it does not follow that because one or two particular epistles are not alluded to, they were unknown to the author. Rather, the use of a substantial number of epistles suggests possession of the entire Corpus." Donald Alfred Hagner, *The Use of the Old and New Testaments in Clement of Rome* (Leiden: E. J. Brill, 1973), 321.

[3] Robert M. Grant, *The Formation of the New Testament* (New York: Harper & Row, 1965), 102-103.

[4] John Knox, *Marcion and the New Testament: An Essay in the Early History of the Canon* (Chicago: The University of Chicago Press, 1942), 172-173.

[5] Many consider it probable that Polycarp would have had access to the entire thirteen letter collection, including (but not limited to) Burnett Hillman Streeter, *The Primitive Church* (New York: The Macmillan Company, 1929), 167; Adolf von Harnack, "Lightfoot on the Ignatian Epistles: II. Genuineness and Date of the Epistles," *The Expositor*, 3rd series, vol. 3 (1886): 186 and *Miscellen zu den apostolischen Vätern, den Acta*

Paul's letters were neglected during the early and middle parts of the second century.[6] Polycarp not only used Paul's writings, he enthusiastically commended their use (Pol. *Phil.* 3.2). Lindemann accurately observes, "All that we can say is this: in the first half of the second century, some Christian authors did make explicit use of the Pauline letters and of Pauline theological themes, and others did not."[7]

6. *Imitation.* Polycarp, as a Hellenistic writer in the early second century, was influenced by a strong literary impulse to imitate earlier literary authorities. The general value accorded imitation can be observed in the writings of Graeco-Roman rhetoricians roughly contemporaneous with Polycarp. Polycarp modeled his own letter after the letters of Paul because he was writing to a church founded by Paul. In addition, Polycarp enjoined imitation of the ethical character of Paul whom he highly regarded.

7. *Simpleton.* The widespread and oft-repeated idea that Polycarp was uncreative and a simpleton is untenable when Polycarp is judged by the standards of his day. He wrote a letter which would have been effective to its purpose. Polycarp demonstrates awareness of the way he has structured his letter and crafted his argument so as to elicit the desired response from his readers.

8. *Clusters.* There is a marked tendency in Pol. *Phil.* to cluster allusions to Paul's writings around the mention of Paul's name. Other less dramatic clusters also exist in the Pol. *Phil.*, but none so convincing as

---

Pauli, Apelles, dem Muratorischen Fragment, den pseudocyprianischen Schriften und Claudianus Marmertus, TU 2-20/3b (Leipzig: J. C. Hinrichs, 1900), 89; Charles M. Nielsen, 'Polycarp, Paul and the Scriptures,' *ATR* 47 (1965): 208-210; Albert E. Barnett, *Paul Becomes a Literary Influence* (Chicago: The University of Chicago Press, 1941), 171; Hagner, *Use*, 314-331; Bruce M. Metzger, *The Canon of the New Testament: Its Origin, Development, and Significance* (Oxford: Clarendon Press, 1987), 259; E. Randolf Richards, 'The Codex and the Early Collection of Paul's Letters,' *BBR* 8 (1998): 151-166. It is less likely that Marcion was responsible for the collection of Paul's letters, as Balás observes, "Since he [Marcion] considered it necessary to eliminate large portions of several of Paul's epistles and to alter or expurgate individual verses, in order to fit Paul into his own mold of thought, it is somewhat difficult to imagine him collecting for the first time documents he then was prepared to mutilate." David L. Balás, 'Marcion Revisited: A "Post-Harnack" Perspective,' in *Texts and Testaments: Critical Essays on the Bible and Early Church Fathers*, ed. W. Eugene March (San Antonio: Trinity University Press, 1980), 103.

[6] Hans von Campenhausen, *The Formation of the Christian Bible*, trans. J. A. Baker (Philadelphia: Fortress Press, 1972), 177-178.

[7] Andreas Lindemann, 'Paul in the Writings of the Apostolic Fathers,' in *Paul and the Legacies of Paul*, ed. William S. Babcock (Dallas: Southern Methodist University Press, 1990), 27. Note that those who did not use Paul were mostly apologists for whose purposes Paul was not germane.

those congregated around the name of Paul.

9. *Pastorals and Paul.* Citations from 1 Timothy and 2 Timothy are included within the first two of the three Pauline clusters. The fact that Polycarp clustered Pauline references around the name of Paul indicates that he considered those references to be Pauline. The presence of quotations from 1 and 2 Timothy in those clusters argues that he considered those also to have been written by Paul. Thus, Polycarp has become the earliest external testimony to the Pauline authorship of 1 and 2 Timothy.

10. *Authorities.* Polycarp drew upon three streams of authority, the OT Scriptures, the teaching of Christ, and the apostolic writings (among which the Pauline writings are used the most). He considered all three streams to be authoritative. He did not seem to yet be asking the question of whether the apostolic writings were on the same level as the OT, though he clearly considered them binding upon his own actions and those of his readers.

11. *Theology.* Polycarp depended upon Paul for a great many pieces of his theological puzzle, but overall lacked some of Paul's fundamental structures (see full discussion in ch. 5). This is particularly noticeable in Polycarp's distance from Paul's organic, redemptive-historical (and Jewish) framework. Polycarp passed over any mention of the Holy Spirit, and did not develop concepts of imputed sin, sin as a cosmic principle of the old age, or union with Christ – all topics of central importance for Paul. Polycarp's eschatological expectation was not as intense as that of Paul, though certainly more than some later writers. His primarily futuristic eschatology contrasts with the emphasis upon both futuristic and realized eschatological elements in Paul's letters. Polycarp appears to have emphasized more the human response in salvation (while still affirming God's grace), whereas Paul emphasized more the divine initiative. Theologically, Paul's primary (though not sole) influence upon Polycarp was ethical.

Polycarp of Smyrna and the Apostle Paul, each important church leaders in their generations, have been inextricably linked by Pol. *Phil.*. Polycarp's letter bears the indelible marks of the great Apostle.

SUMMARIES OF POLYCARP'S CITATIONS, ALLUSIONS, AND REMINISCENCES

In chapter 2, Polycarp's citations, allusions and reminiscences of biblical and extra-biblical literature were delineated, weighed and categorized. They were judged to be either almost certain, probable, or possible (i.e. seriously possible). Included here are summaries in various categories of the conclusions made there.

Summary According to the Order of Pol. Phil.

Summary of Salutation: No dependence can be demonstrated.

Summary of 1.1: A possible allusion to Phil 4:10 and 2:17. A possible dependence upon Johannine language in general. A possible reminiscence of Ign. *Smyrn.* 11.1 and Ign. *Eph.* 11.2.

Summary of 1.2: A possible reminiscence of Paul's many commendations to the Philippian church. An almost certain loose citation of Acts 2:24 from the Western textual tradition.

Summary of 1.3: An almost certain loose citation of 1 Pet 1:8. A probable allusion to 1 Pet 1:12 in form but influenced in content from the sayings of the Lord (as represented by Matt 13:17; Luke 10:2 and Matt 25:21, 23). An almost certain true (though compressed) citation of Eph 2:5, 8, 9.

Summary of 2.1: A probable allusion to 1 Pet 1:13 combined with a possible allusion to Eph 6:14. A probable allusion to Ps 2:11. A probable loose citation of 1 Pet 1:21. A possible allusion to Phil 3:21 and 2:10. A possible allusion to Acts 10:42.

Summary of 2.2: A possible loose citation of 2 Cor 4:14. An almost certain true citation of 1 Pet 3:9. A probable reminiscence of the Lord's teaching such as is found in Luke 6:28-29 and Matt 5:39, but whether through an oral or written medium is unclear.

Summary of 2.3: Probable general dependence upon *1 Clem.* 13.1-2 for the *fact* but less for the *form* of the introductory formula and the four maxims. Possible correction toward Matt 7:1 in maxim #1 and toward Luke 6:38 in maxim #4. Possible influence also from the oral tradition. Probable citation (conflation) of Luke 6:20 (cf. Matt 5:3) with Matt 5:10.

Summary of 3.1: There are no allusions to earlier writings in 3.1.

Summary of 3.2: A possible reminiscence of *1 Clem.* 47.1. A possible reminiscence of Phil 1:27. A probable allusion to a Pauline expression ('the word of truth') though no specific text is identifiable.

Summary of 3.3: A probable allusion to Gal 4:26 with possible influence from Rom 4:16. A probable allusion to 1 Cor 13:13. A probable reminiscence of Paul's use of the Jesus tradition in Rom 13:8-10 and/or Gal 5:14 (cf. 6:2).

Summary of 4.1: An almost certain allusion to 1 Tim 6:10 followed by an almost certain loose citation of 1 Tim 6:7. An almost certain allusion to the general Pauline metaphor 'weapons of righteousness' and probably an allusion to 2 Cor 6:7.

Summary of 4.2: A probable general dependence in Pol. *Phil.* 4.2-6.2 upon the *Haustafeln* of 1 Timothy. A probable allusion to *1 Clem.* 1.3. A probable loose citation of *1 Clem.* 21:6.

Summary of 4.3: A possible reminiscence of the widow Anna (cf. Luke 2:37). A possible allusion to Ignatius's figurative use of 'altar' (as in Ign. *Eph.* 5.2; *Magn.* 7.2; *Trall.* 7.2; *Rom.* 2.2) or to Paul's idea in Philippians of a person's actions being a sacrifice to God (Phil 2:17; 4:18). A possible allusion to *1 Clem.* 41.2. A probable loose citation of *1 Clem.* 21.3. A probable allusion to 1 Cor 14:25.

Summary of 5.1: An almost certain true citation of Gal 6:7.

Summary of 5.2: A possible allusion to Mark 9:35. A possible dependence upon the Johannine tradition that Christ promised to raise us from the dead (cf. John 5:21, 25; 6:44). A probable allusion to Phil 1:27 (in form possibly influenced by *1 Clem.* 21.1). A probable allusion to 2 Tim 2:12.

Summary of 5.3: A probable loose citation of 1 Pet 2:11 (with possible influence from Gal 5:17 for πνεύματος). An almost certain compressed citation of 1 Cor 6:9-10. A possible influence of Ignatius on the thought of Polycarp that one should submit to one's leaders as to God and Christ. A possible allusion to *1 Clem.* 1.3.

Summary of 6.1: A possible allusion to Ezek 34:4. A probable loose citation of Prov 3:4 (possibly mediated through 2 Cor 8:21). A possible reminiscence of 1 Tim 5:19. A probable allusion to the Lord's Prayer (mediated orally?) with possible theological indebtedness to Paul.

Summary of 6.2: A probable allusion to Matt 6:12, 14-15. An almost certain loose citation of Rom 14:10, 12 with probable influence on the form from 2 Cor 5:10.

Summary of 6.3: A probable allusion to Ps 2:11.

Summary of 7.1: An almost certain compressed citation of 1 John 4:2-3. A possible reminiscence of 1 John 5:6-9. A probable allusion to 1 John 3:8. A possible reminiscence of 1 John 3:12.

Summary of 7.2: A probable loose citation of 1 Pet 4:7. A possible borrowing of the word παντεπόπτην from *1 Clem.* 55.6; 64.1. An almost certain true citation of the Lord's Prayer with Matt 6:13 as its probable source. An almost certain true citation of the words of the Lord with Matt 26:41 its probable source.

Summary of 8.1: Probable allusions to Paul's equating of Christ with hope (cf. 1 Tim 1:1; Col 1:27) and Paul's use of the word ἀρραβών (cf. 1 Cor 1:22; 5:5; Eph 1:14), though a specific passage cannot be demonstrated. An almost certain loose citation of 1 Pet 2:24. An almost certain exact citation of 1 Pet 2:22 (which is itself a citation of the LXX of Isa 53:9b).

Summary of 8.2: A probable allusion to 1 Pet 2:21. A possible allusion to 1 Pet 4:16.

Summary of 9.1: A possible allusion to Heb 5:13. A possible reminiscence of Phil 1:29-30.

Summary of 9.2: A probable loose citation of Phil 2:16. A possible reminiscence of Rom 8:17. An almost certain loose citation of 2 Tim 4:10. A possible loose citation of 2 Cor 5:15.

Summary of 10.1: A probable allusion to a Pauline phrase either from 1 Cor 15:58 or Col 1:23. A possible allusion to 1 Pet 2:17 or 3:8. Two probable allusions to Rom 12:10. A possible allusion to 2 Cor 10:1.

Summary of 10.2-3: A possible reminiscence of Prov 3:27 or Sir 29:8-9. An almost certain true citation of Tob 4:10 and/or Tob 12:9. A possible loose citation of Eph 5:21, 1 Pet 5:5, *1 Clem. 38.1*, or Ign. *Magn.* 13.2. An almost certain loose citation of 1 Pet 2:12. A probable loose citation of Isa 52:5 with possible influence from Ign. *Trall.* 8.2 and Rom 2:24.

Summary of 11.1: A possible citation of 1 Thess 5:22.

Summary of 11.2: A possible reminiscence of 1 Tim 3:5. A possible reminiscence of Eph 5:5 or Col 3:5. A probable allusion to Jer 5:4-5. An almost certain, true citation of 1 Cor 6:2.

Summary of 11.3: A possible reminiscence of Phil 4:15 or 2 Cor 3:2. A probable allusion to 2 Thess 1:4.

Summary of 11.4: A possible allusion to 2 Tim 2:25. A probable loose citation of 2 Thess 3:15. A probable reminiscence of Paul's body metaphor (cf. esp. 1 Cor 12:12-27; Rom 14:4-8; Eph 4:4-13) with possible influence from *1 Clem.* 37.5.

Summary of 12.1: A probable true citation of Ps 4:5a (with awareness of Eph 4:26a) followed by a probable true citation of Eph 4:26b (with awareness of Ps 4:5b).

Summary of 12.2: A possible allusion to the conception of Christ as 'eternal high priest' and 'son of God' by the author of Hebrews (cf. Heb 4:14; 6:20; 7:3). A possible loose citation of Gal 1:1.

Summary of 12.3: A possible abbreviated citation of Eph 6:18. A possible loose citation of 1 Tim 2:2. A possible conflated citation of Matt 5:44 and Luke 6:27. A probable allusion to Phil 3:18. A possible allusion to Matt 5:48.

Summary of 13-14: There appear to be no literary connections in chs. 13-14.

Summary According to Degree of Probability

Almost Certain
1.2 Loose citation of Acts 2:24.
1.3 Loose citation of 1 Pet 1:8.
1.3 True (though compressed) citation of Eph 2:5, 8, 9.
2.2 True citation of 1 Pet 3:9.
4.1 Allusion to 1 Tim 6:10.
4.1 Loose citation of 1 Tim 6:7.
4.1 Allusion to the general Pauline metaphor 'weapons of righteousness' (probably an allusion to 2 Cor 6:7).
5.1 True citation of Gal 6:7.
5.3 Compressed citation of 1 Cor 6:9-10.
6.2 Loose citation of Rom 14:10, 12.
7.1 Compressed citation of 1 John 4:2-3.
7.2 True citation from the Lord's Prayer (Matt 6:13 its probable source).
7.2 True citation of the words of the Lord (Matt 26:41 its probable source).
8.1 Loose citation of 1 Pet 2:24.
8.1 Exact citation of 1 Pet 2:22 (which is itself a citation of the LXX of Isa 53:9b).
9.2 Loose citation of 2 Tim 4:10.
10.2 True citation of Tob 4:10 and/or Tob 12:9.

10.2 Loose Citation of 1 Pet 2:12.

11.2 True citation of 1 Cor 6:2.

Probable

1.3 Allusion to 1 Pet 1:12 in form but influenced in content from the sayings of the Lord (as represented by Matt 13:17; Luke 10:2 and Matt 25:21, 23).

2.1 Allusion to 1 Pet 1:13.

2.1 Allusion to Ps 2:11.

2.1 Loose citation of 1 Pet 1:21.

2.2 Reminiscence of the Lord's teaching such as is found in Luke 6:28-29 and Matt 5:39.

2.3 General dependence upon *1 Clem.* 13.1-2 for the *fact* but less for the *form* of the introductory formula and the four maxims.

2.3 Citation (conflation) of Luke 6:20 (cf. Matt 5:3) with Matt 5:10.

3.2 Allusion to a Pauline expression ('the word of truth') though no specific text is identifiable.

3.3 Allusion to Gal 4:26.

3.3 Allusion to 1 Cor 13:13.

3.3 Reminiscence of Paul's use of the Jesus tradition in Rom 13:8-10 and/or Gal 5:14 (cf. 6:2).

4.2-6.2 General dependence upon the *Haustafeln* of 1 Timothy.

4.2 Allusion to *1 Clem.* 1.3.

4.2 Loose citation of *1 Clem.* 21:6.

4.3 Allusion to 1 Cor 14:25.

5.2 Allusion to Phil 1:27.

5.2 Allusion to 2 Tim 2:12.

5.3 Loose citation of 1 Pet 2:11.

6.1 Loose citation of Prov 3:4.

6.1 Allusion to the Lord's Prayer (mediated orally?).

6.2 Allusion to Matt 6:12, 14-15.

6.2 Probable influence on the form of the almost certain loose citation of Rom 14:10 by 2 Cor 5:10.

6.3 Allusion to Ps 2:11.

7.1 Allusion to 1 John 3:8.

7.2 Loose citation of 1 Pet 4:7.

7.2 Matt 6:13 the probable source of the almost certain citation of the Lord's Prayer.

7.2 Matt 26:41 the probable source of the almost certain true citation of the words of the Lord.

8.1 Allusion to Paul's equating of Christ with hope (cf. 1 Tim 1:1; Col 1:27) and Paul's use of the word ἀρραβών (cf. 1 Cor 1:22; 5:5; Eph 1:14), though a specific passage cannot be demonstrated.
8.2 Allusion to 1 Pet 2:21.
9.2 Loose citation of Phil 2:16.
10.1 Allusion to a Pauline phrase either from 1 Cor 15:58 or Col 1:23.
10.1 Allusion to Rom 12:10.
10.1 Another allusion to Rom 12:10.
10.2-3 Loose citation of Isa 52:5 (with possible influence from Ign. *Trall.* 8.2 and Rom 2:24).
11.2 Allusion to Jer 5:4-5.
11.3 Allusion to 2 Thess 1:4.
11.4 Loose citation of 2 Thess 3:15.
11.4 Reminiscence of Paul's body metaphor (cf. esp. 1 Cor 12:12-27; Rom 14:4-8; Eph 4:4-13) (with possible influence from *1 Clem.* 37.5).
12.1 True citation of Ps 4:5a (with awareness of Eph. 4:26a).
12.1 True citation of Eph 4:26b (with awareness of Ps 4:5b).
12.3 Allusion to Phil 3:18.

Possible
1.1 Allusion to Phil 4:10 and 2:17.
1.1 Johannine language in general.
1.1 Reminiscence of Ign. *Smyrn.* 11.1 and Ign. *Eph.* 11.2.
1.2 Reminiscence of Paul's commendations of the Phil. church.
2.1 Allusion to Eph 6:14.
2.1 Allusion to Phil 3:21 and 2:10.
2.1 Allusion to Acts 10:42.
2.2 Loose citation of 2 Cor 4:14.
2.3 Correction toward Matt 7:1 in maxim #1 and toward Luke 6:38 in maxim #4.
3.2 Reminiscence of *1 Clem.* 47.1.
3.2 Reminiscence of Phil 1:27.
3.3 Possible influence from Rom 4:16 on the probable allusion to Gal 4:26.
4.3 Reminiscence of the widow Anna (cf. Luke 2:37).
4.3 Allusion to Ignatius's figurative use of 'altar' (as in Ign. *Eph.* 5.2; *Magn.* 7.2; *Trall.* 7.2; *Rom.* 2.2l) or to Paul's idea in Philippians of a person's actions being a sacrifice to God (cf. Phil 2:17; 4:18).
4.3 Allusion to *1 Clem.* 41.2.
5.2 Allusion to Mark 9:35.

5.2 Dependence upon the Johannine tradition that Christ promised to raise us from the dead (cf. John 5:21, 25; 6:44).

5.2 Influence upon form of probable allusion to Phil 1:27 by *1 Clem.* 21.1.

5.3 Influence upon form of probable loose citation of 1 Pet 2:11 from Gal 5:17.

5.3 Influence of Ignatius upon the thought of Polycarp that one should submit to one's leaders as to God and Christ.

5.3 Allusion to *1 Clem.* 1.3.

6.1 Allusion to Ezek 34:4.

6.1 Mediation of the probable loose citation of Prov 3:4 through 2 Cor 8:21.

6.1 Reminiscence of 1 Tim 5:19.

6.1 Theological influence from Paul on the probable allusion to the Lord's Prayer.

7.1 Reminiscence of 1 John 5:6-9.

7.1 Reminiscence of 1 John 3:12.

7.2 Borrowing of the word παντεπόπτην from *1 Clem.* 55.6; 64.1.

8.2 Allusion to 1 Pet 4:16.

9.1 Allusion to Heb 5:13.

9.1 Reminiscence of Phil 1:29-30.

9.2 Reminiscence of Rom 8:17.

9.2 Loose citation of 2 Cor 5:15.

10.1 Allusion to 1 Pet 2:17 or 3:8.

10.1 Allusion to 2 Cor 10:1.

10.2 Reminiscence of Prov 3:27 or Sir 29:8-9.

10.2 Loose citation of Eph 5:21, 1 Pet 5:5, *1 Clem.* 38.1, or Ign. *Magn.* 13.2.

10.2-3 Influence from Ign. *Trall.* 8.2 and Rom 2:24 upon the probable loose citation of Isa 52:5.

11.1 Citation of 1 Thess 5:22.

11.2 Reminiscence of 1 Tim 3:5.

11.2 Reminiscence of Eph 5:5 or Col 3:5.

11.3 Reminiscence of Phil 4:15 or 2 Cor 3:2.

11.4 Allusion to 2 Tim 2:25.

11.4 Influence from *1 Clem.* 37.5 on the probable reminiscence of Paul's body metaphor.

12.2 Allusion to the conception of Christ as 'eternal high priest' and 'son of God' by the author of Hebrews (cf. Heb 4:14: 6:20: 7:3).

12.2 Loose citation of Gal 1:1.

12.3 Abbreviated citation of Eph 6:18.
12.3 Loose citation of 1 Tim 2:2.
12.3 Conflated citation of Matt 5:44 and Luke 6:27.
12.3 Allusion to Matt 5:48.

Summary According to Source

Psalms
2.1 Probable allusion to Ps 2:11.
6.3 Probable allusion to Ps 2:11.
12.1 Probable true citation of Ps 4:5a (with awareness of Eph 4:26a).

Proverbs
6.1 Probable loose citation of Prov 3:4.
10.2 Possible reminiscence of Prov 3:27 or Sir 29:8-9.

Isaiah
10.2-3 Probable loose citation of Isa 52:5 (with possible influence from Ign. *Trall.* 8.2 and Rom 2:24).

Jeremiah
11.2 Probable allusion to Jer 5:4-5.

Ezekiel
6.1 Possible allusion to Ezek 34:4.

Sirach
10.2 Possible reminiscence of Prov 3:27 or Sir 29:8-9.

Tobit
10.2 Almost certain true citation of Tob 4:10 and/or Tob 12:9.

Matthew
6.2 Probable allusion to Matt 6:12, 14-15.
7.2 Matt 6:13 the probable source of the almost certain citation of the Lord's Prayer.
7.2 Matt 26:41 the probable source of the almost certain true citation of the words of the Lord.
2.3 Possible correction toward Matt 7:1 in maxim #1.
12.3 Possible conflated citation of Matt 5:44 and Luke 6:27.

12.3 Possible allusion to Matt 5:48.

Mark
5.2 Possible allusion to Mark 9:35.

Luke
2.3 Probable citation (conflation) of Luke 6:20 (cf. Matt 5:3) with Matt 5:10.
2.3 Possible correction toward Luke 6:38 in maxim #4.
4.3 Possible reminiscence of the widow Anna (cf. Luke 2:37).
12.3 Possible conflated citation of Matt 5:44 and Luke 6:27.

John
5.2 Possible dependence upon the Johannine tradition that Christ promised to raise us from the dead (cf. John 5:21, 25; 6:44).

Acts
1.2 Almost certain loose citation of Acts 2:24.
2.1 Possible allusion to Acts 10:42.

Romans
6.2 Almost certain loose citation of Rom 14:10, 12.
3.3 Probable reminiscence of Paul's use of the Jesus tradition in Rom 13:8-10 and/or Gal 5:14 (cf. 6:2).
10.1 Probable allusion to Rom 12:10.
10.1 Another probable allusion to Rom 12:10.
3.3 Possible influence from Rom 4:16 on the probable allusion to Gal 4:26.
9.2 Possible reminiscence of Rom 8:17.
10.2-3 Possible influence from Rom 2:24 upon the probable loose citation of Isa 52:5.

1 Corinthians
5.3 Almost certain compressed citation of 1 Cor 6:9-10.
11.2 Almost certain true citation of 1 Cor 6:2.
3.3 Probable allusion to 1 Cor 13:13.
4.3 Probable allusion to 1 Cor 14:25.
10.1 Probable allusion to a Pauline phrase either from 1 Cor 15:58 or Col 1:23.
11.4 Probable reminiscence of Paul's body metaphor (cf. esp. 1 Cor

12:12-27; Rom 4:4-8; Eph 4:4-13) (with possible influence from *1 Clem.* 37.5).

2 Corinthians
4.1 Almost certain allusion to the general Pauline metaphor 'weapons of righteousness' (probably an allusion to 2 Cor 6:7).
6.2 Probable influence on the form of the almost certain loose citation of Rom 14:10 by 2 Cor 5:10.
2.2 Possible loose citation of 2 Cor 4:14.
6.1 Possible mediation of the probable loose citation of Prov 3:4 through 2 Cor 8:21.
9.2 Possible loose citation of 2 Cor 5:15.
10.1 Possible allusion to 2 Cor 10:1.
11.3 Possible reminiscence of Phil 4:15 or 2 Cor 3:2.

Galatians
5.1 Almost certain true citation of Gal 6:7.
3.3 Probable allusion to Gal 4:26.
3.3 Probable reminiscence of Paul's use of the Jesus tradition in Rom 13:8-10 and/or Gal 5:14 (cf. 6:2).
5.3 Possible influence upon form of probable loose citation of 1 Pet 2:11 from Gal 5:17.
12.2 Possible loose citation of Gal 1:1.

Ephesians
1.3 Almost certain true (though compressed) citation of Eph 2:5, 8, 9.
12.1 Probable true citation of Eph 4:26b (with awareness of Ps 4:5b).
2.1 Possible allusion to Eph 6:14.
10.2 Possible loose citation of Eph 5:21, 1 Pet 5:5, *1 Clem.* 38.1, or Ign. *Magn.* 13.2.
11.2 Possible reminiscence of Eph 5:5 or Col 3:5.
12.3 Possible abbreviated citation of Eph 6:18.

Philippians:
Note that Polycarp explicitly mentions Paul's letter-writing activity to the Philippians in 3.2 making knowledge of the letter almost certain.
5.2 Probable allusion to Phil 1:27.
9.2 Probable loose citation of Phil 2:16.
12.3 Probable allusion to Phil 3:18.
1.1 Possible allusion to Phil 4:10 and 2:17.

1.2 Possible reminiscence of Paul's commendations of the Phil. church.
2.1 Possible allusion to Phil 3:21 and 2:10.
3.2 Possible reminiscence of Phil 1:27.
4.3 Possible allusion to Paul's idea in Philippians of a person's actions being a sacrifice to God (cf. Phil 2:17; 4:18).
9.1 Possible reminiscence of Phil 1:29-30.
11.3 Possible reminiscence of Phil 4:15 or 2 Cor 3:2.

Colossians
10.1 Probable allusion to a Pauline phrase either from 1 Cor 15:58 or Col 1:23.
11.2 Possible reminiscence of Eph 5:5 or Col 3:5.

1 Thessalonians
11.1 Possible citation of 1 Thess 5:22.

2 Thessalonians
11.3 Probable allusion to 2 Thess 1:4.
11.4 Probable loose citation of 2 Thess 3:15.

1 Timothy
4.1 Almost certain allusion to 1 Tim 6:10.
4.1 Almost certain loose citation of 1 Tim 6:7.
4.2-6.2 Probable general dependence upon the *Haustafeln* of 1 Timothy.
6.1 Possible reminiscence of 1 Tim 5:19.
11.2 Possible reminiscence of 1 Tim 3:5.
12.3 Possible loose citation of 1 Tim 2:2.

2 Timothy
9.2 Almost certain loose citation of 2 Tim 4:10.
5.2 Probable allusion to 2 Tim 2:12.
11.4 Possible allusion to 2 Tim 2:25.

Hebrews
9.1 Possible allusion to Heb 5:13.
12.2 Possible allusion to the conception of Christ as 'eternal high priest' and 'son of God' by the author of Hebrews (cf. Heb 4:14; 6:20; 7:3).

1 Peter
1.3 Almost certain loose citation of 1 Pet 1:8.

2.2 Almost certain true citation of 1 Pet 3:9.

8.1 Almost certain loose citation of 1 Pet 2:24.

8.1 Almost certain true citation of 1 Pet 2:22 (which is itself a citation of the LXX of Isa 53:9b).

10.2 Almost certain loose citation of 1 Pet 2:12.

1.3 Probable allusion to 1 Pet 1:12 in form but influenced in content from the sayings of the Lord (as represented by Matt 13:17; Luke 10:2 and Matt 25:21, 23).

2.1 Probable allusion to 1 Pet 1:13.

2.1 Probable loose citation of 1 Pet 1:21.

5.3 Probable loose citation of 1 Pet 2:11.

7.2 Probable loose citation of 1 Pet 4:7.

8.2 Probable allusion to 1 Pet 2:21.

8.2 Possible allusion to 1 Pet 4:16.

10.1 Possible allusion to 1 Pet 2:17 or 3:8.

10.2 Possible loose citation of Eph 5:21, 1 Pet 5:5, *1 Clem.* 38.1, or Ign. *Magn.* 13.2.

1 John

7.1 Almost certain compressed citation of 1 John 4:2-3.

7.1 Probable allusion to 1 John 3:8.

7.1 Possible reminiscence of 1 John 5:6-9.

7.1 Possible reminiscence of 1 John 3:12.

1 Clement

2.3 Probable general dependence upon *1 Clem.* 13.1-2 for the *fact* but less for the *form* of the introductory formula and the four maxims.

4.2 Probable allusion to *1 Clem.* 1.3.

4.2 Probable loose citation of *1 Clem.* 21:6.

3.2 Possible reminiscence of *1 Clem.* 47.1.

4.3 Possible allusion to *1 Clem.* 41.2.

5.2 Possible influence upon form of probable allusion to Phil 1:27 by *1 Clem.* 21.1.

5.3 Possible allusion to *1 Clem.* 1.3.

7.2 Possible borrowing of the word παντεπόπτην from *1 Clem.* 55.6; 64.1.

10.2 Possible loose citation of Eph 5:21, 1 Pet 5:5, *1 Clem.* 38.1, or Ign. *Magn.* 13.2.

11.4 Possible influence from *1 Clem.* 37.5 on the probable reminiscence of Paul's body metaphor.

Letters of Ignatius
1.1 Possible reminiscence of Ign. *Smyrn.* 11.1 and Ign. *Eph.* 11.2.
4.3 Possible allusion to Ignatius's figurative use of 'altar' (as in Ign. *Eph.*
5.2; *Magn.* 7.2; *Trall.* 7.2; *Rom.* 2.2l).
5.3 Possible influence of Ignatius upon the thought of Polycarp that
one should submit to one's leaders as to God and Christ.
10.2 Possible loose citation of Eph 5:21, 1 Pet 5:5, *1 Clem.* 38.1, or Ign.
Magn. 13.2.
10.2-3 Possible influence from Ign. *Trall.* 8.2 upon the probable loose
citation of Isa 52:5.

Cumulative Results

The following two charts display the probability (given as a number
expressed in percent) that Polycarp depended upon a given piece of
literature. These charts represent a simple statistical analysis of the
material already detailed. There is no intention of making the conclusions elicited in ch. 2 appear 'scientific'. There remains, of course, a
strong intuitive element in any study of this nature. Nevertheless, there
is value in such a statistical analysis. The value of these charts is in
recognizing that the cumulative effect of Polycarp's knowledge and
dependence upon a given source is substantially stronger than the likelihood of his dependence upon a source in any individual instance.

The method employed was as follows. A scale of one to ten was
used. *Ten* represented absolute certainty of dependence, *zero* represented
absolute certainty that dependence did not exist. Dependencies judged
'almost certain' were assigned the conservative value of *eight* on the
scale of one to ten. Those judged 'probable' were assigned the conservative value *six*. Those deemed 'possible' were assigned a *three*, unless
two sources were joined by an 'or' in which case they were assigned
either a *two* or *one*.

Once such values were assigned, a simple statistical analysis was per-
formed in order to calculate the probabilities that Polycarp *did* depend
on each given source.

The analysis consisted of first calculating the probabilities that
Polycarp *did not* depend upon a given source in a given instance. This is
equal to one minus the probability that he did.

Cumulative probabilities then were calculated. The *cumulative* probability that he did *not* depend on a source is the product of all the probabilities that he did not depend on that source. Conversely, the prob-

ability that he *did* depend upon that source is equal to one minus the cumulative probability that he did not depend on that source.

For example, if a source was deemed possible in four instances (each assigned the value 3) and deemed probable in one instance (assigned the value 6), then the calculation would be $1-[(1-.6) \times (1-.3) \times (1-.3) \times (1-.3) \times (1-.3)] = .903$ a result in excess of 90% confidence that he was influenced by that source. This is much stronger than the 60% in the single instance.

The statistics were calculated using the aid of an Excel computer program. The results appear on the following charts.

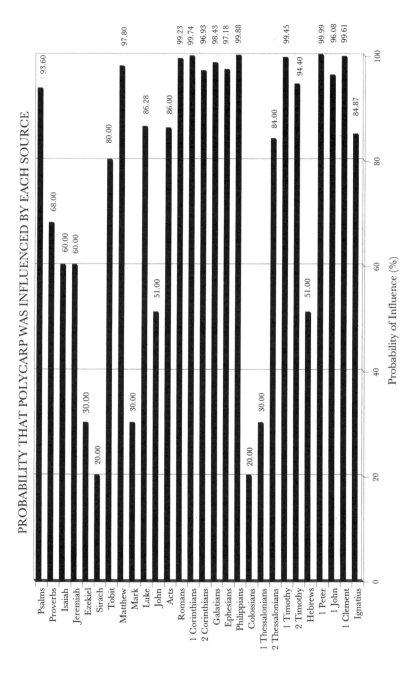

PROBABILITY THAT POLYCARP WAS INFLUENCED BY EACH SOURCE

Probability of Influence (%)

Psalms	93.60
Proverbs	68.00
Isaiah	60.00
Jeremiah	60.00
Ezekiel	30.00
Sirach	20.00
Tobit	80.00
Matthew	97.80
Mark	30.00
Luke	86.28
John	51.00
Acts	86.00
Romans	99.23
1 Corinthians	99.74
2 Corinthians	96.93
Galatians	98.43
Ephesians	97.18
Philippians	99.88
Colossians	20.00
1 Thessalonians	30.00
2 Thessalonians	84.00
1 Timothy	99.45
2 Timothy	94.40
Hebrews	51.00
1 Peter	99.99
1 John	96.08
1 Clement	99.61
Ignatius	84.87

PROBABILITY THAT POLYCARP WAS INFLUENCED BY EACH SOURCE
(sorted by probability)

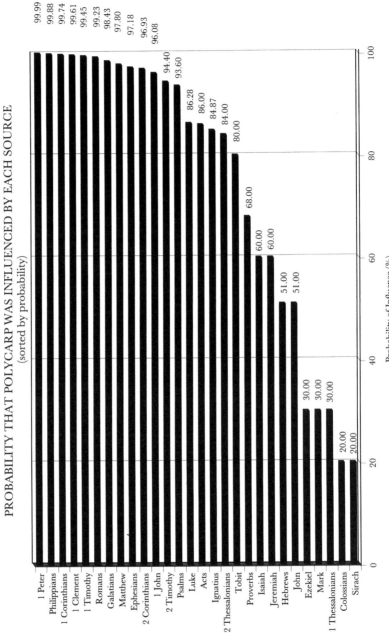

BIBLIOGRAPHY

Altaner, Berthold. *Patrology*. Translated by Hilda C. Graaf. Freiburg: Herder and Edinbugh-London: Nelson, 1960.

Aune, David E. *The New Testament in Its Literary Environment*. Philadelphia: The Westminster Press, 1987.

Avis, Paul, ed. *The History of Christian Theology*. Vol. 2. *The Study and Use of the Bible*, by John Rogerson, Christopher Rowland and Barnabas Lindars SSF. Basingstoke: Marshall Pickering and Grand Rapids: Wm. B. Eerdmans Publishing Co., 1988.

Babcock, William S., ed. *Paul and the Legacies of Paul*. Dallas: Southern Methodist University Press, 1990.

Bailey, Kenneth E. 'Informal Controlled Oral Tradition and the Synoptic Gospels.' *Asia Journal of Theology* 5 (1991): 34-54.

Balás, David L. 'Marcion Revisited: A 'Post-Harnack' Perspective.' In *Texts and Testaments: Critical Essays on the Bible and Early Church Fathers*. Edited by W. Eugene March. San Antonio: Trinity University Press, 1980.

Bardenhewer, Otto. *Geschichte der Altkirchlichen Literatur*. Vol. 1. Frieburg: Herdersche Verlagschandlung, 1913.

Bardsley, H. J. 'The Testimony of Ignatius and Polycarp to the Writings of St John.' *Journal of Theological Studies* 14 (1913): 207-220.

Barnard, L. W. *Studies in the Apostolic Fathers and Their Backgrounds*. Oxford: Basil Blackwell, 1966.

Barnes, Timothy D. 'A Note on Polycarp.' *Journal of Theological Studies* 18 (1967): 433-437.

Barnett, Albert E. *Paul Becomes a Literary Influence*. Chicago: The University of Chicago Press, 1941.

Barrett, C. K. *The Pastoral Epistles*. Oxford: Clarendon Press, 1963.

——. 'Pauline Controversies in the Post-Pauline Period.' *New Testament Studies* 20 (1974): 229-245.

Batiffol, Pierre. 'Polycarp.' In *Dictionary of the Apostolic Church*. Vol. 2. Edited by James Hastings. Edinburgh: T. & T. Clark, 1918.

Bauer, Johannes Bapt. *Die Polykarpbriefe*. Göttingen: Vandenhoeck & Ruprecht, 1995.

Bauer, Walter. *Die apostolischen Väter II: Die Briefe des Ignatius von Antiochia und der Polykarpbrief*. Tübingen: J. C. B. Mohr (Paul Siebeck), 1920.

——. *A Greek-English Lexicon of the New Testament and Other Early Christian Literature*. Translated and Adapted by William F. Arndt and F. Wilbur Gingrich. Second edition revised and augmented by F. Wilbur Gingrich and Frederick W. Danker. Chicago and London: The University of Chicago Press, 1979.

——. *Orthodoxy and Heresy in Earliest Christianity*. Second German edition, with added appendices, by Georg Strecker. Translated by a team from the Philadelphia Seminary on Christian Origins. Edited by Robert A. Kraft and Gerhard Krodel. Philadelphia: Fortress Press, 1971; repr., Mifflintown, Pa.: Sigler Press, 1996.

Baur, Ferdinand Christian. *The Church History of the First Three Centuries*. Translated by Allan Menzies. London: Williams and Norgate, 1978.

Beckwith, Roger. *The Old Testament Canon of the New Testament Church and its Background in Early Judaism*. Grand Rapids: William B. Eerdmans Publishing Company, 1985.

Beker, Johan Christiaan. *Heirs of Paul: Paul's Legacy in the New Testament and in the Church Today*. Minneapolis: Fortress Press, 1991.

——. 'Prophecy and the Spirit in the Apostolic Fathers.' Ph.D. diss., The University of Chicago, 1955.

Berding, Kenneth. 'Polycarp of Smyrna's View of the Authorship of 1 and 2 Timothy.' *Vigiliae Christianae* 53 (1999): 349-360.

Bernard, J. H. *The Pastoral Epistles*. Cambridge: Cambridge University Press, 1899; repr., Grand Rapids: Baker Book House, 1980.

Boismard, M. -E. 'Critique Textuelle et Citations Patristiques.' *Revue Biblique* 57 (1950): 388-408.

Bovon-Thurneysen, Annegreth. 'Ethik und Eschatologie im Philipperbrief des Polykarp von Smyrna.' *Theologische Zeitschrift* 29 (1973): 241-256.

Brodie, Thomas Louis. 'Greco-Roman Imitation of Texts as a Partial Guide to Luke's Use of Sources.' In *Luke-Acts: New Perspectives from the Society of Biblical Literature Seminar*. Edited by Charles H. Talbert. New York: Crossroad, 1984.

Brown, Harold O. *Heresies: The Image of Christ in the Mirror of Heresy and Orthodoxy from the Apostles to the Present*. Garden City, N.Y.: Doubleday & Company, 1984.

Brown, Raymond E. *An Introduction to the New Testament*. New York: Doubleday, 1997.

Bruce, F. F. 'Eschatology in the Apostolic Fathers.' In *The Heritage of the Early Church: Essays in Honor of Georges Vasilievich Florovsky*. Edited by David Neiman and Margaret Schatkin. Rome: Pont. Institutum Studiorum Orientalium, 1973.

Buschmann, Gerd. *Das Martyrium des Polykarp*. Translation and Commentary. Göttingen: Vandenhoeck and Ruprecht, 1998.

Cadoux, Cecil John. *Ancient Smyrna: A History of the City from the Earliest Times to 324 A.D.* Oxford: Basil Blackwell, 1938.

——. Review of *Polycarp's Two Epistles to the Philippians*, by P. N. Harrison. *The Journal of Theological Studies* 38 (1937): 267-270.

Campenhausen, Hans von. *Ecclesiastical Authority and Spiritual Power in the Church of the First Three Centuries*. Translated by J. A. Baker. Stanford: Stanford University Press, 1953.

——. *The Formation of the Christian Bible*. Translated by J. A. Baker. Philadelphia: Fortress Press, 1972.

——. 'Polycarp von Smyrna und die Pastoralbriefe.' Chap. in *Aus der Frühzeit des Christentums: Studien zur Kirchengeschichte des ersten und zweiten Jahrhunderts*. Tübingen: J. C. B. Mohr (Paul Siebeck), 1963.

Carrington, Philip. *The Early Christian Church*. 2 Vols. Cambridge: Cambridge University Press, 1957.

Carroll, Howard. 'Polycarp of Smyrna – With Special Reference to Early Christian Martyrdom.' Ph.D. diss., Duke University, 1946.

Carson, D. A., Douglas J. Moo, and Leon Morris. *An Introduction to the New Testament*. Grand Rapids: Zondervan Publishing House, 1992.

Castelli, Elizabeth A. *Imitating Paul: A Discourse of Power*. Louisville, Ky.: Westminster/John Knox Press, 1991.

Clark, Donald Lemen. 'Imitation: Theory and Practice in Roman Rhetoric.' *The Quarterly Journal of Speech* 37 (1951): 11-22.

Collins, Raymond F. *Introduction to the New Testament*. Garden City, N.Y.: Doubleday & Company, 1983.

Cotterill, J. M. 'The Epistle of Polycarp to the Philippians and the Homilies of Antiochus Palaestinensis.' *The Journal of Philology* 19 (1891): 241-285.

Cross, F. L. *The Early Christian Fathers*. London: Gerald Duckworth & Co. Ltd., 1960.

Cruttwell, Charles Thomas. *A Literary History of Early Christianity: Including the Fathers and the Chief Heretical Writers of the Ante-Nicene Period*. Vol. 1. New York: AMS Press, repr., 1971.

Dahl, Nils Alstrup. 'Der Erstgeborene Satans und der Vater des Teufels (Polyk. 7, und Joh 8₄₄).' In *Apophoreta: Festschrift für Ernst Haenchen*. Berlin: Verlag Alfred Töpelmann, 1964.

Daley, Brian E. *The Hope of the Early Church: A Handbook of Patristic Eschatology*. Cambridge: Cambridge University Press, 1991.

Danker, Frederick W. 'Bridging St. Paul and the Apostolic Fathers: A Study in Reciprocity.' *Currents in Theology and Mission* 15 (1988): 84-94.

DeBoer, Martinus C. 'Images of Paul in the Post-Apostolic Period.' *Catholic Biblical Quarterly* 42 (1980): 359-80.

Dehandschutter, Boudewijn. 'Polycarp's Epistle to the Philippians: An Early Example of "Reception".' In *The New Testament in Early Christianity: La réception des écrits néotestamentarios dans le christianisme primitif*. Edited by Jean-Marie Sevrin. Leuven: Leuven University Press, 1989.

Derrett, J. Duncan M. 'Scripture and Norms in the Apostolic Fathers.' In *Principat 27,1: Religion*. Edited by Wolfgang Haase. Berlin and New York: Walter de Gruyter, 1993.

Dibelius, Martin. *A Fresh Approach to the New Testament and Early Christian Literature*. New York: Charles Scribner's Sons, 1936.

Dimant, Devorah. 'Use and Interpretation of Mikra in the Apocrypha and Pseudepigrapha.' In *Mikra: Text, Translation, Reading and Interpretation of the Hebrew Bible in Ancient Judaism and Early Christianity*. Edited by Martin Jan Mulder. Assen/Maastricht: Van Gorcum and Minneapolis: Fortress Press, 1990.

Dockery, David S. *Biblical Interpretation Then and Now: Contemporary Hermeneutics in the Light of the Early Church*. Grand Rapids: Baker Book House, 1992.

Ehrhardt, Arnold. 'Christianity before the Apostles' Creed.' *Harvard Theological Review* 55 (1962): 73-119.

Ehrman, Bart D. *The New Testament: A Historical Introduction to the Early Christian Writings*. New York and Oxford: Oxford University Press, 1997.

——. *The New Testament and Other Early Christian Writings: A Reader*. Oxford: Oxford University Press, 1998.

Fantham, Elaine. 'Imitation and Decline: Rhetorical Theory and Practice in the First Century after Christ.' *Classical Philology* 73 (1978): 102-116.

Farkasfalvy, Denis M. '"Prophets and Apostles": The Conjunction of the Two Terms before Irenaeus.' In *Texts and Testaments: Critical Essays on the Bible and Early Church Fathers*. Edited by W. Eugene March. San Antonio: Trinity University Press, 1980.

Fee, Gordon D. 'The Text of John in *The Jerusalem Bible*: A Critique of the Use of Patristic Citations in New Testament Textual Criticism.' *Journal of Biblical Literature* 90 (1971): 163-173.

——. 'The Use of Greek Patristic Citations in New Testament Textual Criticism: The State of the Question.' In *Studies in the Theory and Method of New Testament Textual Criticism*, by Eldon Jay Epp and Gordon D. Fee. Grand Rapids: William B. Eerdmans Publishing Company, 1993.

Feldman, Louis H. 'Use, Authority and Exegesis of Mikra in the Writings of Josephus.' In *Mikra: Text, Translation, Reading and Interpretation of the Hebrew Bible in Ancient Judaism and Early Christianity*. Edited by Martin Jan Mulder. Assen/Maastricht: Van Gorcum and Minneapolis: Fortress Press, 1990.

Fischer, Joseph A. *Die Apostolischen Väter*. Darmstadt: Wissenschafliche Buchgesellschaft, 1976.

Flora, Jerry R. 'A Critical Analysis of Walter Bauer's Theory of Early Christian Orthodoxy and Heresy.' Th.D. diss., Southern Baptist Theological Seminary, 1972.

Gamble, Harry Y. *Books and Readers in the Early Church: A History of Early Christian Texts.* New Haven, Conn. and London: Yale University Press, 1995.

——. 'The Canon of the New Testament.' In *The New Testament and Its Modern Interpreters*. Edited by Eldon Jay Epp and George W. MacRae. Philadelphia: Fortress Press and Atlanta: Scholars Press, 1989.

Garrison, Roman. *The Graeco-Roman Context of Early Christian Literature*. Journal for the Study of the New Testament Supplement Series 127. Sheffield: Sheffield Academic Press, 1997.

Gerhardsson, Birger. *Memory and Manuscript: Oral Tradition and Written Transmission in Rabbinic Judaism and Early Christianity*. Translated by Eric J. Sharpe. Uppsala: Almqvist & Wiksells, 1961.

Giordani, Igino. *The Social Message of the Early Church Fathers*. Translated by Alba I. Zizzamia. Patterson, N.J.: St. Anthony Guild Press, 1944.

Glasson, T. F. 'Hort's Renderings of Passages from Ignatius and Polycarp.' *Church Quarterly Review* 167 (1966): 302-309.

Gloucester, A. C. 'The Epistle of Polycarp to the Philippians.' *The Church Quarterly Review* 141 (1945): 1-25.

Gokey, Francis X. *The Terminology for the Devil and Evil Spirits in the Apostolic Fathers*. Washington, D.C.: The Catholic University of America Press, 1961.

Goodspeed, Edgar J. *The Apostolic Fathers: An American Translation*. New York: Harper & Brothers, 1950.

——. *The Formation of the New Testament*. Chicago: The University of Chicago Press, 1926.

——. *A History of Early Christian Literature*. Revised and enlarged by Robert M. Grant. Chicago: The University of Chicago Press, 1966.

——. *New Solutions of New Testament Problems*. Chicago: The University of Chicago Press, 1927.

Goulder, Michael D. 'Ignatius' "Docetists".' *Vigiliae Christianae* 53 (1999): 16-30.

Grant, Robert M. *After the New Testament*. Philadelphia: Fortress Press, 1967.

——. *The Formation of the New Testament*. New York: Harper & Row, 1965.

——. *An Introduction*. Vol. 1. The Apostolic Fathers: A New Translation and Commentary. Edited by Robert M. Grant. New York: Thomas Nelson & Sons, 1964.

——. 'Polycarp of Smyrna.' *Anglican Theological Review* 28 (1948): 137-148.

—— and David Tracy. *A Short History of the Interpretation of the Bible*. Second Edition. Philadelphia: Fortress Press, 1984.

Greer, Rowan A. 'The Christian Bible and Its Interpretation.' In *Early Biblical Interpretation*, by James L. Kugel and Rowan A. Greer. Philadelphia: The Westminster Press, 1986.

Hagner, Donald Alfred. 'The Sayings of Jesus in the Apostolic Fathers and Justin Martyr.' In *Gospel Perspectives: The Jesus Tradition Outside the Gospels*. Vol. 5. Edited by David Wenham. Sheffield: JSOT Press, 1984.

——. *The Use of the Old and New Testaments in Clement of Rome*. Leiden: E. J. Brill, 1973.

Hahn, Ferdinand. *The Worship of the Early Church*. Translated by David E. Green. Edited by John Reumann. Philadelphia: Fortress Press, 1973.

Hanson, R. P. C. *Tradition in the Early Church*. Philadelphia: The Westminster Press, 1962.

Harnack, Adolf von. *Die Briefsammlung des Apostels Paulus und die anderen vorkonstantinischen christlichen Briefsammlungen*. Leipzig: J. C. Hinrichs, 1926.

———. *History of Dogma*. Vol. 1. Translated by Neil Buchanan. London: Williams & Norgate, 1905.

———. 'Lightfoot on the Ignatian Epistles: II. Genuineness and Date of the Epistles.' *The Expositor*. Third Series, vol. 3 (1886): 175-192.

———. *Miscellen zu den apostolischen Vätern, den Acta Pauli, Apelles, dem Muratorischen Fragment, den pseudocyprianischen Schriften und Claudianus Marmertus*. Texte und Untersuchungen zur Geschichte der altchristlichen Literatur 2-20/3b. Leipzig: J. C. Hinrichs, 1900

———. *The Origin of the New Testament and the Most Important Consequences of the New Creation*. Translated by J. R. Wilkinson. New York: The Macmillan Company, 1925.

Harrison, P. N. *Paulines and Pastorals*. London: Villiers Publications, 1964.

———. *Polycarp's Two Epistles to the Philippians*. Cambridge: Cambridge University Press, 1936.

———. *The Problem of the Pastoral Epistles*. London: Oxford University Press, 1921.

Hawkin, David J. 'A Reflective Look at the Recent Debate on Orthodoxy and Heresy in Earliest Christianity.' *Église et Théologie* 7 (1976): 367-378.

Hefele, Carolus Iosephus. *Patrum Apostolicorum Opera*. Tubingae: Henrici Laupp, 1855.

Hemer, Colin J. *The Letters to the Seven Churches of Asia in their Local Setting*. Journal for the Study of the New Testament Supplement Series 11. Sheffield: JSOT Press, 1986.

Hernando, James Daniel. 'Irenaeus and the Apostolic Fathers: An Inquiry into the development of the New Testament Canon.' Ph.D. diss., Drew University, 1990.

Hill, Charles E. 'The *Epistula Apostolorum*: An Asian Tract from the Time of Polycarp.' *Journal of Early Christian Studies* 7 (1999): 1-53.

Hillmer, Melvyn Raymond. 'The Gospel of John in the Second Century.' Ph.D. diss., Harvard University, 1966.

Hodgson, Richard G. 'The Doctrine of Salvation in the Second-Century Church.' Th.M. thesis, Westminster Theological Seminary, 1966.

Holmes, Michael W. 'A Note on the Text of Polycarp *Philippians* 11.3' *Vigiliae Christianae* 51 (1997): 207- 210.

———. 'Polycarp of Smyrna.' In *Dictionary of the Later New Testament & Its Developments*, ed. Ralph P. Martin and Peter H. Davids. Downers Grove and Leicester: InterVarsity Press, 1997.

Hort, Fenton John Anthony. *Six Lectures on the Ante-Nicene Fathers*. London: Macmillan and Co., 1895.

Hübner, Reinhard M. 'Thesen zur Echtheit und Datierung der sieben Briefe des Ignatius von Antiochien.' *Zeitschrift für Antikes Christentum* 1 (1997): 44-72.

Jacquier, E. *Le Nouveau Testament dans L' Église Chrétienne*. Vol. 1. Paris: Libraire Victor Lecoffre, J. Gabalda, 1911.

Jay, Eric G. 'From Presbyter-Bishops to Bishops and Presbyters. Christian Ministry in the Second Century: a Survey.' *Second Century* 1 (1981): 125-162.

Jefford, Clayton N. *Reading the Apostolic Fathers: An Introduction*. Peabody, Mass.: Hendrickson Publishers, 1996.

Johnson, Sherman E. 'Unsolved Questions about Early Christianity in Anatolia.' In *Studies in New Testament and Early Christian Literature: Essays in Honor of Allen P. Wikgren*. Edited by David Edward Aune. Leiden: E. J. Brill, 1972.

Joly, Robert. *Le Dossier d'Ignace d'Antioche*. Université libre de Bruxelles, Faculté de Philosophie et Lettres 69. Brussells: Éditions de l'Université de Bruxelles, 1979.

Kelly, J. N. D. *Early Christian Doctrines*. 5th rev. ed. London: Adam & Charles Black, 1958; repr. 1980.

Kennedy, George. *The Art of Rhetoric in the Roman World 300 B.C.- A.D. 300.* Princeton: Princeton University Press, 1972.

———. *Classical Rhetoric and Its Christian and Secular Tradition from Ancient to Modern Times.* Chapel Hill: The University of North Carolina Press, 1980.

Kinzig, Wolfram. 'The Greek Christian Writers.' In *Handbook of Classical Rhetoric in the Hellenistic Period 330 B.C.- A.D. 400.* Edited by Stanley E. Porter. Leiden: Brill, 1997.

Kleist, James A. *The Didache, the Epistle of Barnabas, the Epistle and the Martyrdom of St. Polycarp, the Fragments of Papias, the Epistle to Diognetus.* Vol. 6. Ancient Christian Writers. Edited by Johannes Quasten and Joseph C. Plumpe. Westminster, Md.: The Newman Press, 1948.

Knight III, George W. *The Pastoral Epistles: A Commentary on the Greek Text.* The New International Greek Testament Commentary. Grand Rapids: William B. Eerdmans Publishing Company and Carlisle: The Paternoster Press, 1992.

Knox, John. *Marcion and the New Testament: An Essay in the Early History of the Canon.* Chicago: The University of Chicago Press, 1942.

Koester (Köster), Helmut. *Ancient Christian Gospels: Their History and Development.* London: SCM Press Ltd and Philadelphia: Trinity Press International, 1990.

———. *History and Literature of Early Christianity. Vol. 2: Introduction to the New Testament.* Philadelphia: Fortress Press and Berlin: Walter de Gruyter, 1982.

———. *Synoptische Überlieferung bei den apostolischen Vätern.* Berlin: Akademie-Verlag, 1957.

Koskenniemi, Heikki. *Studien zur Idee und Phraseologie des griechischen Briefes bis 400 n. Chr.* Soumalaisen Tiedekatemian Toimituksia; Annales Academiae Scientarium Fennicae 102.2. Helsinki: Akateeminen Kirjakauppa, 1952.

Kreitzer, Larry J. 'Eschatology.' In *Dictionary of Paul and His Letters.* Edited by Gerald F. Hawthorne, Ralph P. Martin and Daniel E. Reid. Downers Grove, Ill. and Leicester: InterVarsity Press, 1993.

Krüger, Gustav. *History of Early Christian Literature.* Translated by Charles R. Gillett. New York: The Macmillan Company, 1897.

Kugel, James L. 'Early Interpretation: The Common Background of Later Forms of Biblical Exegesis.' In *Early Biblical Interpretation*, by James L. Kugel and Rowan A. Greer. Philadelphia: The Westminster Press, 1986.

Kümmel, Werner Georg. *Introduction to the New Testament.* Rev. ed. Translated by Howard Clark Kee. Nashville: Abington, 1975.

Lake, Kirsopp, *The Apostolic Fathers.* Vol. 1. Cambridge University Press and London: William Heinemann Ltd, 1912; repr. 1977.

———. Review of *Polycarp's Two Epistles to the Philippians*, by P. N. Harrison. In *Journal of Biblical Literature* 56 (1937): 72-75.

Latourette, Kenneth Scott. *A History of Christianity.* New York: Harper & Brothers Publishers, 1953.

Leaney, A. R. C. *The Jewish and Christian World 200 BC to AD 200.* Vol. 7. Cambridge Commentaries on Writings of the Jewish and Christian World 200 BC to AD 200. Cambridge: Cambridge University Press, 1984.

Lightfoot, J. B. *The Apostolic Fathers: Clement, Ignatius, and Polycarp.* Second Edition. 2 Parts in 5 Vols. London: Macmillan and Co., 1890; repr., Peabody, Mass.: Hendrickson Publishers, 1989.

———, J. R. Harmer and Michael W. Holmes, trans. and eds. *The Apostolic Fathers: Greek Texts and English Translations of Their Writings.* Second Edition. Grand Rapids: Baker Book House, 1992.

Lindemann, Andreas. 'Der Apostel Paulus im 2. Jahrhundert.' In *The New Testament in Early Christianity: La réception des écrits néotestamentarios dans le christianisme primitif.* Edited by Jean-Marie Sevrin. Leuven: Leuven University Press, 1989.

———. 'Paul in the Writings of the Apostolic Fathers.' In *Paul and the Legacies of Paul.* Edited by William S. Babcock. Dallas: Southern Methodist University Press, 1990.

———. *Paulus im ältesten Christentum: Das Bild des Apostels und die Rezeption der paulinischen Theologie in der frühchristlichen Literatur bis Marcion.* Beiträge zur historichen Theologie 58. Tübingen: J. C. B. Mohr (Paul Siebeck), 1979.

Lovering, Eugene Harrison. 'The Collection, redaction, and early circulation of the corpus Paulinum.' Ph.D. diss, Southern Methodist University, 1988.

MacDonald, Dennis Ronald. *The Legend and the Apostle: The Battle for Paul in Story and Canon.* Philadelphia: The Westminster Press, 1983.

Mackinnon, James. *The Gospel in the Early Church: A Study of the Early Development of Christian Thought.* London: Longmans, Green, and Co., 1933.

Maier, Harry O. 'Purity and Danger in Polycarp's Epistle to the Philippians: The Sin of Valens in Social Perspective.' *Journal of Early Christian Studies* 1 (1993): 229-247.

Malherbe, Abraham J. *Moral Exhortation, A Greco-Roman Sourcebook.* Philadelphia: The Westminster Press, 1986.

Massaux, Édouard. *The Influence of the Gospel of Saint Matthew on Christian Literature before Saint Irenaeus. Book 2: The Later Christian Writings.* Translated by Norman J. Belval and Suzanne Hecht. Edited by Arthur J. Bellinzoni. Macon, Ga.: Mercer University Press, 1990.

McDonald, Lee M. *The Formation of the Christian Biblical Canon.* Peabody, Mass.: Hendrickson Publishers, 1995.

McNatt, Charles William. 'An Investigation of Old Testament Usage in the Pastoral Epistles and Selected Apostolic Fathers.' Ph.D. diss., Southwestern Baptist Theological Seminary, 1972.

Metzger, Bruce M. *The Canon of the New Testament: Its Origin, Development, and Significance.* Oxford: Clarendon Press, 1987.

———. 'Patristic Evidence and the Textual Criticism of the New Testament.' *New Testament Studies* 18 (1971- 1972): 379-400.

Miller, W. London. 'An Anthology of the Theology of the Apostolic Fathers.' Ph.D. diss., Southwestern Baptist Theological Seminary, 1948.

Moore, Edward Caldwell. *The New Testament in the Christian Church.* New York: The Macmillan Company, 1924.

Morgan, Richard Lyon. 'Regula Veritatis: A Historical Investigation of the Canon in the Second Century.' Ph.D. diss., Union Theological Seminary in Virginia, 1966.

Mowry, Lucetta. 'The Early Circulation of Paul's Letters.' *Journal of Biblical Literature* 63 (1944): 73-86.

Nautin, Pierre. *Lettres et Écrivains Chrétiens des IIe et IIIe Siecles.* Paris: Cerf, 1961.

Nestle, Eberhard. 'Two Interesting Biblical Quotations in the "Apostolic Constitutions."' *The Expository Times* 9 (1897-1898): 13-15.

Nielsen, Charles M. 'Polycarp and Marcion: A Note.' *Theological Studies* 47 (1986): 297-299.

———. 'Polycarp, Paul and the Scriptures.' *Anglican Theological Review* 47 (1965): 199-216.

Norris, Frederick W. 'Asia Minor before Ignatius: Walter Bauer Reconsidered.' In *Studia Evangelica.* Vol. 7. Papers presented to the Fifth International Congress on Biblical Studies (1973). Edited by Elizabeth A. Livingstone. Texte und Untersuchungen zur Geschichte der altchristlichen Literatur 126. Berlin: Akadamie- Verlag, 1982.

———. 'Ignatius, Polycarp, and I Clement: Walter Bauer Reconsidered.' *Vigiliae Christianae* 30 (1976): 23-44.

Olbricht, Thomas H. 'Exegesis in the Second Century.' In *Handbook to Exegesis of the New Testament*. Edited by Stanley E. Porter. Leiden: Brill, 1997.
Osburn, William. *Doctrinal Errors of the Apostolic and Early Fathers*. London: Hamilton, Adams, and Co.; Hatchard and Son; and Seely and Son, 1835.
Oxford Society of Historical Theology. *The New Testament in the Apostolic Fathers*. Oxford: The Clarendon Press, 1905.

Pagels, Elaine Hiesey. *The Gnostic Paul: Gnostic Exegesis of the Pauline Letters*. Philadelphia: Fortress Press, 1975.
Patzia, Arthur G. *The Making of the New Testament: Origin, Collection, Text & Canon*. Downers Grove, Ill.: InterVarsity Press, 1995.
Paulsen, Henning. *Die Brief des Ignatius von Antiochia und der Brief des Polykarp von Smyrna: Zweite, neubearbeitete Auflage der Auslegung von Walter Bauer*. Tübingen: J. C. B. Mohr (Paul Siebeck), 1985.
———. *Zur Literatur und Geschichte des frühen Christentums*. Wissenschaftliche Untersuchungen zum Neuen Testament 99. Tübingen, J. C. B. Mohr (Paul Siebeck), 1997.
Payne, J. Barton. 'The Biblical Interpretation of Irenaeus.' In *Inspiration and Interpretation*. Edited by John F. Walvoord. Grand Rapids: Wm. B. Eerdmans Publishing Co., 1957.
Pérès, Jacques -Noël. *L'Épître des apôtres accompagnée du Testament de notre Seigneur et notre Sauveur Jésus- Christ*. Apocryphes, vol. 5. Turnhout: Brepols, 1994.
Petersen, William L. 'Can ΑΡΣΕΝΟΚΟΙΤΑΙ be translated by "Homosexuals"? (1 COR. 6.9; 1 TIM. 1.10).' *Vigiliae Christianae* 40 (1986): 187-191.
Pfleiderer, Otto. *Primitive Christianity: Its Writings and Teachings in their Historical Connections*. Translated by W. Montgomery. Vol. 3. London: Williams & Norgate and New York: G. P. Putnam's Sons, 1910.
Prior, Michael. *Paul the Letter-Writer and the Second Letter to Timothy*. Journal for the Study of the New Testament Supplement Series 23. Sheffield: Sheffield Academic Press, 1989.
Prostmeier, Ferdinand R. 'Zur Handschriftlichen Überlieferung des Polykarp – Und des Barnabasbriefes. Zwei nicht beachtete Deszendenten des Cod. Vat. Gr. 859.' *Vigiliae Christianae* 48 (1994): 48-64.

Quasten, Johannes. *Patrology. Vol 1: The Beginnings of Patristic Literature*. Westminster, Md.: The Newman Press and Ultrecht-Brussels: Spectrum Publishers, 1951.

Renan, Ernest. *Histoire des Origines du Christianisme*. Vol. 6, *L'Eglise Chrétienne*. Paris: Calmann Lévy, 1899.
Rensberger, David K. 'As the Apostle Teaches: The Development of the Use of Paul's Letters in Second- Century Christianity.' Ph.D. diss, Yale University, 1981.
Richards, E. Randolph. 'The Codex and the Early Collection of Paul's Letters.' *Bulletin for Biblical Research* 8 (1998): 151-166.
Ridderbos, Herman. *Paul: An Outline of His Theology*. Translated by John Richard de Witt. Grand Rapids: William B. Eerdmans Publishing Company, 1975.
Roberts, C. H., ed. *An Unpublished Fragment of the Fourth Gospel in the John Rylands Library*. Manchester: The Manchester University Press, 1935.
Roberts, J. H. and A. B. Du Toit. *Guide to the New Testament*. Vol. 1. Translated by D. Roy Briggs. Pretoria: N. G. Kerkboekhandel Transvaal, 1979.
Robinson, Thomas A. *The Early Church: An Annotated Bibliography of Literature in English*. Metuchen, N.J.: The American Theological Library Association, 1993.

Sanday, W. *The Gospels in the Second Century*. London: Macmillan and Co., 1876.

Sanders, J. N. *The Fourth Gospel in the Early Church*. Cambridge: Cambridge University Press, 1943.

Schaff, Philip. *History of the Christian Church*. Vol. 2, *Ante-Nicene Christianity: A.D. 100-325*. Grand Rapids: Wm. B. Eerdmans Publishing Company, 1910.

Schnider, Franz and Werner Stenger. *Studien zum neutestamentlichen Briefformular*. New Testament Studies XI. Leiden: E. J. Brill, 1987.

Schoedel, William R. 'The Apostolic Fathers.' In *The New Testament and Its Modern Interpreters*. Edited by Eldon Jay Epp and George W. MacRae. Philadelphia: Fortress Press and Atlanta: Scholars Press, 1989.

——. 'Polycarp, Epistle of.' In *The Anchor Bible Dictionary*. Vol. 5. New York: Doubleday, 1992.

——. *Polycarp, Martyrdom of Polycarp, Fragments of Papias*. Vol. 5 of *The Apostolic Fathers: A New Translation and Commentary*. Edited by Robert M. Grant. Camden, N.J.: Thomas Nelson & Sons, 1967.

——. 'Polycarp's Witness to Ignatius of Antioch.' *Vigiliae Christianae* 41 (1987): 1-10.

Schubert, Paul. *Form and Function of the Pauline Thanksgivings*. Berlin: Töpelmann, 1939.

Schwegler, Albert. *Das nachapostolische Zeitalter*. Vol. 2. Tübingen: Ludwig Friedrich Fues, 1846.

Schweizer, Eduard. 'Der zweite Thessalonicherbrief ein Philipperbrief?' *Theologische Zeitschrift* 1 (1945): 90-105.

Shepherd, Massey Hamilton, ed. and trans. 'The Letter of Polycarp, Bishop of Smyrna, to the Philippians.' In *Early Christian Fathers*. Edited by Cyril C. Richardson. New York: Collier Books, 1970.

Stark, Alonzo Rosecrans. *The Christology in the Apostolic Fathers*. Chicago: The University of Chicago Press, 1912.

Steinmetz, Peter. 'Polykarp von Smyrna über die Gerechtigkeit.' *Hermes* 100 (1972): 63-75.

Stirewalt, M. Luther. 'Paul's Evaluation of Letter-Writing.' In *Search the Scriptures: New Testament Studies in Honor of Raymond T. Stamm*. Edited by J. M. Myers, O. Reimherr and H. N. Bream. Leiden: E. J. Brill, 1969.

——. *Studies in Ancient Greek Epistolography*. Atlanta: Scholars Press, 1993.

Stonehouse, N. B. 'The Authority of the New Testament.' In *The Infallible Word*. Edited by N. B. Stonehouse and Paul Wooley. Philadelphia: Presbyterian and Reformed Publishing Company, 1946.

Stowers, Stanley K. *Letter Writing in Greco-Roman Antiquity*. Philadelphia: The Westminster Press, 1986.

Streeter, Burnett Hillman. *The Primitive Church*. New York: The Macmillan Company, 1929.

Stuckwisch, D. Richard. 'Saint Polycarp of Smyrna: Johannine or Pauline Figure?' *Concordia Theological Quarterly* 61 (1997): 113-125.

Suggs, M. J. 'The Use of Patristic Evidence in the Search for a Primitive New Testament Text.' *New Testament Studies* 4 (1957-1958): 139-147.

Swete, Henry Barclay. *The Holy Spirit in the Ancient Church: A Study of Christian Teaching in the Age of the Fathers*. London: Macmillan and Co., 1912.

——. An Introduction to the Old Testament in Greek. Revised by Richard Rusden Ottley. Cambridge: Cambridge University Press, 1914; repr. Peabody, Mass.: Hendrickson Publishers, 1989.

Tajra, Harry W. *The Martyrdom of St. Paul*. Wissenschaftliche Untersuchungen zum Neuen Testament 2. Reihe 67. Tübingen: J. C. B. Mohr (Paul Siebeck), 1994.

Taylor, Stephen S. 'One Way to Categorize Patristic Citations.' Unpublished paper, Westminster Theological Seminary, 1998.

Thompson, J. David and J. Arthur Baird. *A Critical Concordance to the Epistle of Saint Polycarp to the Philippians*. Edited by J. Arthur Baird and David Noel Freedman. n.p.: Biblical Research Associates, 1996.

Torrance, Thomas F. *Divine Meaning: Studies in Patristic Hermeneutics*. Edinburgh: T & T Clark.

——. *The Doctrine of Grace in the Apostolic Fathers*. n.p.: Oliver and Boyd Ltd., 1948; repr.: Pasadena: WIPF & Stock Publishers, 1996.

Towner, Philip H. *The Goal of our Instruction: The Structure of Theology and Ethics in the Pastoral Epistles*. Journal for the Study of the New Testament Supplement Series 34. Sheffield: Sheffield Academic Press, 1989.

Trigg, Joseph W. *Biblical Interpretation*. Vol. 9. Message of the Fathers of the Church. Wilmington, Del.: Michael Glazier, 1988.

Trobisch, David. *Paul's Letter Collection: Tracing the Origins*. Minneapolis: Fortress Press, 1994.

Turner, H. E. W. *The Pattern of Christian Truth: A Study in the Relations between Orthodoxy and Heresy in the Early Church*. London: A. R. Mowbray & Co. Limited, 1954.

Weidmann, Frederick W. *Polycarp & John: The Harris Fragments and Their Challenge to the Literary Traditions*. Notre Dame, Ind: University of Notre Dame Press, 1999.

Weiss, Bernard. *A Manual of Introduction to the New Testament*. Vol. 1. Translated by A. J. K. Davidson. New York: Funk & Wagnalls, n.d.

Welsford, A. E. *Life in the Early Church: A.D. 33 to 313*. London: National Society and S.P.C.K., 1951.

Westcott, Brook Foss. *A General Survey of the History of the Canon of the New Testament*. Cambridge and London: Macmillan and Co., 1881.

White, John L. 'New Testament Epistolary Literature in the Framework of Ancient Epistolography.' In *Aufstieg und Niedergang der Römischen Welt* 25.2. Edited by H. Temporini and W. Haase, 1730-1756. Berlin: Walter de Gruyter, 1984.

——. 'Saint Paul and the Apostolic Letter Tradition.' *The Catholic Biblical Quarterly* 45 (1983): 433-444.

White, Newport J. D. *The First and Second Epistles to Timothy and The Epistle to Titus*. The Expositor's Greek Testament IV. New York: George H. Doran Company, 1897; repr., Grand Rapids: Wm. B. Eerdmans Publishing Company, 1974.

Wiles, Maurice F. *The Divine Apostle: The Interpretation of St. Paul's Epistles in the Early Church*. Cambridge: Cambridge University Press, 1967.

Wilken, Robert L. 'Diversity and Unity in Early Christianity.' *Second Century* 1 (1981): 101-110.

Williams, C. S. C. 'The History of the Text and Canon of the New Testament to Jerome.' In *Cambridge History of the Bible*. Vol. 2. *The West from the Fathers to the Reformation*. Edited by G. W. H. Lampe. Cambridge University Press, 1969.

Wisse, Frederik. 'The Use of Early Christian Literature as Evidence for Inner Diversity and Conflict.' In *Nag Hammadi, Gnosticism, and Early Christianity*. Edited by Charles W. Hedrick and Robert Hodgson, Jr. Peabody, Mass.: Hendrickson Publishers, 1986.

Wright, David F. 'Homosexuals or Prostitutes: The Meaning of ΑΡΣΕΝΟΚΟΙΤΑΙ (1 Cor. 6:9, 1 Tim. 1:10).' *Vigiliae Christianae* 38 (1984): 125-153.

——. 'Translating ΑΡΣΕΝΟΚΟΙΤΑΙ (1 COR. 6:9; 1 TIM. 1:10).' *Vigiliae Christianae* 41 (1987): 396-398.

Wright, Leon E. *Alterations of the Words of Jesus: As Quoted in the Literature of the Second Century*. Cambridge, Mass.: Harvard University Press, 1952.

Young, Frances M. *Biblical Exegesis and the Formation of Christian Culture*. Cambridge: Cambridge University Press, 1997.

Zahn, Theodor. *Introduction to the New Testament*. Translated from the third German edition by John Moore Trout, William Arnot Mather, Louis Hodous, Edward Strong Worcest, William Hoyt Worrell, and Rowland Backus Dodge. 3 Vols. Grand Rapids: Kregel Publications, 1953.
———. *Ignatii et Polycarpi epistulae martyria fragmenta*. Patrum Apostolicorum Opera II. Lipsiae: J. C. Hinrichs, 1876.
Ziegler, Joseph, ed. *Isaias*. Septuaginta. Göttingen: Vandenhoeck & Ruprecht, 1983.

INDEX OF NAMES

INDEX OF SOURCES

BIBLE

OLD TESTAMENT

NEW TESTAMENT